Understanding Dutch Law

Understanding Dutch Law

Sanne Taekema (editor)

Boom Juridische uitgevers
Den Haag
2004

ISBN 90 5454 432 5
NUR 820
www.bju.nl

Preface

The idea for this book grew over the last few years as a result of teaching a course on Dutch law to foreign students at Tilburg University. In discussions with students, I found that they were curious not only about the typical legal institutions of the Netherlands, but also about the social and cultural context and development of Dutch law. I hope this book is able to satisfy that curiosity and will be interesting and useful for students of Dutch law.

I want to thank the colleagues who were kind enough to contribute to this book for their efforts. Special thanks are due to Hildegard Penn and Ineke Sijtsma, who corrected the English of a number of chapters, and who were always ready to answer questions about terminology and usage. I also want to thank the Erasmus students and other foreign students at the Faculty of Law over the last three autumn semesters for their discussions about Dutch law.

Tilburg, December 2003

Sanne Taekema

Table of Contents

List of Contributors

Maria IJzermans is Assistant Professor of Jurisprudence at Tilburg University.

Randall Lesaffer is Professor of Legal History at Tilburg University, and Professor of Law at the Catholic University of Leuven.

Sanne Taekema is Assistant Professor of Jurisprudence at Tilburg University.

Peter J.P. Tak is Professor in the Department of Criminal Law at the University of Nijmegen.

Maarten van Dijck is a Ph.D. candidate in Jurisprudence/Criminal Law at Tilburg University.

Bart van Klink is Associate Professor of Jurisprudence at Tilburg University.

Paul Vlaardingerbroek is Professor in Family and Juvenile law at Tilburg University and Deputy Judge in the Court of Appeal in 's-Hertogenbosch and in the District Court of Rotterdam.

Willem J. Witteveen is Professor of Jurisprudence at Tilburg University and member of the First Chamber of the Dutch Parliament.

Part I

General Topics

1 Introducing Dutch Law*

Sanne Taekema

1 Introduction

Law is an important phenomenon in modern society: it influences people's lives in more ways than they probably realize. It proclaims certain conduct illegal, but it also makes things possible by creating legal means to achieve them. Many of the central elements in law can be found in the vast majority of legal systems: there is usually a court system, citizens have certain rights, the government enforces aspects of law. Every legal system, however, has its own mechanisms and institutions, its particular prohibitions and principles. One important way in which legal systems differ is in the language they use: the official language (or languages) of a country will also be the language of the law. This means that the statutory rules, court proceedings and most of the literature about the legal system are also in the country's official language.

If one is interested in another legal system, this poses a problem. The legal system of the Netherlands, for instance, is almost impossible to understand for someone without knowledge of the Dutch language. There are few translations of Dutch laws in other languages and court cases are only published in Dutch. This book tries to make the law of the Netherlands accessible to foreigners who do not speak Dutch.

In order to gain knowledge of a legal system, it is not enough to be told about the existing rules in the major fields of law. It is vital to combine knowledge of the rules with an understanding of the way the rules came about and of the context in which the rules function. The aim of this book is to give insight into the historical, political and cultural context of Dutch law as well as the main legal rules and institutions. This chapter is devoted to some basic features of Dutch law and its context.

2 Dutch law as a European legal system

The Netherlands are a country on the European continent. This simple observation is the key to a number of basic characteristics of the Dutch legal system, two of which will be discussed here: the character of Dutch law in comparison to other legal systems and the influence of European law on the Dutch system.

---

* Many thanks to Roland Pierik for his helpful comments.

2.1 A comparative perspective

In the theory of comparative law, it is customary to classify the legal systems of the world as part of legal families. The members of a legal family share particular features, such as their history, the style of legal thought, specific legal institutions, the choice of sources of law and methods of interpretation, and ideology.[1] In the Western world, the greatest difference is between common law and civil law systems.

Common law systems, such as English and American law, are characterized by case-by-case reasoning, typical institutions such as the trust, and an emphasis on judge-made law. Civil law systems are characterized by abstract reasoning and an emphasis on statutory law. Although the systems of continental Europe can all be regarded as civil law systems, there are important differences which justify a subdivision into smaller legal families.[2] Therefore, a subdivision can be made between the Romanistic, the Germanic and the Nordic legal families. The central system of the Romanistic family is the French legal system; among the other legal systems belonging to this family are the Italian and the Spanish system. The central system of the Germanic family is the German system, and of the Nordic family, the Swedish and Danish systems.

Traditionally, the Dutch system has been classified as a Romanistic system. The most important reason for this classification is that the Netherlands were briefly occupied by France when Napoleon was in power, a period in which the French legal codes were introduced in the Netherlands. The later Dutch codes were modelled on the French originals, and this has given the Dutch system a number of typically Romanistic institutions. For instance, the existence of cassation as the highest instance of court proceedings has a French origin.[3]

More recently, however, changes in Dutch law have not been exclusively modelled on the French system. One of the most important changes, the recodification of civil law in the new Civil Code, was inspired by German legal thinking: the structure of the code, moving from more general to more specific rules, is comparable to the German *Bundesgesetzbuch*. The new code also introduced particularly Dutch elements: for instance, it codified the major developments in Dutch case law throughout the 20th century. In general, one can say that law reform in the Netherlands draws on different legal systems and that Dutch law can no longer be classified as clearly Romanistic.

2.2 The Netherlands in the European Union

The Netherlands have always been an enthusiastic supporter of European cooperation. It was one of the six countries that formed the first European community, the European Coal and Steel Community in 1951. Since then, the

---

1. Zweigert and Kötz, *Introduction to Comparative Law*, Oxford: Clarendon 1998 (3rd edition), p. 68.
2. This is the division made by Zweigert and Kötz; not all comparatists agree on the criteria and number of legal families, see Zweigert and Kötz, p. 64-65, see note 2.
3. See also Chapter 3.2.

Netherlands have been party to all the treaties establishing closer ties between the countries of Europe. The pro-European attitude of the Netherlands has had profound influence on the law: most fields of law are affected by rules and regulations from Brussels. In some fields, for instance environmental law and consumer law, the majority of the rules are either European or national rules adopted to conform to European law. European community law takes precedence over national law.[4] Because European rules are made by supra-national bodies, the European Council, Commission and Parliament, national sovereignty, the power of the national government and Parliament to legislate and execute legal rules as they see fit, has seriously diminished. Now that the European Union is expanding, the influence of the Dutch government on European issues diminishes even further. Although not everyone is completely happy about this, many people acknowledge that a small country such as the Netherlands cannot achieve much, economically or politically, on its own.

In addition to the law stemming from the European Communities, and now the European Union, there is a pervasive influence of the European Convention on Human Rights in Dutch law. The Netherlands ratified the European Convention in 1954. As a consequence, Dutch citizens can take their complaints about the violation of the Convention to the European Court of Human Rights, after they have exhausted national remedies. Although the general opinion in the Netherlands is that Dutch human rights protection is very good, the European Court has on a number of occasions ruled that the Dutch state violated a provision of the European Convention. One of the articles for which the Netherlands were at fault in the past is article 6: the right to a fair trial. A famous case which was reason for profound changes in procedural administrative law was the *Benthem* case.[5] The question was whether appeal to the Judicial Division of the Council of State, as it then functioned, and appeal to the Crown, should be regarded as a hearing by an impartial and independent tribunal in the sense of article 6. Because the Division of the Council of State could only give an advice, not a decision, and because the Crown was a part of the government and not independent, the European Court ruled that these proceedings violated article 6. As a result, Dutch administrative law has been reformed so that the appeal to the Crown was abolished and the Judicial Division of the Council of State now gives decisions as the final court of appeal. The *Benthem* case can be regarded as an example of the - sometimes more, sometimes less profound - changes in the Dutch legal system that originated from rulings of the European Court of Human Rights.

3 Sources of law

As most legal systems today, Dutch law recognizes a number of different sources of law. Of course, legal rules can be found in various types of enacted law, but case law,

---

4. This is not problematic within the Dutch legal system, which contains the more general constitutional rule that treaties precede national law. See also the next section.
5. ECHR 23 October 1985, 8848/80.

customary law, and principles of law are recognized sources as well. All of these sources are subject to certain conditions of validity: when does a rule from that source count as a *legal* rule, i.e. as a source of legal obligations? For some sources, there is the additional problem of knowing exactly what the rule is: how do we know which legal rules the source contains? These are questions that can be asked about each source separately, while there is also the overarching question of the relation between the different sources: which is the more important? In case of conflict, which source prevails? Many of the Dutch solutions will seem familiar to students of other Continental European systems: with respect to the sources of law, the Netherlands do not differ hugely from other civil law countries.

3.1   Enacted law

Enacted law, i.e. law made by a body invested with the power of law-making, can be divided into four main categories: treaties (including international law made by supra-nation bodies), the constitution, statutes, and other regulations by government bodies.

1. *Treaties*. As was pointed out in the previous section, treaties and other international rules have steadily become a more important source of law over the last century. In general, the procedure by which a treaty becomes part of Dutch law is simple. Whenever the Dutch government is party to a treaty and the treaty is ratified (by Parliament), it only needs to be published in order to attain the status of a source of law. This means that the Dutch system is a monistic system: treaties are part of the law automatically. By contrast, a dualistic system makes it necessary to transform international rules separately into national law by an act of law.[6] There are some international rules, however, that do need to be transformed, regardless of the monistic system, notably European directives that explicitly leave it to the Member States themselves to incorporate the content of the directive in the way they see fit.

   Although the basic idea of treaties as a source of law is straightforward, there is a complication when an individual citizen wants to appeal to a treaty before a Dutch court of law. For such cases, the Dutch Constitution prescribes that only the provisions of treaties that are directly addressed to citizens can be invoked in court (article 93). Clear examples of such provisions are the human rights guaranteed by the European Convention: these are often invoked before, and regularly applied by, the Dutch courts. Many treaty provisions are less clear in this respect, so that the courts themselves have to determine whether a particular provision is eligible for direct application.

2. *Constitution*. The highest national law in the Netherlands is the Constitution, last changed profoundly in 1983 when the catalogue of basic rights was expanded and compiled to form the first chapter. The Constitution grants basic rights to citizens and provides the basis for governmental organization: it establishes the

---

6. Among the countries with a more dualistic system are Germany and Italy.

independent judiciary, the process of elections, and the different governmental bodies and their rule-making powers, such as the Parliament, provinces and municipalities. As the foundation of Dutch law, the Constitution is subject to a stricter procedure for amendment than regular statutes.[7]

3. *Statutes.* The bulk of enacted Dutch law is formed by Acts of Parliament or statutes, made by the government and Parliament together. The Dutch constitutional system aims to respect legality: the government may only limit the freedom of the citizens on the basis of general, public laws. Although this principle is most relevant to criminal law *(nulla poena sine lege)*, it is more generally applicable: all government action must have a basis in statutory law. As a consequence, there are Acts of Parliament in all areas of law, which provide the general rules for that field. This does not mean, however, that all general rules can be found in Acts of Parliament.

4. *Governmental regulations.* Often, the powers to make additional rules are delegated by the statute to other government bodies, giving rise to regulations by these bodies. Sometimes, the statute is no more than a framework for a series of more detailed regulations by the government or by particular ministers. In some areas, these government bodies have independent rule-making powers, awarded by the Constitution. For instance, the municipal council such as the city council of Amsterdam has the power to make regulations or by-laws (article 127 Constitution). Such independent rule-making powers have been awarded to the government, the provincial states, municipal councils, district water boards,[8] and specialized public bodies for professions and trades.[9]

Within the category of enacted law, there is a clear hierarchy of sources: whenever there is a conflict between rules, the higher rule precedes the lower. Thus, as is shown in figure 1, treaties precede the Constitution, which precedes Acts of Parliament, which precede other government regulations. There is one peculiar aspect to this hierarchical system: although the Constitution precedes Acts of Parliament, the courts are not allowed to invalidate a statute because it conflicts with the Constitution (article 120 Constitution). It is the sole responsibility of the democratic Parliament to ensure that its Acts are in accordance with the Constitution. However, this ban on the judicial review of statutes does not mean that Dutch statutes are never declared invalid by a judge: when a statutory rule conflicts with a rule of international law, it can be declared invalid. This has happened on numerous occasions, especially on the basis of the European Convention on Human Rights, which contains many provisions that are in substance the same as the Dutch constitutional rights.

---

7. See section 2.2 of the chapter on legislation for a description of constitutional amendment.
8. Water boards are historically important in the Netherlands because such a large part of the country is below sea level: water boards are responsible for the upkeep of dykes, the prevention of floods and all other matters concerning water, such as clean drinking water.
9. Such bodies can make rules for an area of trade, such as rules for the clothing industry, or for a certain profession, such as disciplinary rules for lawyers.

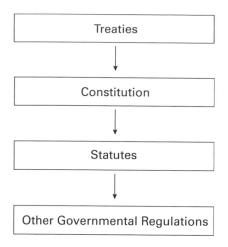

Figure 1 – Hierarchy of Sources: Enacted Law

3.2 Case law

An important additional source of law is formed by judicial decisions. What is peculiar about this source is that the rules contained in judicial cases are always made in relation to a concrete case. This has the consequence that the general rule to be applied in later cases is not always clearly formulated as such. Furthermore, case law always builds upon other sources: it concerns the interpretation of legal rules to be applied in the case at hand. In the Dutch system, case law is primarily seen as supplementing enacted law. Court decisions are a source of case law if they provide a novel interpretation that can be applied in other cases. The most important court in this respect is the Dutch Supreme Court. It has explicitly been given the task to ensure the unity of Dutch law.

Dutch courts are not formally obligated to follow earlier (Supreme Court) decisions. This means that there is no principle of precedent or *stare decisis* as known in common law countries *(stare decisis* is the idea that lower courts must abide by the rulings of higher courts). In fact, however, Dutch courts do follow Supreme Court decisions: when a court's decision goes against a Supreme Court ruling, it is possible to appeal to a higher court and, in the last instance, the Supreme Court, which will not usually overrule its own previous decision. Thus, in practice, lower courts use the Supreme Court's decisions as an authoritative source.

In cases of conflict between case law and enacted law, it is usually the most recent source that is followed. The Supreme Court has in some cases refrained from applying statutory rules because they were no longer in accordance with widespread social practice or opinion. If the legislator, on the other hand, makes new legislation which overturns Supreme Court rulings, such legislation takes precedence.

3.3 Unwritten law

There are also sources of law that are not laid down in written documents. Present Dutch law recognizes two of these: customary law and general principles of law.

1. *Customary law.* Custom is the traditional source of unwritten law. If a certain rule has been practiced uniformly and constantly and if the rule is regarded as required by law, such an unwritten rule is regarded as valid customary law. The two conditions are referred to as *usus* and *opinio necessitatis*,[10] respectively.

   Dutch law used to contain the provision that a custom was only a source of law if it was recognized as such in a statute. This did not stop the Dutch courts from recognizing customary rules that were independent of statutory provisions. In 1992, the rule requiring a statutory foundation for custom was abolished and judicial practice was formally recognized. However, one should not conclude that custom is therefore an important source of law in its own right. It is often invoked as a last resort, i.e. when no other source of law provides a basis for a satisfactory solution. We do find scattered customary rules throughout Dutch law. For example, the rule that the government must resign if it no longer has the trust and support of the Second Chamber of Parliament is an unwritten, customary rule. The most important role of customary law is not within Dutch law but in international law.

2. *General principles of law.* A second source of unwritten law is formed by the general principles of law: abstract norms that refer to basic legal values and underlie the whole of the legal system or large parts of it. Like customary law, legal principles are found throughout the Dutch legal system. However, because they are regarded as foundational, they are often invoked in court not only to supplement the written legal rules, but also to support particular interpretations of the rules. For example, in private law, the freedom of contract is regarded as one of the implicit principles of the law of obligations, which can be used to justify respecting particular contractual obligations and to interpret restrictively legal rules that limit such freedom.[11]

   Perhaps the most influential set of legal principles have been the general principles of good governance, which were developed as broad norms for administrative action. Whenever a governmental agency takes a decision concerning particular citizens, it has to ensure that the general principles of good governance are respected. Among other things, the agency has to honor its earlier promises, it has to take care in fact-finding before taking the decisions, etc. The courts have made extensive use of these principles to judge the administration's behaviour.[12]

---

10. Sometimes, this condition is called the *opinio juris* (or *opinio juris sive necessitatis*): it has the same meaning, namely the conviction that the custom is required by law.
11. A recent example, is the Supreme Court decision HR 27 September 2002, NJ 2003, 139. For further discussion of the freedom of contract and the kinds of restrictions that Dutch law imposes, see Chapter 8.4.
12. See further Chapter 4.5.

4 Dutch law in context

If one wants to gain a more profound insight into the character of Dutch law, it is essential to examine more than the structure and rules of positive law. To know what a legal system is really like, one has to consider the context in which the legal rules function. How are the rules applied? What values is law supposed to serve? What is typical of the society which the law is supposed to regulate? Some knowledge of the cultural background of Dutch law is necessary. One way to gain such knowledge is by getting some first-hand experience of Dutch society, but even then it may be helpful to have some background information. I will discuss three typical features of the context of Dutch law.

4.1 Religious and cultural diversity

For many centuries, the Netherlands were a place of refuge for people with religious beliefs that were outlawed in other countries, such as the French Huguenots and Portugese Jews. Because of this hospitality to other religions and because of the free press, the country had a reputation for tolerance. Since the Reformation, there had been religious diversity among the Dutch population as well: many remained Roman Catholics, many others turned to Calvinist protestantism. Although Catholicism was officially forbidden in the 17th and 18th centuries, toleration of Catholic beliefs was a matter of practical policy: as long as the churches were not too obvious, nothing was done to ban them actively.[13]

During the 19th century, when the Protestant church once again divided, the more orthodox Reformed Churches separated from the official Dutch Reformed Church. Their leader, Abraham Kuyper, also started a political party and a number of other projects, such as a university: the Free University in Amsterdam, founded in 1878. At the same time, a political battle started over the public funding of schools: on the one hand, the liberals only wanted to fund public schools, without any religious affiliation, on the other hand, Catholics and Protestants wanted funding for schools with a religious character as well. It was a long and heated battle, but the issue was finally resolved with a compromise in 1917 that started the development in the Netherlands of a characteristic political system: the accommodation of four blocks or 'pillars'.[14]

The system of pillarization depended on the separate functioning of four blocks in society: Catholics, orthodox Protestants, socialists and a general liberal group (which was more heterogeneous consisting of non-church going groups and liberal Protestants). Each had its own schools, political parties, newspapers, radio and

---

13. Hence, the existence of many clandestine churches ('schuilkerken'), such as Ons' Lieve Heer op Solder in Amsterdam, now a museum.
14. See A. Lijphart, *The Politics of Accommodation: Pluralism and Democracy in the Netherlands*, Berkeley: University of California Press 1968. He uses the term 'block' to translate the Dutch term 'zuil', which literally means 'pillar'.

television associations, etc. Contact between people in the different pillars was scarce; it was only at the level of the leadership of the organizations, especially the political parties, that there was much interaction. This led to a 'politics of accommodation', the leaders of national politics worked out compromise solutions for political problems, which were deferentially accepted by the broad population.

The system of pillarization started to break down at the end of the 1960s, when church membership became less important and Dutch society became more individualistic. The rise of television made it easier to learn about the ideas from other pillars. At present, people are less loyal to one political party and membership of the different pillarized organizations has declined. In some respects, however, the remnants of the system are still visible. Most of public television is still run by the associations that were once part of the four pillars. Many of the socio-economic policies of the government are still decided in consultation with the leaders of employers' organisations and trade unions that used to belong to the pillars.

In the same period, the end of the 1960s, Dutch society became more culturally diverse: so-called guest workers from the south of Europe, Morocco and Turkey arrived, and after the independence of the Dutch colony of Surinam in 1975, many chose to move to the Netherlands. Immigration is still an important phenomenon: about 18% of the population have at least one non-Dutch parent.[15] In many inner-city schools, more than half the students belong to such immigrant groups. We can say that the religious diversity of old has changed into cultural diversity, although there is a religious component too: Islam is a growing religion in the Netherlands now. The old animosity between Catholic and Protestant groups has, however, faded, because the majority of the Dutch population is no longer actively religious. Only 25% of the population still go to church regularly, although about 60% still consider themselves as belonging to a religion.[16]

4.2   A pragmatic attitude

One of the reasons why the politics of accommodation developed as it did was that none of the political parties of the four blocks ever commanded a majority of the electorate. As a result, the national government always consisted of parties from different blocks forming a coalition: sometimes a socialist-Catholic coalition or a Catholic-Protestant-liberal coalition. This reinforced the need to compromise and settle for pragmatic solutions. Sometimes, this meant accepting that a more principled solution was not feasible. One of the reasons why, for example, the law on euthanasia was gradually developed by the courts was that there was no political majority in favour of changing the statutory rules nor was there a majority in favour

---

15. Of these, about half are of non-Western descent, 1,6 million, according to statistics of the CBS (Centraal Bureau voor de Statistiek, report Allochtonen in Nederland 2002).
16. 31% Roman Catholic, 14% Dutch Reformed, 7% Reformed Churches, 5% Islam, 3% other religions (CBS 2000).

of strictly enforcing the criminal law forbidding euthanasia. The result was that a viable system was developed in case law, which was finally laid down in a statute when a political majority could be found.[17]

The attitude of (temporarily) accepting a solution that may not be very elegant or principled is one that is shared by politicians and jurists alike. Because politics and law are connected spheres of society, this is not surprising: in the case of euthanasia, something had to be done by jurists to overcome the disagreement that made a political solution impossible. There had already been a discussion among doctors about conditions under which they thought euthanasia was medically and ethically permissible, which also gave rise to the opinion that it should not be illegal. The solution that the courts chose was to consider the practice of euthanasia as a situation of necessity under certain conditions. After the Public Prosecution Service had adopted the policy of non-prosecution if these conditions were met, the call for legislation was renewed. Finally, in 2002, the system as developed in case law was made part of the Criminal Code. Among the reasons that made possible a change in statutory law was the coalition of a social-democratic and two liberal parties with a majority in Parliament: this made it possible to resolve an issue that had always been very sensitive for Christian political parties.

Although the Dutch legal system is notorious for its practice of regulated tolerance, or *gedogen*, in criminal matters such as drugs, prostitution and euthanasia, there is not a widespread condoning of this practice.[18] It is best seen as a phase in a dynamic process of coping with changing circumstances and opinions in society. Regulated tolerance is a reaction that stems from the realistic attitude that the problematic phenomenon will not simply go away. As Chrisje Brants points out in relation to prostitution, once the view takes hold that the criminal law cannot solve the social problem, the pragmatic attitude demands that other tactics be pursued.[19] Regulated tolerance means following a clear policy of not prosecuting certain offences; in the Dutch context, it is usually a combination of administrative policies by the local government and criminal policies by the public prosecution office. Similarly to the case of euthanasia, regulated tolerance with regard to prostitution was a step on the way to legalization: in 2000, prostitution was made legal by a change in the Criminal Code.

The practice of regulated tolerance is one of the indications that the Dutch legal culture is pragmatic, i.e. the focus is on finding a good solution instead of following the rules for their own sake.[20] It is important to note, however, that this is a characteristic of the *internal* legal culture, being the attitudes and values of the people working in the legal profession. It should not be confused with the attitudes about law in society, the *external* legal culture. The general public is less lenient about

---

17. For a thorough discussion of the development of the euthanasia law, see Griffiths et al., *Euthanasia & Law in the Netherlands*, Amsterdam: Amsterdam University Press 1998.
18. The third case, Dutch drugs policy, is treated extensively in Chapter 7.
19. Chrisje Brants, 'The Fine Art of Regulated Tolerance: Prostitution in Amsterdam', *Journal of Law and Society* (25) 1998, p. 621-635, at 624.
20. See Freek Bruinsma, *Dutch Law in Action*, Ars Aequi Libri 2000, p. 15-19.

following the rules and their expectations about what can be achieved by legislation are higher.

To understand the way the Dutch legal system functions, a grasp of the internal legal culture has to be combined with an understanding of the legal institutions, the infrastructure that makes the rules work. The informal, pragmatic attitude of the Dutch jurists is reinforced by the legal infrastructure: the legal system is organized in such a way that informal solutions are fairly easily achieved. A key factor are the many alternatives to formal court procedures.[21]

4.3   Limits on tolerance: the debate on safety

Although I have so far emphasized the tolerant and pragmatic side of the Dutch legal and political culture, this is not the whole story. These tendencies are counteracted by the need felt in society for 'law and order', a stricter enforcement of the rules to achieve a more orderly society. This tendency can be most clearly witnessed in the debates about issues of public safety.

In 2000 and 2001, there were two disasters that shocked Dutch society: on 13 May 2000, a major explosion at a fireworks factory killed 22 people; on New Year's night, a fire in a bar caused the death of 14 people. In the discussion about the causes of these events, the questions arose whether the safety rules had been adequate and whether they had been adequately enforced. An independent committee, led by former Ombudsman Oosting, investigated the causes of the fireworks explosion and found that different government agencies had indeed been too lenient towards the factory and had not enforced the rules as strictly as they should have. Not only has the effect been that tolerating the transgression of safety rules has met with widespread disapproval, it has also led to the recommendation that government agencies should be criminally liable if they have not enforced the rules and this non-enforcement results in damage.

A second issue concerns safety in public places, especially in the large cities. Because more people feel unsafe, especially in inner-city neighbourhoods, there has been an extension of the number of police and of police powers. For instance, in a number of designated problem areas, police are now authorized to search all persons for weapons without suspecting them of a crime. Dutch public opinion, which is in favour of individual freedom in matters of sexual orientation and private opinion, has become stricter when the value of freedom has to be balanced against safety and public order: restrictions on civil rights in the interest of safety, to prevent crime or terrorism, are more easily accepted now than they used to be.

The criminologist Boutellier has called this longing for safety a utopian desire: implicit in our culture, there is the desire to be completely safe.[22] In this respect, one might say that Dutch culture is a typically Western culture: since 11 September 2001 the importance of safety, and the difficulty of achieving it, has been widely felt throughout the Western world.

---

21. See Chapter 3 and Bruinsma, *Dutch Law in Action*.
22. Hans Boutellier, *De veiligheidsutopie*, Den Haag: Boom Juridische uitgevers 2002.

5   The structure of Dutch law and this book

This book is structured in such a way that the reader will not only become acquainted with the general features of the main areas of Dutch law, but will also understand the way Dutch law works with respect to certain specific themes. By more detailed discussion of the context and development of specific areas of Dutch law, it will be easier to understand the particular character of Dutch law. Such knowledge cannot be comprehensive, but the reader will be acquainted with the style and background of the Dutch legal system. The book is divided into four parts, following traditional distinctions to structure Dutch law.

The **first** part, **General Topics**, continues with **Chapter 2** on the legal history of the Netherlands to provide a general background to Dutch law. It is followed by a chapter on procedural law. One common way of subdividing the law is to distinguish between substantive law and procedural law. The first consists of the rules establishing rights and duties; the second, of rules regulating the procedures by which rights and duties can be enforced. For instance, the right to get married and the prohibition of murder are part of substantive law (private and criminal law respectively). The requirements for bringing a case to court, or rules about hearing witnesses are rules of procedural law. **Chapter 3** gives an introduction to the Dutch court system and discusses the basic principles of procedural law.

The most common way of dividing national Dutch law is into public and private law. The main criterion for this division is the involvement of government: if a legal relationship only concerns citizens, it is subject to the rule of private law; if the government is one of the parties involved, it is a matter of public law. However, the distinction cannot be applied so simply. The idea behind the distinction is that there should be one set of rules for situations where parties act as equals to further their own, private interests, and where they themselves can take the initiative to enforce the law, and a different set of rules for the unequal relationships between government and citizens, for the furthering of the general interest, which is reason to give government the initiative for law enforcement. The difficulty is that sometimes a government body can act as if it is a private party, for instance, when it enters into a contract of sale. In such a case, the rules of private law apply, even though the government is involved. It has become generally accepted that there are situations in which government bodies can best serve the general good by using private law rules.

Public law is usually subdivided into three fields: constitutional law, administrative law and criminal law. Constitutional law is the part of law that organizes the state and the different bodies that form its components. Strictly speaking, constitutional law is a slightly too narrow term, it is more correct to speak of the law of the state: the constitution establishes public bodies and their fundamental powers, while other more specific laws provide the details of their organization and powers. All of these laws are usually grouped together. The main difference between constitutional law and administrative law is that the former concerns government as such and the relationships between different governmental bodies, while the latter governs the way governmental bodies act towards citizens. Administrative law gives the rules for giving out permits and subsidies, for levying taxes and award social security benefits. The general rules for administrative law have recently been gathered together and restructured into one code: the General Administrative Law Act.[23] Criminal law is primarily characterized by the role of the government, i.e. the police and the public prosecutor, in the enforcement of the law. The values which the criminal law aims to protect, like the right to life and property, are of such fundamental and general interest that their enforcement cannot be entrusted to the citizens themselves.

In the **second** part of the book, entitled **Constitutional Law**, **Chapter 4** is a general chapter about the principles of constitutional law and its founding ideas regarding the *rechtsstaat*. It is followed by **Chapter 5** on the specific topic of legislation, in which the nature of the legislative process is discussed and the development towards a more communicative model of legislation. In the **third** part, **Criminal Law**, **Chapter 6** is about general features of substantive and procedural criminal law, followed by **Chapter 7** about the specific topic of Dutch drug policy. In this chapter, the legal and social context of the Dutch policy of tolerance towards drugs is presented in order to give an insight into the different considerations of policy making in the field of criminal law.

Private law is characterized by the general assumption of equality and private initiative: it was traditionally founded on the principle that citizens should be able to shape their own legal relationships provided they do not harm others. To a large extent, substantive private law recognizes the rules made by private individuals themselves, such as contractual rules, and it supplements these rules when necessary. Procedural private law will not be discussed further, but here too, the basic structure is dependent upon private initiative: most importantly, it is up to the individual to judge whether a legal problem is serious enough to take it to court.

Substantive **private law** is discussed in the **fourth** and final part of the book. **Chapter 8** is a general chapter about substantive private law, containing the basics of Dutch patrimonial law and more extensive discussion of contract and tort. **Chapter 9** gives a detailed account of recent developments of Dutch family law, in which the influence of European law is highlighted.

---

23. *Algemene wet bestuursrecht*, in force since 1 January 1994. There is no separate chapter about administrative law in this book, although the development of principles of administrative law is treated in Chapter 4. For an overview of Dutch administrative law, see: J. Chorus et al., *Introduction to Dutch Law*, The Hague [etc.]: Kluwer Law International, Chapter 17.

2 A Short Legal History of the Netherlands

Randall Lesaffer

1 Introduction

Before the Dutch revolt of the 16th century, the territories of what is now the Kingdom of the Netherlands were never independent and united at the same time. Dutch law, as an autonomous system of law, can by no means be traced back further than the early modern period. However, as the modern Dutch system of law is part of the civil law tradition that dominates all of continental Europe, the earlier history of the law in the Northern Netherlands is to a large extent similar to that in the rest of Western Europe. During most of the Middle Ages, before the successful secession from Habsburg authority, the northern provinces of the Low Countries had political and legal institutions that were quite comparable to those of the Southern Netherlands.[1] One cannot but include some remarks on the general legal history of continental Europe in general and the Low Countries in particular when discussing the medieval and 16th century Northern Netherlands.

The legal history of the Netherlands can be understood in terms of a gradual process of centralization of political power and of unification of the law. It took about four hundred years (16th to 18th centuries) for the modern sovereign state to arise out of the multitude of feudal and ecclesiastical lordships and to overcome the diversity of law systems that marked the later medieval period. Though the sovereign state has been severely challenged over the last fifty years, both through the European integration as well as through far reaching decentralization in many European countries, to this day, the Netherlands remain one of the most centralized states in Western Europe. The recent re-codification of civil law, an exceptional feature in Europe, is after all an act of re-unification of Dutch law.

2 The later Middle Ages (1000-1400)

2.1 The feudal lordships

Out of the political chaos that followed the fall of the Carolingian dynasty and the collapse of royal authority in Western Europe, arose a multitude of feudal 'states', both great and small. Through the Treaty of Meersen (870), the Netherlands became part of the Kingdom of East Francia or Germany. The northern provinces of the Low

---

1. For a brief survey on the legal history of Belgium: Dirk Heirbaut, 'The Belgian Legal Tradition: does it exist?', in: Hubert Bocken & Walter de Bondt (eds.), *Introduction to Belgian Law*, Bruxelles/The Hague: Bruylant/Kluwer Law International 2001, p. 1-22.

Countries remained under the supreme authority of the Emperor of the Holy Roman Empire for the rest of the Middle Ages and beyond.

During the 10th and 11th centuries, the Ottonian dynasty succeeded in restoring royal power in most of the German empire and asserted its suzerainty over the Kingdom of Italy. Otto the Great (936-973) was the first of the German kings who, after the example of Charlemagne (768-814) had himself crowned Roman Emperor by the Pope. Otto and his heirs attempted to curtail the power of the great dukes and lords of the Kingdom and closely associated the high clergy to their power. They bestowed secular power over important parts of the Empire upon bishops and abbots. This gave rise to the great ecclesiastical lordships such as the bishoprics of Utrecht and Liège in the Low Countries. Theoretically, the Low Countries were part of the Duchy of Lorraine, one of the five great Duchies of the German Kingdom. However, the Dukes of Lorraine failed to vest their authority in the Netherlands. Smaller feudal lords and ecclesiastical princes hardly took account of the Duke and often treated directly with the Emperor.[2]

The Investiture Controversy between the Emperor and the Pope over the autonomy of the Church was instrumental in the breakdown of imperial power in Germany and thus in the Netherlands. By the end of the 13th century, the regional lordships in the Low Countries had attained a high degree of independence and held few obligations towards the Emperor, their feudal suzerain. By 1400, the most important lordships of the Northern Netherlands were the Duchy of Gueldres, the Counties of Holland and Zealand and the Bishopric of Utrecht. To the north lay the Frisian territories, where the feudal system never really took hold and which for a long time had no overlord. The different local circles of Frisia continued to enjoy their autonomy under the theoretical sovereignty of the Emperor.[3] The present Dutch province of Brabant was part of the great Duchy of Brabant while present-day Limburg was divided over several lordships, among them the Bishopric of Liège.

Secular princes such as the Duke of Brabant or the Count of Holland held their territories as vassals to the German King, the Emperor. In most cases, feudal dynasts had great difficulty in affirming their hold over their lands. Their power was constantly challenged, sometimes by rival dynasties and claimants to the throne, but more often by local powers such as the feudal nobility, the town and rural communities. Most of the great lordships were construed by bringing several of the old Carolingian *pagi* or counties and other entities under one ruler. In reality, those old juridical circles held on to their judicial institutions and their customs and were a real check on the freedom of the princes.

2. W. Kienast, *Der Herzogstitel in Frankreich und Deutschland (9. bis 12. Jahrhundert)*, Munchen: Oldenbourg 1968.
3. K. von Richthofen, 'The relation between Frisia and the Empire from 800-1500 in the light of the eighth of the 17 Statutes', *Amsterdamer Beiträge zur älteren Germanistik* 49 (1998), p. 1-76.

2.2 The learned ius commune and the reality of the iura propria

The rediscovery of the *Digest* of Justinian (527-565) and the beginning of the study of Roman law in Italy at the end of the 11th century constitute a fundamental caesura in European legal history. With the recuperation of Roman law, the history of Western legal science truly begins. By the end of the 14th century, there were faculties of civil law all over Europe, here, the *Digest* and the other parts of what later was to become known as the *Corpus iuris civilis* of Justinian were analyzed, commented upon and taught. From the Low Countries, where there was no university prior to 1425, students went to places like Orleans, Montpellier, Bologna, or after 1388, Cologne. In the old Roman texts, the glossators and commentators found a law system that was much more sophisticated than the medieval laws in force.

After their victory over the Emperor in the Investiture Controversy, the Popes greatly strengthened their position within the Church and shaped it into a central monarchy. To this effort, the elaboration of a complex system of law was essential. Around 1140, Gratian, an Italian monk, made a collection of canon law texts, the *Decretum Gratiani*, which eventually gained papal sanction. During the 12th, 13th and 14th centuries a lot of new papal and conciliar laws or decretals saw the light, which were gradually compiled in official codifications as the *Liber extra* (1234) and the *Liber sextus* (1298). These texts were studied at the faculties of canon law in a similar way as the Roman law was at the civil law faculties.

The learned Roman and canon law of the Middle Ages were not two completely separate. Under the late Roman Empire, the Church had adopted institutions and rules from Roman law. Now, as many scholars studied at both law faculties, the two legal sciences became intertwined. Baldus de Ubaldis (1327-1400), one of the greatest jurists of the Middle Ages, often considered both Roman and canon law arguments when discussing a particular point of law. Out of the science of Roman and canon law emerged a new body of law, the so-called *ius commune*, that was an amalgam of both laws and that was common to the whole of the Latin West.[4]

In the greatest part of Europe, this *ius commune* was nothing more than a professorial law, a science of law. The canon law was of course the applicable law of the Church and its ecclesiastical courts. As those enjoyed extensive jurisdiction, both in the personal sense – for all cases involving clerics – as well as the material sense – e.g. marital law, contract law, treaty law – canon law functioned as a kind of common law of the West, notwithstanding the many local customs and differences that were as real. To the contrary, leaving aside some territories to the south of Europe, Roman law was not the applicable law.

Opposite the universality of the learned *ius commune* stood the reality of many hundreds, if not thousands of regional and local law systems with all their

---

4. On the *ius commune* in the Middle Ages: Manlio Bellomo, *The Common Legal Past of Europe, 1000-1800*, Washington: The Catholic University of America Press 1995; Harold Berman, *Law and Revolution. The Formation of the Western Legal Tradition*, Cambridge, Mass./London: Harvard University Press 1983.

particularities and disparities that were applied by the many thousands of courts and councils: the so-called *iura propria*. In this respect, the Netherlands were no different from most of Europe. Each lordship, each juridical circle, each town or city had its own courts where justice was rendered according to the local law system. To this territorial diversity, personal diversity was added. The *iudicium parium* principle granted each estate, each class of the population, the right to be judged by its own courts and according to its own laws. Clerics enjoyed the *privilegium fori* to be sentenced before an ecclesiastical court; the burghers brought their cases before the aldermen of their town while feudal courts were competent for all disputes between feudal lords and their vassals.

In the Netherlands, the applicable law of most of these courts and juridical circles was for the greater part customary law. Germanic in origin, the laws and customs had been developed and made more sophisticated over the ages by the courts. Though there was no formal doctrine of *stare decisis* as in the modern English common law, the logic of a customary system caused the courts to sustain their older judgements. As representatives of the King, the dukes, counts and lords acted as the highest judicial authority within their lands. This meant that in principle, vassals and subjects could turn to their overlord to demand justice. Though proper appeal procedures did not exist as yet, the lord and his *curia* held some authority over the lower courts, just as the courts of a larger town could have over smaller towns and villages. The most important of these control mechanisms was the *hoofdvaart* or *recours au chef de sens* by which a court asked the advice of a more important one. This and other mechanisms helped to harmonize the different law systems within a certain region or even lordship.

Like any other feudal lord, the 'sovereign' lords of the Low Countries such as the Dukes of Brabant and Gueldres and the Counts of Flanders, Holland and Zealand ruled with the help of a *curia* or council, consisting of the most powerful vassals and prelates of their territory. These *curiae* advised the lord in all matters, judicial, political, military as well as financial. Together with the gatherings of the estates – the representatives of the nobility, the clergy and the third estate – which were only very loosely structured and the organization of which varied for the different territories of the Northern Netherlands before the 15th and 16th centuries, the *curiae* embodied the principle of dualism. This implied that the prince ruled in cooperation with the estates of the realm. Around 1400, the judicial activities of the *curiae* had become so extensive that it proved expedient to split the council. Thus emerged high courts in Flanders (1386), Holland-Zealand (1428, the two counties since long formed a personal union) and Brabant (1430). Though in theory the prince continued to preside over these Councils and judgement was rendered in his name, in practice, the princes were more often than not absent. The new Councils were not packed any longer with members of the nobility and the clergy *qualitate qua*. These were now driven out of the princely courts by professional councillors, appointed and paid by the prince. Most of these had studied law at the civil or canon law faculties and held university degrees.

This brings us back to the *ius commune* and more particularly, the learned Roman law. What was, as Roman law was not the applicable law in most parts of the Latin West, its significance? Why was it, that although this knowledge would serve only a very limited practical purpose at first sight, many young students from all over Europe chose to study Roman law for years on end, often far away from home?

Roman law may not have been applied directly in most courts of the Latin West, this did not mean that it held no real significance. The Latin West was politically divided in many kingdoms, feudal and ecclesiastical lordships, local communities and towns. Nevertheless, it was also considered to be a religious, cultural and, to a certain extent, political and legal unity – the *respublica christiana* – under the supreme, if largely theoretical leadership of the Pope and Emperor. Just as the ideal of Christian unity balanced the divisions of real political life, so the *ius commune* balanced the diversity of the law. Though the effective significance and influence of the learned law upon 'real' law varied all over Europe, it was everywhere considered a kind of ideal law system that stood above all *iura propria*. As such, it functioned as a kind of compass, a lighthouse that lawyers and rulers steered towards when developing and reforming their own law. In the long run, the *ius commune* gained the statue of a supplementary law that was looked to when the *ius proprium* did not provide a satisfactory solution.

As mentioned above, the effective impact of Roman law varied greatly. Generally speaking, it held more sway in the south of Europe than in the north. In Italy and Southern France, Roman law was considered to be *lex scripta* or supplementary law in the technical sense of the word. Every time the local law proved unsatisfactory, the courts had to apply the Justinian laws as if they were the law of the land. To the north, Roman law never gained this position and was only relevant as *ratio scripta*, offering inspiration when justice was not felt to be ensured by the local laws.

In general, it has to be said that Roman law gained ground in the Northern Netherlands at a later state than in France or even the Southern Netherlands. Before 1388, when the University of Cologne was founded, there was no law faculty closer than France or England. Nevertheless, well before 1400, young people from the Netherlands had studied abroad and obtained law degrees. Some had made it to councillors in the service of their princes. But until the 15th century, the material impact of Roman law remained rather small.[5]

Nevertheless, the rise of the learned law did influence the legal culture, even in the late medieval Netherlands. Two main examples should be cited. First, in contradiction to customary law, the *ius commune* was a written law. Its influence proved to be instrumental in the gradual but steady rise of the use of the written word in customary law. While it took up to the 16th century before the princes made any serious attempt to codify customary law in the Netherlands, there are some examples of the writing down of existing customs in Frisia (13th century), Utrecht (1396) or Drente (1412). Some of these compilations gained statutory value. During the late Middle Ages, this process hardly involved an attempt of systematization or harmonization. Furthermore, some individual practitioners took to writing down or even collecting judgements of one of the courts. The most famous example from the

---

5. Robert Feenstra, 'Zur Rezeption in den Niederlanden', in: Wolfgang Kunkel et al., *L'Europa e il diritto romano. Studi in memoria di P. Koschaker*, Milan: Giuffrè 1953, p. 243-268; B.H.D. Hermesdorf, *Römisches Recht in den Niederlanden*, Mediolani: Giuffrè 1968.

Northern Netherlands is the *Book of Den Briel*, compiled by Jan Matthijsen, secretary of the town of Den Briel (around 1404).[6] The so-called *Sachsenspiegel*, compiled in the 13th century by the German knight Eike von Repgau, had great influence in the Northern Netherlands. The growing importance of writing was also reflected in the rise of the romano-canonic procedure that was first used in the Church, but later on also in the secular courts and that made extensive use of written documents, as well as in the rise of public notaries.

Second, from the 13th century on, for the first time since the Carolingian days, legislation gained ground. Though it was not the only factor causing this, the example of the Roman Emperor Justinian as a law-maker was certainly an inspiration to emperors, kings and princes. The Roman law, as it was laid down in the Justinian code, reflected a political and juridical system in which the power of the monarch was almost absolute. This proved attractive to the medieval princes. In the Empire, France and Castile, Roman lawyers helped to redefine the royal powers and overcome the limits of feudal suzerainty. In Holland, Philip of Leyden (1326-1382) was the first to write a treatise defending the authority of the Count using arguments from Roman law.[7] An important form of princely legislation in the Middle Ages were the privileges the princes granted to the towns of their realm, in which they determined the competences of the town's aldermen and the relations between the prince and the towns. These privileges were often not considered to be the result of a one-sided decision by the prince, but were seen as a contract between the ruler and his subjects. As such, they were irrevocable and the rights accorded through them were inalienable.[8] More generally, the statutory law tended to concentrate on matters of criminal and procedural law. Legislative activities were not limited to princes. In the Netherlands, some towns – like Amsterdam or Haarlem – and even rural communities obtained the right to promulgate statutes themselves. From the 14th to the 16th centuries, these local statutes gained ground and became an important instrument of policy and law-making in the Netherlands.

3   The Burgundian and Habsburg Netherlands (1400-1581)

3.1   *The attempt at centralization by the Burgundians and the Habsburgs*

The 15th century saw a dramatic change in the political constellation of the Netherlands. By his marriage to Margaret, daughter of the Count of Flanders, the French prince Philip the Bold, younger son of the French King and Duke of

---

6. For more examples: U.D. von Oppitz, *Deutsche Rechtsbücher des Mittelalters* 3, Cologne/Vienna: Böhlau 1990-1992.
7. Robert Feenstra, *Philip of Leyden and his treatise 'De cura republicae et sorte principantis'*, Glasgow: University of Glasgow 1970; Piet Leupen, *Philip of Leyden. A fourteenth century jurist. A study of his life and treatise 'De cura rei publicae et sorte principantis'*, The Hague/Zwolle: Leiden University Press 1981.
8. J.J. Woltjer, 'Dutch privileges, real and imaginary', in: J.S. Bromley & E.H. Kossmann (ed.), *Britain and the Netherlands*, vol. 5, The Hague: Nijhoff 1975, p. 19-35.

Burgundy (1363-1404), became Count of Flanders, Artois and the Franche-Comté in 1384. His son and grandson, John the Fearless (1404-1419) and Philip the Good (1419-1467) extended their power over most of the Netherlands adding the Duchies of Brabant (1430), Limburg (1430) and Luxemburg (1451) as well as the Counties of Hainaut, Namur, Holland and Zealand (1433) to their lands. By getting close relatives elected, among which some of his many bastard sons, to the sees of Utrecht, Liège, Tournai and Cambrai, Philip also gained temporary control over the ecclesiastical territories in the Netherlands. Philip's son and heir Charles the Bold (1467-1477) tried to expand his inheritance further and temporarily conquered Gueldres and Lorraine, thus making the bridge between the *pays de par deçà* in the Low Countries with the *pays de par delà*, Burgundy and the Franche-Comté. After his violent death at the Battle of Nancy in 1477, these new territories were quickly lost while his heiress Mary of Burgundy (1477-1482) could not prevent the French annexation of the Duchy of Burgundy itself.

Needful of a powerful ally against France, Mary went through with the marriage her father had already arranged for her to Maximilian of Habsburg, son to the Emperor Frederick III (1440-1493), who would later become Emperor himself (1493-1519). By this marriage, the Burgundian Netherlands became part of the Habsburg power complex that already consisted of the Austrian hereditary lands. Maximilian later married his children Philip (1478-1506) and Margaret (1480-1530) to the children of the Spanish Kings Ferdinand of Aragon (1479-1516) and Isabelle of Castile (1474-1504). Upon the death of Philip in 1506, his oldest son Charles (1500-1558) became heir to the combined territories of his four grandparents. By 1519, Charles V was Emperor and King of Germany, King of Spain (with its territories in Italy and the New World), Archduke of Austria and lord of the Burgundian Netherlands. From this position of power and ruthlessly abusing his authority as Emperor, he succeeded in subjecting the whole of the Netherlands – except Liège and Cambrai – including Gueldres (1543), Frisia (1524), Groningen and even the ecclesiastical territories of Tournai (1521) and Utrecht with Drente and Overijssel (1528).

The Burgundian Dukes initiated a policy of centralization and bureaucratization, which was pursued by their Habsburg successors. As their forefathers and cousins the Kings of France had done, the Dukes of Burgundy tried to construe a central bureaucracy staffed with university trained clerics and scholars they could freely appoint and dismiss. Through this, they further curbed the power of the feudal nobility and the high clergy. Shortly after his accession as Count of Flanders, Philip the Bold in 1386 installed the Council of Flanders in Lille and split it up in a judiciary and a financial division *(Chambre de Comptes)*. In 1407, the judiciary Council of Flanders would finally move to Ghent.[9] Under Flemish-Burgundian influence, some of the other (future) Burgundian lands also established a provincial

---

9. On the role of the Council of Flanders in the centralisation of the Netherlands by Charles V: Paul Van Petegem, *De Raad van Vlaanderen en staatsvorming onder Karel V (1515-1555). Een publiekrechtelijk onderzoek naar centralisatiestreven in de XVII Provinciën*, Nijmegen: Gerard Noodt Instituut 1990.

Council or High Court. In 1428, Philip the Good forced the installation of the High Court of Holland and Zealand.[10] Brabant followed suit with the Council of Brabant in 1430.[11] Other territories like Utrecht (1530) and Gueldres (1547) only got a provincial high court under Charles V, after earlier attempts had met with failure due to staunch local resistance.[12]

The Burgundian and Habsburg Netherlands never became a unified 'state'. Strictly speaking, they were a personal union of eventually seventeen lordships that all had the same prince. Until the Pragmatic Sanction of 1549, it was not even certain that this state of affairs would hold as each lordship had its own rules of succession. Through this Pragmatic Sanction, Charles V ensured that the seventeen 'provinces' would remain under the same lord.

The Burgundian Dukes had however already started an attempt of construing a central 'government' over their different territories. Whereas before his accession, Flanders, Artois and the Franche-Comté each had their own chancellors to head the central administration, Philip the Bold appointed a chancellor for all his territories. Next to the *Chambre des Comptes* in Lille, new *chambres* were installed in Dijon, Brussels and The Hague (1447). The Dukes also began to convene one High Council, one *curia*, for all their lands consisting of clergymen, nobles and university trained jurists. From the 1440s on, the council was gradually split into specialized divisions. One of these, the *Grand Conseil de la Justice souveraine*, became the high court of the Burgundian lands (1445). In 1473, Charles the Bold reformed this Council into the *Parlement de Malines*, thus giving the court a permanent seat. Charles aspired to creating a true 'royal' court, as was the *Parlement de Paris* in France, subjecting all other courts in his territories to its control and its appellate procedure. This step met with a lot of resistance from the 'provincial' Councils and the estates of the different territories and upon the death of her father in 1477, Mary had to give in and abolished the *Parlement*. She had to revert to the situation before 1473 with an ambulant *Grand Conseil*.[13] As the *Grand Conseil* held the same competences as the *Parlement*, this setback was largely of a symbolic and political nature. Nevertheless, it was an important indication for the failures central government could encounter. In the end, it took up to 1504 before the Archduke Philip could reinstitute a permanent high court with its own seat, now choosing for the less offending name of *Grand Conseil de Malines*. Some of the provincial courts would never recognize the sovereign authority of the *Grand Conseil* and refused to allow their subjects to take their appeal to Malines.[14]

---

10. Christel Verhas, *De beginjaren van de Hoge Raad van Holland, Zeeland en West-Friesland*, The Hague: Algemeen Rijksarchief 1997.
11. Philippe Godding, *Le conseil de Brabant sous le règne de Philippe le Bon (1430-1467)*, Brussels: Classe des Lettres, Académie Royale de Belgique 1999.
12. North-eastern provinces like Drente and Overijssel had to await the 18th century.
13. *Jan van Rompaey, De grote raad van de hertogen van Boergondië en het parlement van Mechelen*, Brussel: Paleis der Academiën 1973.
14. On the *Grand Conseil*: C.H. van Rhee, *Litigation and Legislation. Civil Procedure at First Instance in the Great Council of the Netherlands in Malines (1522-1559)*, Brussels: Archives Générales du Royaume et Archives de l'Etat dans les Provinces 1997.

Thanks to his ruling all of the seventeen provinces of the Netherlands – only the bishoprics of Liège and Cambrai escaped direct Habsburg rule – and thanks to his position as Emperor, Charles V was the most successful in centralizing government in the Low Countries. In 1531, while present in the Netherlands, Charles V took extensive measures to that extent. He replaced the old central institutions with the so-called Collateral Councils: the Council of State, the Privy Council and the Council of Finance.[15] In 1548, he saw that a Treaty was accepted by the Diet of the Empire in Augsburg that assembled all his 'Belgian' lands into one *Kreits* or juridical circle of the Empire and exempted the Netherlands from the authority of the imperial court, the *Reichskammergericht* in Spiers. In consequence of this treaty, the *Grand Conseil de Malines* was now a truly sovereign court.[16] The suzerainty of the Empire in the Netherlands was limited to a mutual obligation of defence and a small imperial tax.

Powerful though the Burgundian and Habsburg princes were, especially Charles V, compared to their medieval predecessors, they were not wholly successful in overcoming the defence of traditional local and provincial rights and freedoms by the estates of each lordship. The Burgundians and Habsburgs were true dynasts who submitted the interests of their subjects to the power and glory of their dynasties and whose economic, financial and institutional policies where more often than not instrumental to their territorial and foreign ambitions. By consequence, at almost no point did a true and stable alliance of interests emerge between the greater local powers – especially the rich industrial, maritime and commercial towns of Flanders, Brabant, Holland and Zealand – and the sovereigns. Insurrections and their bloody quelling – like the revolts of Ghent in 1453 and 1539-1540 – marked this continuous struggle.[17] The attempts to form a 'national identity' did not go much further than the anyhow international circles of the higher nobility and clergy. The knighthood of the *Toison d'Or* founded by Philip the Good in 1430 was a symbol of this state of affairs: as European as it was 'Burgundian', it never achieved more than strengthening the loyalty of some members of the higher nobility to the prince.

The Burgundian and Habsburg rulers could neither make a clear break with dualism and the participation in government by the estates. To the contrary, most territories during the 15th and 16th centuries saw the formation of representative institutions that came to be known as the provincial estates. They were convened by the prince and held on to their privileges, among which the right to grant and refuse taxes. In the Northern Netherlands, the constitution of these estates was different for

---

15. Michel Baelde, *De Collaterale Raden onder Karel V and Filips II, 1531-1578*, Brussels: Paleis der Academiën 1965; idem, 'Les conseils collatéraux des anciens Pays-Bas. Résultats et problèmes, 1531-1794', *Revue du Nord* 50 (1968), p. 203-212.

16. Paul L. Nève, *Het Rijkskamergerecht en de Nederlanden,* Assen: Van Gorcum 1972. Through the Peace Treaties of Madrid (1526) and Cambrai (1529), the French King had already accepted that the County of Flanders was no longer a fief of the French crown so that the authority of the *Parlement de Paris* over the Council of Flanders ceased to exist.

17. Jan Dumolyn, 'The legal repression of the revolts in late medieval Flanders', *Tijdschrift voor Rechtsgeschiedenis* 68 (2000), p. 479-521.

each of the provinces. In the Western provinces, the representatives of the towns were dominant, while in the eastern parts of the Netherlands, the rural communities or the nobility held sway. After the Reformation, the clergy rapidly lost its representation. Philip the Good and Charles the Bold also tried to stimulate the union of their lands by convening the Estates General, a gathering of the delegates from the estates of all their territories. The first of these meetings took place in 1464. Under the Habsburg monarchs, the Estates General became increasingly important.[18] As much as the establishment of the Estates General was an element for centralization, they also became a powerful instrument for challenging princely authority. At her accession in 1477, Mary of Burgundy had to grant the *Grand Privilege* to the Estates in which she promised wide-ranging concessions in order to be recognized as Duchess by the Estates.[19]

The fact that through Charles V the Netherlands became part of the immense Habsburg power complex, held advantages as well as disadvantages. On the economic and commercial side, the benefits were apparent. And it was also thanks to the Habsburg political and military power that Flanders could gain independence and security from France. But on the other hand, the enormous power of Charles V and his son and heir, King Philip II of Spain (1555-1598), also allowed them to impose a policy of centralization and overcome much of the resistance by their subjects. In the long run, this would prove to be unproductive.

After his coming to power in Spain in 1516/1517, Charles V was absent from the Low Countries for most of his reign. Philip II ruled almost permanently from his new capital Madrid. During their absence, the Habsburg princes appointed a Governor General for the Netherlands, who was always a member of the Habsburg family. In the different provinces, they nominated a Governor or Stadholder to represent them.

The permanent tension between the local and provincial powers and the prince greatly increased during the last decades of Charles V's rule and under his son Philip II. The spread of Lutheranism and Calvinism in both the northern and southern provinces and the harsh repression of the new religions by the Habsburgs, offer only part of the explanation for the revolt of the 1560s that led to the Eighty Years War (1568-1648) and the final secession of the Northern Netherlands from the Habsburg-Spanish empire. Other factors that triggered the Revolt were the centralization policy, the bureaucratization and the loss of influence by the higher nobility, the curbing of local and provincial rights, the high level of taxes due to the endemic warfare of a great empire and the alienation of the 'natural prince' from his people.

The revolt began in earnest when Philip II sent the Duke of Alva (1507-1582) with an army to the Netherlands in 1567 in reaction to several rebellions of a

---

18. H.G. Koenigsberger, *Monarchies, States Generals and Parliaments. The Netherlands in the Fifteenth and Sixteenth Centuries*, Cambridge: Cambridge University Press 2001.
19. F.W.N. Hugenholze, 'The 1477 Crisis in the Burgundian duke's dominions', *Britain and the Netherlands* 2 (1962), p. 33-46.

religious and a social nature.[20] Although most of the nobles initially aided the Governor General in his attempt to restore order, the brutal actions of Alva alienated many of them. William of Orange (1533-1584), the richest and most powerful of the nobles in the Netherlands, had already fled the country and run to Germany in 1567. One year later, he invaded the Netherlands. The Eighty Years war had begun.

After some very harsh years and major setbacks, the rebellion suddenly gained ground in 1572. The capture of Den Briel proved to be a turning point. The massacre of thousands of Calvinists in Paris and France the same year strengthened the international solidarity among Protestants and this eventually aided the Dutch in winning international support. By 1575/1576, the Spanish military power had been temporarily quelled and royal authority was in deep crisis in the whole of the Low Countries. In 1576, the Estates General announced religious tolerance and many thought the Estates were in a strong position to force the King to accept their demands. The religious, linguistic and economical divisions now proved advantageous to the intransigent Philip II. By 1579, the new Spanish Governor Alessandro Farnese (1545-1592) had regained a strong foothold in the Walloon provinces in the south and in parts of Flanders and Brabant. In that year, seven northern provinces – Holland, Zealand, Utrecht, Gueldres, Overijssel, Frisia and Groningen – allied themselves in the Union of Utrecht.[21] Two years later, they deposed Philip II as their prince in the *Akte van Verlating*. After two unsuccessful attempts, the United Provinces finally gave up the ambition to find a new prince. Later on, they became known as the Republic. By 1609, the first year of the Twelve Years Truce, it was clear to almost everybody that the secession of the Northern Netherlands would be very hard to undo. Through the Treaty of Münster of 1648, the Spanish King Philip IV (1621-1665) finally accepted that he was no longer prince over the now eight – with Drente – northern provinces. Some years later, the last effective obligations to the Holy Roman Empire disappeared.[22]

3.2   The codification and homologation of customary law

The establishment of the first university of the Netherlands in Leuven in 1425 did a great deal to enhance the influence and significance of Roman law in the Low

---

20. Phyllis M. Crew, *Calvinist preaching and iconoclasm in the Netherlands, 1544-1569*, Cambridge: Cambridge University Press 1978.
21. J.C. Boogman, 'The Union of Utrecht: Its Genesis and Consequences', *Bijdragen en Mededelingen betreffende de Geschiedenis der Nederlanden* 94 (1979), p. 377-407.
22. On the Revolt in the Netherlands and the Eighty Years War: A. Duke, *Reformation and Revolt in the Low Countries*, London/Ronceverte: The Hambledon Press 1990; M. van Gelderen, *The Political Thought of the Dutch Revolt, 1555-1590*, Cambridge: Cambridge University Press 1992; idem, *The Dutch Revolt*, Cambridge: Cambridge University Press 1993; Pieter Geyl, *The Revolt in the Netherlands 1555-1609*, London: Benn 1932; Geoffrey Parker, *The Dutch Revolt*, London: Allen Lane 1977; idem, *Spain and the Netherlands 1559-1659. Ten studies*, London: Collins 1979; Robert Feenstra, 'A quelle époque les Provinces Unies sont-elles devenues indépendantes en droit à l'égard du Saint Empire?', *Tijdschrift voor Rechtsgeschiedenis* 20 (1952), p. 30-63.

Countries. The first Leuven jurists were commentators. As true scholastics, they accepted the Justinian code to be of authoritative value and the Roman law to be universal and timeless. The commentators were not only concerned with understanding and interpreting the Justinian texts, they also turned to Roman law to address contemporary legal problems. In doing so, the commentators started building a bridge between the *iura propria* and the *ius commune*. Commentators like the great Bartolus of Sassoferrato (1314-1357) and the afore cited Baldus de Ubaldis, produced an enormous amount of *consulta* in which they offered a solution from Roman law to the most diverse problems and cases.

The 16th century saw the rise of a new tendency in the study of Roman law that challenged the supremacy of the *mos italicus* of the commentators: the humanistic jurisprudence. Early on, the humanists gained a foothold in the Netherlands. Among the early humanists Gabriel Mudaeus (1501-1561), Nicolaus Everardus (1461-1532), Viglius van Aytta (1507-1577), Petrus Peckius (1529-1589) and Matthaeus Wesenbeckius (1531-1586) should be mentioned. As opposed to their predecessors and competitors – the commentators –, the humanists were more concerned with a correct understanding of Roman law as a historic legal system and less with its application as a universal, timeless ideal system of law. While in the short run, this led to a more esoteric and less practical approach of Roman law, in the long run, this paradoxically helped to tear down the walls between Roman jurisprudence and the *iura propria*. The historical approach to Roman law led to the watering down of its almost absolute authority, its universality and timelessness and by comparison increased the standing of other systems of law. From the 16th century on, the *iura propria* became the object of treatises in which the scientific methods and terminology of the *ius commune* were used to create a jurisprudence for the applicable law. This 'scientification' of law would turn out to be a process of many centuries and had in fact already begun with the writing down of customary law during the late Middle Ages. Some of the first important and more or less systematic treatises of law in the Netherlands, next to Philip of Leyden's work, were Philip Wielant's (1441-1520) books on civil and criminal procedure.[23] His work however only gained notoriety through the Latin version, published in his own name, by the Bruges humanist Joost de Damhouder (1507-1581). These treatises would deeply influence lawyers from the Netherlands as well as from other parts of Europe.

To these mostly unofficial endeavours of writing down and commenting upon the *iura propria*, the Habsburgs added their efforts. Their purpose was to strengthen their control over the local laws and where possible, to harmonize and unify the law. Inspired by the examples of the Valois Kings of France (the Ordinance of Montil-lez-Tours of 1454), Charles V in 1531 ordered all customs to be written down and sent to Brussels in order to be promulgated. Though this would give the local customs statutory authority, it also offered Charles the opportunity to 'correct' them before he homologated them. The codification and homologation could be an instrument of harmonization of the law. In truth, of the 700 customs that were written down and

---

23. *Practijcke civile* and *Pracktijcke criminele*.

sent to the prince, 600 were abolished. Of these 700, less than 100 stemmed from the northern Netherlands. The lack of success of Charles' initiative was also made clear by the continuous restating of the Ordinance of 1531. Anyway, at the beginning of the Revolt, the law of the northern provinces was largely uncodified. Where the law was codified and homologated, the spontaneous evolution of the local customary law was frozen. In the long run, this would necessitate more legislation.

As lords over the seventeen provinces of the Netherlands, the Habsburg princes Charles V and Philip II proved to be active legislators. Though they had to promulgate their laws seventeen times – as Duke of Brabant, Count of Flanders, Count of Holland etc. – they used statutory law as a means of unification for the whole of the Netherlands. Whereas most acts were rather limited in scope and only contained some very specific measures or rules, some were more ambitious and covered a whole subject. By the Ordinances of 1531 and 1570, Charles V and Philip II codified criminal procedure.

The establishment of a supreme court in each province and the foundation of the *Grand Conseil de Malines* were essential to the centralization of government and the unification of the law. The southern provinces and some of the northern ones like Holland and Zealand or Frisia (1499) already had a provincial court from the 15th century. In other provinces, a provincial court was created under Charles V: Utrecht in 1530, Gueldres in 1547, Overijssel in 1553. These courts were supreme in the sense that they controlled the lower courts within the province. They also functioned as the highest appellate court of the lordship. In general, they adopted the procedures of the French higher courts, which in turn were inspired by Roman law. By consequence, the provincial courts did a great deal to further the reception of Roman law in the Netherlands. The same was true for the *Grand Conseil de Malines*. This council, just as the *Parlement de Malines*, was intended to be the supreme and sovereign court of the Netherlands having appellate jurisdiction over all provincial courts.[24] In truth, some of these refused to recognize the authority of Malines in this respect and considered themselves to be sovereign. It is just another indication that even the most powerful princes like Charles V and Philip II were only partly successful in vesting their authority over the Netherlands.

4   The Dutch Republic

4.1   A loose confederation of states

When in 1648 the Spanish King Philip IV agreed to the Peace Treaty of Münster with the Estates General of the Republic and renounced his claims to the northern provinces, he did nothing else than confirm a situation that had been in place for decades. After the Twelve Years Truce (1609-1621), Spain never seriously hoped to regain the Northern Netherlands. In the three decades of war, it even lost important

---

24. From 1495 to 1548 the Netherlands were subjected to the appellate jurisdiction of the imperial *Reichskammergericht.*

places like Den Bosch (1629), Maastricht (1632) and Breda (1637). Through these and other conquests, the Dutch Republic now did not only control the historical territories of the eight provinces – Holland, Zealand, Utrecht, Gueldres, Frisia, Groningen, Overijssel and Drente – but also had to administer conquered lands such as the northernmost parts of the Duchy of Brabant (with Breda and Den Bosch) and of the County of Flanders (with Sluys, Hulst and Aardenburg). Moreover, the war had not been limited to Europe. Dutch privateers and traders had roamed the seas and attacked the ships and trade of their Spanish and Portuguese enemies. By the 1630s, the Dutch were on their way to establish a powerful commercial and colonial empire in the Eastern and Western Indies.[25]

In historiography, the 17th century became known as the Dutch Golden Age. By 1648, the Republic was, notwithstanding its small territory and population, one of the most powerful and influential maritime, commercial, military and political powers in Western Europe. After the rise of its Stadholder William III (1672-1702) to the thrones of England, Scotland and Ireland in 1689, it would however quickly lose its pivotal role as a leading Protestant power in Europe and fall back to a diplomatic and military position that was more in line with its demographic potential. On the high seas, the Republic had to cede its supremacy to the British.

Revolting against the 'natural prince' may not have been exceptional in 16th and 17th century Europe, the outcome of the rebellion was. The Dutch Revolt was in the first place a conservative revolution of the privileged classes in order to preserve their traditional rights and liberties against the onslaughts of regal absolutism. Such revolts, which often also had a religious or regionalist dimension, were common in Europe between 1500 and 1660. Medieval dualism fell victim to this struggle. But whereas in most countries civil strife between the monarch and the estates ended in royal victory and the power of the estates was curbed, such was not the case in the Netherlands. Here, the monarchy disappeared from the equation.

Even when they deposed the Spanish King in 1581, the Dutch provinces did not envision becoming a Republic without a prince. It was only in 1585, after the second failure to find a new overlord that they gave in to the idea of not having a monarch anymore. More generally, the new state that arose from the Revolt was not the result of conscious state building.

The Revolt was a conservative undertaking and no attempt was made to establish a set of new institutions. The Dutch made do with the institutions as they existed, although their respective roles and competences changed over time.

The closest thing to a constitutive Act the Republic had was the Union of Utrecht of 1579. This was in fact a treaty of permanent alliance between the then seven provinces – Drente would enter the alliance later. It involved a promise to stand by each other in the war against Spain and it regulated the joint war effort. In order to wage the war successfully and organize joint military and diplomatic actions, the seven sovereign provinces conserved some of the central institutions from the Burgundian and Habsburg period. But the Republic was in fact no more than a loose confederation of 'sovereign' states, be they still part of the Holy Roman Empire.

---

25. C.R. Boxer, *The Dutch Seaborne Empire, 1600-1800*, London: Hutchinson 1965.

Now that the prince was deposed, the sovereignty in each of the eight provinces fell to the provincial Estates. The composition of those differed. In each province, the daily business of government was delegated to a small group of members of the Estates, the *Gedeputeerde Staten*.

The highest authority in the Union was the Estates General, consisting of the representatives of the seven original provinces. Drente, which soon became part of the Republic, was not represented in this august body. Though the Estates General were called 'sovereign' in Europe, it was not they that held sovereignty but the Provincial Estates they represented.

Whereas before the Estates General only convened when convoked by the King, they now became a permanent institution with a permanent seat, the Binnenhof in The Hague. The Estates General was more of a permanent diplomatic conference of the members of the Union than a Parliament. In all important matters, unanimity between the provinces was obligatory. While in the daily business of the Republic, the ascendancy of Holland and Zealand over the others was great, the unanimity rule proved an effective means to curb the power of Holland and Zealand in crucial political questions.[26] The assembly held the highest authority in all matters concerning the union: warfare and the organization of the army and fleet, foreign relations, the administration of the conquered territories (the so-called *Generaliteitslanden*), the control over the East and West Indian Companies which ruled the colonial empire and the finances of the Union.[27] The most important functionary within the Estates was the Grand Pensionary of Holland, who acted as the effective minister of foreign affairs and leader of the Estates General. Famous historical leaders of the Republic like Johan van Oldenbarneveldt (1547-1619), Johan de Witt (1625-1672) and Simon van Slingelandt (1664-1736) held this position.[28]

Another Habsburg institution that endured was the Council of State. Historically, this most august of the Collateral Councils of Charles V, was an advisory body that was concerned with high politics. As such, it seemed to have the best position to become the true government of the Union. But it did not. The Estates General curbed its power and degraded it to a kind of permanent executive secretariat, entrusted with the preparation of its meetings and the execution of its decisions.

That the Dutch did not consciously choose to establish a republic, was made clear by the fact that the provinces continued to appoint a Stadholder. Originally, the

26. J.L. Price, *Holland and the Dutch Republic in the Seventeenth Century*, Oxford: Clarendon Press 1994.
27. On the Estates and the Estates General: J.H. Grever, 'Committees and Deputations in the Assemblies of the Dutch Republic 1666-1668', *Parliaments, Estates, Representations* 1 (1981), p. 13-33; idem, 'The Structure of Decision-Making in the States General of the Dutch Republic 1660-1668', *Parliaments, Estates, Representation* 2 (1982), p. 125-132; idem, 'The States of Friesland: Politics and Society during the 1660s', *Parliaments, Estates, Representation* 9 (1989), p. 1-25.
28. See on de Witt: Herbert H. Rowen, *John de Witt. Grand Pensionary of Holland, 1625-1672*, Princeton: Princeton University Press 1978; idem, *John de Witt: Statesman of the 'true freedom'*, Cambridge: Cambridge University Press 1986.

Stadholders were provincial governors who represented and replaced the Burgundians and Habsburg in each of their lordships during their absence.[29] Therefore, it would have been natural if this institution had disappeared after the deposition of the King. The fact that it had not, indicated that until some years after 1581 the Dutch held on to the idea that there was a throne to be filled and that they needed a replacement in the absence of a true prince. When the ambition to find a new monarch was given up, the Stadholderate was already secure in the hands of Maurice of Nassau (1584-1625), son of the *pater patriae* William of Orange.

Though in the absence of a prince the exact position of the Stadholder was uncertain – all the more since the Estates had taken over sovereignty – it quickly became an important function. It brought a monarchical element in the Republic. The Stadholderate of the most important provinces – among which always Holland and Zealand – was systematically attributed to the leader of the house of Orange-Nassau. In 1748, the Stadholderate of all the provinces became the hereditary right of the princes of Orange. The Republic then seemed on its way to become a monarchy as yet.

As Stadholders of the most powerful provinces, the Orange-Nassaus gained a pivotal role in the Union and its war effort. The Stadholders of the house of Orange were commanders-in-chief of the armies and fleet of the Union. William of Orange and his successors Maurice of Nassau, Frederick Henry (1625-1647) and William III were competent and successful generals who added glory to the reputation of their house. Certainly in times of war, the Orange Stadholders could strengthen their position and from time to time challenged the ascendancy of the Holland and Zealand towns with the help of the other provinces.[30] At other moments, as during the minority of the later William III (1650-1672) and in the early 18th century (1702-1747), there was no Stadholder. In those periods, the Grand Pensionary of Holland and the Estates General ruled more freely.

The Republic was born from a revolt against the centralization policy of the Habsburgs. In consequence, some of their achievements were reversed. Nevertheless, the Republic could not overcome the tensions between centralization and provincial autonomy. While most provinces had little interest in strengthening unity, until 1648 and even after, the Union was the only guarantee for liberty. The central institutions of the Union were themselves remnants of the Burgundian and Habsburg days. This and the ascendancy of two provinces over the others, could not but lead to new tensions between a central 'government' Holland and Zealand often wanted to strengthen and the six other provinces that held on to their autonomy.[31] The checks and balances that were inherent in the complex system of government of

---

29. P. Rosenfeld, 'The Provincial Governors from the Minority of Charles V to the Revolt, *Standen en Landen* 17 (1959), p. 1-53.
30. Herbert H. Rowen, *The princes of Orange. The Stadholders in the Dutch Republic*, Cambridge: Cambridge University Press 1988.
31. For a clear illustration thereof: R. Reitsma, *Centrifugal and Centripetal Forces in the Early Dutch Republic: the States of Overijssel, 1566-1600*, Amsterdam: Rodopi 1982.

the Republic however proved strong enough, if not to overcome the tension, then at least to sustain it.[32]

4.2   The Roman-Hollandic law

The Dutch Revolt led to a clear break with the Habsburg policy of the unification law. With the secession, the *Grand Conseil de Malines* lost its authority in the northern provinces. No new central authority was established. The Council of State in The Hague only had some extraordinary jurisdiction in military and political matters. The highest courts in the Republic were now the provincial courts and only Holland and Zealand had a common court. For the *Generaliteitslanden* in Brabant and Flanders a new Council of Brabant and a Council of Flanders were established in The Hague, as the old Councils were still under Spanish control.

In regaining their political autonomy, the provinces also took back their legal autonomy. In all provinces, the applicable law was a complex body of written and unwritten customary and statutory rules. After the deposition of Philip II, the legislative power fell to the Provincial Estates. In Holland (1580) and Zealand (1583), the assemblies used their new authority to codify and unify a large part of private, and in the case of Holland, procedural law. As was mentioned above, few customs had been sent to Brussels in execution of Charles V's Ordinance of 1531. However, under the Habsburg rule, many towns and localities, mostly in the northern and eastern parts of the later Republic, had written down their customs if not sent them in. During the 17th century, these efforts continued. By the end of the century, some provinces like Groningen had several written customs being applied within their borders.

As the Estates General had only limited power to legislate and as there was no central court, any attempt at harmonizing and unifying the law in the Republic, had to come from jurisprudence. And it did. First of all, the impact of Roman law on the provincial courts increased. The 17th century certainly marked a turning point in the reception of Roman law in the Northern Netherlands. Since the establishment of the *Reichskammergericht* in 1495 and the *Grand Conseil de Malines* in 1504, Roman law had gained recognition as supplementary law in the Low Countries. It continued to have this position under the Republic. Due to the establishment of several universities in the Republic around 1600 – Leyden (1575), Franeker (1585), Harderwijk (1600), Groningen (1614), and Utrecht (1636) – more legal practitioners had a Roman law academic background.

In 1579, the French humanist Hugo Donellus (1527-1591) accepted a chair at Leyden. His arrival stimulated the humanist jurisprudence at the new university.

---

32. S.J. Fockema Andreae, *De Nederlandse staat onder de Republiek*, Amsterdam: Noord-Hollandsche Uitgeversmaatschappij 1961; Robert Fruin, *Geschiedenis van de Staatsinstellingen in Nederland tot de val der Republiek*, 2nd ed., The Hague: Nijhoff 1922; M.C. 't Hart, *The Making of a Bourgeois State: War, Politics and Finance during the Dutch Revolt*, Manchester: Manchester University Press 1993; E.H. Kosmann, *Political Thought in the Dutch Republic. Three Studies*, Amsterdam: Amsterdam-KNAW 2000.

Donellus may be considered the father of the *Hollandse Elegante School*, the Hollandic school of humanist jurisprudence that dominated in the Republic for most of the 17th century.

The Hollandic School did not defend a merely historical approach to Roman law as the first generations of humanists had in the early 16th century. Like their Leuven humanist counterparts, the members of the Hollandic School in fact combined philological and historical correctness in the study of Roman law with a keen interest in contemporary law. They contributed greatly to the construction of a jurisprudence for the applicable law, embedding customary law into the systems and methods of Roman law tradition. In doing this, their work became instrumental to the formation of a Hollandic, and by extension, a Dutch legal system.

In this context, one cannot leave the great Dutch humanist Hugo Grotius (1583-1645) aside.[33] Though never a university professor, his legal thought was among the most influential in Dutch and European legal history. While imprisoned in the castle of Loevenstein for political reasons, Grotius wrote his *Inleidinge tot de Hollandsche Rechts-Geleerdheid*, which was first published in 1631. In this book, Grotius attempted to explain the law of Holland in a systematic way, often referring to Roman law to clarify or supplement the customs and laws of the province. This treatise quickly became the standard textbook of what Simon van Leeuwen (1626-1682) in 1652 coined as the Roman-Hollandic law. The name itself indicated how far the reception of Roman law had gone in the Republic in a few decades time.[34] The School of Holland and the Roman-Hollandic law also gained significance in other provinces of the Republic. The Roman-Hollandic law became a kind of gravitation point for the other provinces.[35]

The Hollandic School did not go unchallenged. There was also some influence of the German *usus modernus pandectarum*, which remained more faithful to the *mos italicus* and which proposed the application of the Justinian code as contemporary law of the Empire regardless of the historical realities behind it. This school held sway in the universities closer to Germany. Johannes Voet (1647-1713) was its most important adherent in the Republic.[36]

---

33. Charles S. Edwards, *Hugo Grotius The Miracle of Holland: A Study in Political and Legal Thought*, Chicago: Nelson-Hall 1981.

34. To this day, the Roman-Hollandic law offers the basis of private law in South Africa. Reinhard Zimmermann & D. Visser (eds.), *Southern Cross. Civil Law and Common Law in South Africa*, Oxford: Clarendon Press 1996.

35. René Dekkers, *Het humanisme en de rechtswetenschap in de Nederlanden*, Antwerpen [etc.]: De Sikkel [etc.] 1938; S.J. Fockema Andreae, *Het burgerlijk recht in de buitengewesten van Nederland*, Amsterdam: Noord-Hollandsche Uitgevers Mij 1955; J.H.A. Lokin, C. Janssen & F. Brandsma, *Het Rooms-Friese recht. De civiele rechtspraktijk van het Hof van Friesland in de 17e en 18e eeuw*, Hilversum: Verloren 1999; Reinhard Zimmermann & Robert Feenstra (eds.), *Das Römisch-Holländische Recht. Fortschritte des Zivilrechts im 17. und 18. Jahrhundert*, Berlin: Duncker & Hunblot 1992.

36. Govaert van den Bergh, *The Life and Works of Gerard Noodt (1647-1725). Dutch Legal Scholarship between Humanism and Enlightenment*, Oxford: Clarendon Press 1988. See on the faculty of Leyden and the different influences: Robert Feenstra & C.J.D. Waal, *Seventeenth-Century Leyden Law Professors. A Study of Bronchorst, Vinnius and Voet*, Amsterdam, Oxford [etc.]: North-Holland Publishing Company 1975.

Grotius not only had merits as the 'founding father' of the Roman-Hollandic law, he can also be considered the father of the modern School of Natural Law. In this respect, his *De jure belli ac pacis libri tres* of 1625 were the most influential. During the second half of the 17th century and the 18th century, the School of Natural Law gained a strong position at the German law faculties. Among its main representatives were Samuel Pufendorf (1632-1694) and Christian Wolff (1679-1754) whose works were also studied at the Dutch law faculties. The natural lawyers questioned the ascendancy of Roman law. They believed that the law had to be based on the moral/juridical premises that were inherent to human nature and rationality. From these first principles, it was possible for human intelligence to perceive or construct a complete, universal and unchangeable system of law without reference to existing historical systems. Though in practice the natural lawyers often had to reach back to existing law and to Roman law, their thought helped in further tearing down the pedestal Roman law traditionally stood on and opened the way for the creation of new legal systems, an ambition that was to materialize in the great codifications of the Revolutionary Era.[37]

One cannot discuss the legal history of the Republic, without at least making a brief reference to the preponderant role Dutch jurists played in the emergence of the modern law of nations. Although his 'fatherhood' of the modern law of nations is now in jeopardy,[38] one cannot deny that Grotius's *De jure belli ac pacis* greatly contributed to the articulation of the law of nations as an autonomous discipline. Grotius did of course draw on the works of his Neo-Scholastic and humanist predecessors and their treatises on aspects of the law of nations. Moreover, his work was not much more comprehensive than some of theirs. Nevertheless, the brilliancy of his synthesis of existing thought, the pragmatism that allowed him to articulate a theory that both legitimated the Dutch Revolt as well as Dutch, French and English colonialism and the high esteem his name was held in all combined to grant his work the stature of the first modern textbook of the law of nations.[39] Furthermore, as Grotius embedded the positive law of nations in a natural law framework, he became an inspiration to both the naturalist and the positive schools of the law of nations that emerged during the second half of the 17th century.[40]

---

37. A. Dufour, 'Grotius et le droit naturel du dix-septième siècle' in: *The World of Hugo Grotius (1583-1645)*, Amsterdam/Maarssen: APA-Holland University Press 1984, p. 25-41; Hendrik van Eikema Hommes, 'Grotius on Natural and International Law', *Netherlands International Law Review* 30 (1983), p. 61-71; K. Haakonssen, ed., *Grotius, Pufendorf and Modern Natural Law*, Aldershot/Sydney: Ashgate/Dartmouth 1999.

38. Wilhelm G. Grewe, 'Grotius – Vater des Völkerrechts', *Der Staat* 23 (1984), p. 161-178.

39. Hedley Bull, Benedict Kingsbury & Adam Roberts (eds.), *Hugo Grotius and International Relations*, Oxford: Clarendon Press 1990; Peter Haggenmacher, *Grotius et la doctrine de la guerre juste*, Paris: Presses Universitaires de France 1983; Richard Tuck, *The Rights of War and Peace. Political Thought and the International Order from Grotius to Kant*, Oxford: Oxford University Press 1999.

40. Another Dutchman, Cornelius van Bynkershoek (1673-1743) is traditionally considered to be one of the foremost representatives of the positivist school. Kinji Akashi, *Cornelius van Bynkershoek and his Role in the History of International Law*, The Hague: Kluwer Law International 1998. Akashi, as other historians of international law have recently done for other writers, warns however not to underestimate the significance of natural law in the thought of Bynkershoek.

5   The Revolutionary Era (1795-1813)

5.1   The French Revolution and the formation of the nation-state[41]

The second half of the 18th century was marked by a growing discontent with the political and legal situation in the Republic. As the ideas of the enlightened *philosophes* won a foothold in the Netherlands, the regime of the Orange Stadholders was increasingly challenged. The political, legal and fiscal privileges of the leading classes in the provinces and the Union were debated; the feudal system was felt to have become obsolete; corruption among public attorneys and other state officials was widespread and the judiciary arbitrariness, especially in criminal procedures, was increasingly criticized. This, together with the demands for more political freedom and democracy, led to a first 'patriotic' revolt in the 1780s. Only with the help of the Prussian King, could the hereditary Stadholder William V of Orange (1751-1795), quell this rebellion in 1787. No less than 6,000 patriots chose exile in France.[42]

When the French Revolution started to spread over Western Europe in the 1790s, the Republic was ripe for it. In 1793, France declared war on Britain and its ally, the Republic. In January 1795, the French general Pichegru invaded the Republic. The Stadholder had to flee to Britain and the patriots returned to the Netherlands. They proclaimed the Batavian Republic and replaced the Estates General by a National Assembly. Inspired by the French Revolution, the Dutch revolutionaries wanted a written constitution, which would include a declaration of fundamental rights and freedoms. A first proposal was however rejected by the overall majority of the electorate in 1797. To overcome the political stand-off that ensued, the more radical unitarists staged a bloodless *coup d'état* and enforced their constitution upon the Republic.

This 1798 Constitution was modelled on the most radical examples from France, the constitutions of the Convention of 1793 and 1795. The farthest-reaching and most permanent change undoubtedly was the fact that sovereignty was taken from the provinces and transferred to the Republic. With one stroke, the Dutch Republic became a unitary and centralized state. The eight provinces were abolished. Eight departments, with new borders, new names and very limited competences let alone autonomy, came in their place. The former *Generaliteitslanden* now became an integral and equal part of the Republic. The departments were under the strict control of the central government.

The 1798 Constitution was heavily influenced by the ideas of the French philosopher Jean-Jacques Rousseau (1712-1778). The Batavian Republic was considered to be one nation and all old divisions and discriminations disappeared. The separation of Church and State was proclaimed and the privileges of the estates and the feudal system were abolished. The Constitution guaranteed some

---

41. *Simon Schama, Patriots and Liberators. Rebellion in the Netherlands 1780-1813*, London: Collins 1977.
42. L. Leonard Leeb, *The Ideological Origins of the Batavian Revolt*, The Hague: Nijhoff 1973.

fundamental rights to the people, equality before the law being foremost among them. The legislative power was vested in the Representative Assembly. The Members of Parliament were considered to the representatives of the whole Dutch nation and not of the department or estates. The Representative Assembly elected and controlled the Executive. Ministerial departments were formed to help the Executive in the daily business of governing. Although the Constitution guaranteed equality, the right to vote was limited. Whole categories of the poorer classes were excluded from this democratic right so that the Batavian Republic became a bourgeois state.

The Constitution of 1798 was amended in 1801. Some of the more radical changes were reversed. The departments regained the old provincial borders and names. Drente was added to Overijssel while Brabant now became the eighth department.

For all practical purposes, the Batavian Republic was a satellite of revolutionary France and its ally – if often an unwilling one – in its wars against Britain. In 1805, the French Emperor Napoleon I (1804-1815) enforced a new regime upon the Republic. The Constitution of 1805 concentrated power in the hands of one state official, the Grand Pensionary. This was to be Napoleon's trustee, the former Dutch ambassador in Paris, Rutger Jan Schimmelpenninck (1761-1825). This change of regime was to guarantee that the Republic would be more loyal to Paris in its struggle with Britain and the counter-revolutionary forces in Europe.

Schimmelpenninck however failed in his assignment as he could not sufficiently get a grasp on affairs in The Hague. Already in 1806, he was deposed. Napoleon now installed his own younger brother Louis as King of Holland in the Netherlands. The fourth Constitution abolished the Republic and turned the Netherlands into a constitutional monarchy. The King ruled, aided by his Ministers. The Council of State, which had been restored in 1805 as an advisory body, now became the place where the King, his Ministers and the Councillors of State met to discuss and prepare legislation. The local and departmental administration was entrusted to appointed state officials instead of locally elected councils. King Louis moved his capital to Amsterdam.

This new regime again proved to be unsatisfactory for the Emperor Napoleon. The Netherlands were still a reluctant and untrustworthy ally and its long coastline continued to be a major weakness in the blockade of Britain. In 1810, Napoleon's patience was exhausted and he decided to take matters into his own hands. That year, he recalled his brother to Paris and annexed the Netherlands to his French Empire. On 1 January 1811, the Netherlands ceased to exist as an independent state. Its now seven departments, with once again new borders and names, were added to France and were administrated by prefects sent from Paris. All local administrators like mayors and local councillors were centrally appointed.

This unsettling situation was not to be imposed for a long time on the Netherlands. In October 1813, Napoleon suffered a crushing defeat at the Battle of Leipzig. In November 1813, William of Orange, son of William V, sailed from England and landed at Scheveningen. Some days later, he was proclaimed Sovereign Prince of the Netherlands and assumed the throne. From then on, he started working to gain recognition by the allied victors of Napoleon, assembled at the Vienna Convention.

5.2   The codification under the French regime

Among the ideas the French Revolution defended, the reform of the legal system held a prominent place. Inspired by the School of Natural Law and the Enlightenment, the revolutionaries dreamt of replacing the inextricable jumble of rules the old system had decayed into by a rational, transparent and unified legal system. In doing so, they hoped to limit the arbitrary power of the myriads of courts and institutions, which were monopolized by the privileged classes. By making the law more transparent, it would become accessible to all and would become an instrument of equality. However democratic and modern these ideals may seem, in truth the bourgeois revolutionaries were only concerned with breaking the power of the traditional privileged classes and not with the fate of the lower classes.

The two main reforms the revolutionaries sponsored in order to achieve these aims were the reform of the judiciary system and the codification of the law. Both reforms were adopted by the Batavian Republic. However, in the matter of judicial reform the Batavian government proved unsuccessful. The plan to abolish all existing courts and replace them by a hierarchy of Courts of First Instance, Departmental Courts and a supreme National Court was only partly executed. Only when the Netherlands became part of the French Empire in 1811, judicial reform could be enforced.

By the annexation to France and the subjection of the Netherlands to the French Constitution and French legislation, all the old and traditional courts all of a sudden disappeared and the French judicial organization was introduced. The territory was divided into *cantons* which each had a justice of the peace who held jurisdiction in smaller cases. Several *cantons* formed an *arrondissement*, the seat of the Court of First Instance which held general and residuary jurisdiction. In each department there was a *Cour d'Assises* where a jury heard cases concerning the most severe crimes. The Courts of First Instance of the departmental capitals also functioned as the Court of Appeal for the whole department. Against the verdicts of the Dutch courts in second or final instance, an appeal in cassation was possible to the French *Cour de Cassation* in Paris. The Imperial Court in The Hague only ensured the disciplinary control over the courts in the Netherlands. By the introduction of this unified and hierarchical court system, the judiciary system could now start to function as a factor of unification and not of diversity and discrimination as the old courts had.

The codification too proved to be a tedious problem. Article 28 of the 1798 Constitution of the Batavian Republic foresaw that the whole civil, criminal and procedural law would be codified by May 1800. This was far too optimistic. In September 1798, a commission of twelve was installed to prepare the codes. The commissioners divided the work over three subcommittees: one for the civil code, one for the penal code and one for the code of procedure. The civil code commission was dominated by Hendrik Constantijn Cras (1739-1820), a staunch defender of natural law. However, he and his colleagues did not believe it feasible to create a whole system of civil law on the basis of the rationalistic natural law and they thought it necessary to refer back to existing law like Roman law and the own 'national' laws. By consequence, it seemed logical to look for inspiration in Grotius's *Inleidinge* as this work itself offered a synthesis of 'natural' principles, Roman law and Hollandic customary law. The civil code subcommittee did not succeed in preparing a draft by 1800, not even by 1806. The only committee to succeed in its task was the one for the code of procedure. Its draft was accepted by the Representative Assembly, but it was not put into effect before the accession of Louis in 1806.

After the coming to power of Napoleon's brother, the codification program was sped up. The Commission of Twelve was sent home. In 1807, the Emperor Napoleon I ordered his brother to introduce his own *Code Civil* or *Code Napoléon* of 1804 in the Kingdom of Holland. Louis, who liked to stress his independence and was keen to strengthen his position in the Netherlands, refused to do so and installed a new commission. He assigned the commission the task to draft a Dutch version of the *Code Civil* and allowed them to use for inspiration the draft Johannes van der Linden had already made for the King. Following this advice, the commission could terminate its work by May 1808 and a year later the *Wetboek Napoleon, ingerigt voor het Koningrijk Holland* became the law of the land. With its introduction, all the traditional laws and law systems were abolished and one of the main ambitions of the Revolution was attained. The *Wetboek Napoleon* was not the only code King Louis could introduce. In 1809, a penal code, the *Crimineel Wetboek voor het Koningrijk Holland*, was accepted as well.

Upon the annexation of the Netherlands by Napoleon, he decreed that all French laws would apply in his new departments. Although the Dutch codes were not explicitly abolished, they were superseded by the Napoleonic codes. This meant that there were now codes for all the main branches of the law. In addition to the *Code Civil* (1804) and the *Code pénal* (1810), also the *Codes de commerce* (1807), the *Code de procédure civile* (1806) and the *Code d'instruction criminelle* (1808) now applied in the Netherlands. After his accession in 1813, Prince William did not strike them off the tables immediately but left them – if temporarily – in force.

6   The Kingdom of the Netherlands (1813-present)

6.1   From nation-state to European integration[43]

The fall of the Napoleonic regime marked the end of the era of the French Revolution and led to the Restoration of many of the European dynasties to their thrones. The Restoration however did not reverse all the achievements of the Revolution. This was also the case in the Netherlands. While the Princes of Orange could restore and even, from a formal point of view, strengthen their position, they left some of the reforms of the Revolution in place. The Netherlands continued on

---

43. P.J. Oud & J. Bosmans, *Staatkundige vormgeving in Nederland*, 2 vol., 11th ed., Assen: Van Gorcum 1995.

as a unified and centralized state – which was only to the advantage of the monarch and of the dominant provinces Holland and Zealand. A new written constitution was introduced which stipulated a limited separation of powers and some fundamental rights and freedoms were safeguarded.

For fifteen years, from 1815 to 1830, the historical unity in the Low Countries was restored. In 1814 and 1815, the great powers of Europe convened at Vienna to redraw the map of Europe. In order to contain France, they wanted to strengthen some of its neighbours. Belgium and the Netherlands were united in what now became the Kingdom of the Netherlands. King William I (1815-1840) of Orange was also raised to the Grand Duchy of Luxemburg that became a member of the Deutsche Bund. Britain, that had occupied and administered most of the Dutch colonies during the Napoleonic wars, now returned them, except for the Cape, Ceylon and part of Guyana. During the 19th century, the Dutch could expand their empire in the Indies, nowadays Indonesia.

The 1814 constitution attributed the executive power to the King. He appointed both the advisory Council of State and his Cabinet Ministers. These were solely responsible to him. The members of the legislative body, the States General (*Staten Generaal*), were elected by the Provincial States. The members of the States General could introduce Bills and Acts themselves but could not force them upon the King. The right to vote was restricted to the upper classes. Upon the unification with the Belgian provinces, the constitution was amended. The freedom of the churches was enlarged, the freedom of the press got into the constitution and the States General now consisted of two Chambers. The members of the First Chamber were appointed by the King.

The religious, economical and linguistic differences made the Dutch-Belgian political marriage a tedious one. The autocratic regime of William I did nothing to relieve the displeasure of the Belgian bourgeoisie. A new revolution in Paris in the summer of 1830 inspired the Belgian liberals and Catholics to revolt themselves. By 1831, the Kingdom of Belgium was a fact and the main European powers accepted its existence. The British imposed a treaty of partition upon both countries whereby the western part of Luxemburg was ceded to Belgium and the Netherlands obtained half of the province of Limburg with Maastricht. William I refused to accept the treaty until 1839.

His refusal to recognize Belgium's independence had isolated the Netherlands internationally and greatly weakened the internal position of William I. In 1840, he amended the constitution and then decided to abdicate and left for Germany. In 1848, his successor William II (1840-1849), wanting to prevent the spread of a new Paris revolt to his country, gave in to the liberal demands and allowed a radical reform of the Dutch constitution.

In 1840, William I had already been forced to cede to some of the liberal demands. Cabinet Ministers were no longer immune from criminal prosecution and the States General from now on had to approve a budget every two years. The liberal leader J.R. Thorbecke (1798-1872) was the architect of the constitutional reform of 1848 that made the Netherlands a true parliamentary monarchy. Some fundamental rights and freedoms as the right of association and assembly were inscribed. Cabinet

Ministers were now subjected to the political control of the States General, who also obtained the right of interpellation. The members of the Second Chamber were elected directly, while the members of the First Chamber were to be appointed by the Provincial States. The position of the Provincial States and local councils was strengthened to the detriment of the Royal Commissioners and the Mayors who were regal appointees. Franchise was extended to a larger number of citizens but was still conditional on paying a minimal amount of taxes. Political life during the second half of the 19th century was dominated by the struggle between liberals and the conservative confessionalist groups of Protestants and Catholics. Once they had regained their religious rights and the hierarchy of the Catholic Church had been restored in the Netherlands (1853), the Catholics soon became a political power to reckon with. In the struggle over the place of religion in education, one of the main issues in the late 19th century, Protestants and Catholics even allied themselves against the liberals. From 1888 to 1891, they formed a Cabinet.

The more autocratic William III (1849-1890) had a hard time accepting parliamentary control over 'his' Cabinets. By 1868, it was however established that a Cabinet that had been rejected by two Parliaments, would be sent home by the King. In 1887, the right to vote was extended once again as the tax condition was dropped. However, the poorer classes could still be excluded in other ways.

At the death of William III in 1890, his daughter Wilhelmina (1898-1948) was the sole heir. As the throne of Luxemburg could not be inherited by a woman at the time, this put an end to the personal union between the Netherlands and Luxemburg.

Though the Netherlands could maintain their neutrality during the Great War (1914-1918), they did not escape all of its economical and political consequences. As in other countries, the political elite deemed it wise to speed up the process of democratization and thus limit the dangers of revolt. In 1917, the Constitution was amended again. General franchise for all male citizens was inscribed. Women had to wait till 1922 to obtain suffrage.[44] The first-past-the-post-system was replaced by a proportional system for the elections of the Second Chamber. These reforms brought the electoral collapse of the liberals and strengthened the hands of the Catholics and the social-democrats. From then onwards, the Netherlands were constantly governed by a coalition of parties. In the period between the World Wars, Cabinets were dominated by the Protestant and Catholic parties.

The Netherlands did not escape World War II (1939-1945). In May 1940, the country was attacked and occupied by Germany. Queen Wilhelmina and her government fled into exile to London. As was the case with most European powers, the war drained most of the economic power of the Netherlands and destroyed its control over its colonial empire. After the liberation in 1945, the Dutch could not regain control over their colonies in the Indies. After a senseless and bloody military repression of the Indonesian rebellion, The Hague had to recognize the independence of the Indonesian Republic in 1949.

---

44. The electoral reform was part of a larger political compromise, which extended to the problems of public and confessional educations.

Like in most countries of Western Europe, the economic and political recovery after 1945 in the mainland was surprisingly swift. In order to contain Soviet expansion, the US chose to maintain a strong military and political presence in Europe. Its Marshall funds helped finance the reconstruction of industry. The Dutch coalition governments – mostly coalitions of the confessional parties with either the social-democrats or the liberals – construed an official network of social protection. The welfare state for the larger part survived the crises of the 1970s and 1980s. Under the socialist-liberal coalitions of the late 1990s (1994-2002), a more liberal economical and social policy was proposed to strengthen the Dutch economy in relation to its main competitors. Though successful in this, the coalition parties took an electoral beating in 2002, partly as a consequence of discontent with budget cuts in the education, social security and justice departments. As in other European countries, four decades of affluence have made it hard to maintain an acceptable balance between economic necessities and the demands of the welfare state and its hedonistic culture.

In the decades following the war, the US supported European integration, both to soothe French fears of a resurrection of Germany and to strengthen the West against a Soviet onslaught. The Netherlands became one of the earliest and staunchest supporters of Atlantic solidarity and European integration. Together with Belgium and Luxemburg, the Netherlands founded the Benelux as a free-trade zone in 1944. The country entered the Council of Europe (1949), Nato (1949) as well as the European Community for Coal and Steel (1951), the European Economic Community (1957) and Euratom (1958). Those last three organizations merged in 1967 to form the European Community (1967), now the European Union (1992). European integration implied that the Netherlands like the other Member States, ceded large parts of its economic, political and juridical autonomy to Brussels.

6.2   The Dutch codifications

One of the revolutionary achievements that were not turned back during the Restoration was the codification of the law. Upon his accession to the throne of the Netherlands, William I expressed the desire to have his own Dutch codes. Article 100 of the 1814 Constitution provided for the re-codification of civil, criminal, commercial and procedural law. Though some prominent lawyers and politicians were content to keep the French codes, the political opposition to everything French was too strong to deny. In April 1814, William I appointed a commission. Joan Melchior Kemper (1776-1824), professor at the Leyden Law Faculty, soon came to dominate his colleagues in the commission. The extensive draft for a civil code of the commission, which was submitted in 1816, was heavily dependent upon the old Roman-Hollandic law. This Dutch bloodline of the proposed code was all the more inconvenient by then since Belgium had now been united with the Netherlands. To overcome Belgian resistance, the King appointed three Belgian jurists to judge the Kemper proposal, among whom the Walloon Judge Pierre Thomas Nicolaï (1736-1836) took precedence. The Belgian commissioners rejected the Kemper draft and

Kemper was forced to amend his proposal. His new code did not make it through Parliament however when it was discussed there in 1820. For the next nine years, Parliament itself worked on a new code. The influence of Nicolaï, now a Member of Parliament, was tantamount. The draft that came out of these parliamentary efforts was very close to the *Code Civil*, though some concessions to both the Dutch and the Belgian old practices were made. The new Code was accepted in Parliament and would have obtained force of law on 1 February 1831. By that time however, Belgium was in revolt and the code's introduction was postponed.

Parliament now decided to rework the 1830 draft and not to return to the 1816 or 1820 'Dutch' drafts by Kemper. By consequence, the Dutch Civil Code of 1838 remained very close to the 1804 Napoleonic code. Twenty years of experience with the French codes had made the Dutch familiar with their relative clarity and brevity. However, important anti-French feelings still existed by the 1830s; the Netherlands held on to the same policies of centralization and economic and social liberalism the French laws incarnated. A return to the more traditional 'Dutch' law would maybe have awakened the desire to restore provincial and local autonomy and diversity. For the same reasons, the French judicial organization was maintained. In place of the Paris *Cour de Cassation*, the *Hoge Raad* (Supreme Court) was founded in The Hague to serve as the Dutch court of cassation.

Not only civil law was re-codified in the 1800s. For commercial and procedural law, drafts had been prepared during the period of the United Netherlands. After revision in the 1830s, the codes of commerce, of criminal and of civil procedure easily made it through Parliament and became applicable as of 1 October 1838. An attempt to make a new criminal code already failed in 1815. Many later reforms to the *Code pénal* failed as well, until a new criminal code made it through Parliament in 1886. This code was far from complete and many supplementary laws had to be added.

By 1838, most of Dutch law had been re-codified. From the second half of the 19th century onwards, it became increasingly clear that the ideals of timelessness and completeness of the code would remain just that. Many amendments had to be made to the codes while whole new branches of law – especially in social security law, labour law, economic law and public law – were developed through parliamentary legislation. The demands of the changing society forced the judiciary as well as doctrine to play a more active and creative role in the interpretation and application of the law.

In France and Belgium, the Exegetic School dominated the scholarly debate. This School defended the strict obedience to the codes and limited the role of doctrine to the interpretation of the codes. The Dutch law faculties were more open to the German jurisprudence of the Historic School of Friedrich Carl von Savigny (1779-1861) and his followers and of the *Interessenjurisprudenz* of Rudolf von Jhering (1818-1892). Both schools had in common that they considered law to be the product of historical circumstances and rejected the claims to absolute validity of the codes in particular and of positive law in general. In the Netherlands, the Utrecht professor Hamaker (1844-1911) severed the links between positive law – the codes and legislation – and the 'natural law' it derived its authority from. He reinstated social relevance of the law as a criterion and revalued the role of the judge in the process of the interpretation and evolution of the law.[45]

These evolutions in legislation, jurisdiction and doctrine greatly diminished the impact of the codes on law and society by 1945. At the end of World War II, the Netherlands however took the surprising step to re-codify civil law. In 1947, the Leyden professor E.M. Meijers (1880-1954) was asked to draft a new code. Though Meijers himself had already done a lot of preparatory work, it took up to 1992 before the new code became law. The new code is in many respects different from the old and thus from the French civil code. It attributes a greater role to considerations of equity than the old code and is much more open to other sources of law than just legislation. As such, it might prove to be more adaptable to the demands of society. If ever a European Civil Code sees the light of day, the Dutch Code might be an inspiration.

45. Egide Spanoghe & Robert Feenstra (eds.), *Honderdvijftig jaar rechtsleven in België en Nederland 1830-1980*, Leyden: Universitaire Pers Leiden 1981; Emile Van Dievoet, *Het burgerlijk recht in België en Nederland van 1800 tot 1940. De rechtsbronnen*, Antwerp/The Hague: De Sikkel/Nijhoff 1943.

3 Dutch Ways of Doing Justice*

Maria IJzermans

1 Dispute resolution

When people have a conflict, there are all kinds of ways to resolve it. The parties could talk it out, fight it out or ignore it. In most societies, parties in a conflict are encouraged to call in a third party – someone who has no part in the conflict – to impose a solution. To resolve conflicts or disputes with legal aspects, the government provides a judicial organization, with judges who are part of an established judiciary, who act according to strict legal rules of procedure and who have the power to enforce the decision: formal justice. In case of legal conflicts, it is often possible to take a less formal course and to call in a different arbiter to reach a solution: informal justice.

1.1 Formal justice

Anyone living in the Netherlands has the right to take a matter to court. The court is still the pre-eminent place in our society where justice is administered by an impartial judge – appointed by the Crown for life – and where strict procedures are used. It is the best way to obtain an enforceable result. This *formal* course takes the opponents to the judicature, whose power is guaranteed in the Constitution *(Grondwet)*. The court system is regulated in the Judiciary Organization Act *(Wet op de rechterlijke organisatie)*. The judiciary is based on the following principles:

Independence
The political organization of the kingdom is based on Montesquieu's *Trias Politica*. There is a system of checks and balances between the three powers of the state, which are in principle attributed to three branches of government: the legislative, executive and judicial power.[1] The judicial power is independent of the other powers. With regard to this independence, the distinction between the two branches of the judiciary – judges and prosecutors – is extremely relevant. Judges are appointed for life, although they have to retire at 70. Judges can only be expelled from office in cases specified by the law, for instance, when convicted of a criminal offence. Their salary is established by law. Prosecutors are subordinate to the Minister of Justice. The Minister can give instructions to the Prosecution concerning how to perform the job. Prosecutors can be fired.[2]

---

* Many thanks to Ineke Sijtsma for her corrections of the English.
1 See also Chapter 4, section 3.2 about the Trias Politica.
2 About the tasks of the prosecutor, see also Chapter 6, section 4.2.

Impartiality

The court should be impartial, which means that a judge cannot give preference to one of the parties. If one party in a court case questions a judge's impartiality, it can challenge him, that is, request that the judge be taken off the case. Then, the proceedings are suspended, so the judge can decide whether he will withdraw from the case or whether he will contest the challenge. In the latter case, the permission to challenge will be handled by a panel of three judges.

Three instances

In principle, justice will be administered in three instances: two factual instances and cassation *(cassatie)* as the final recourse. In first instance and in appeal, the judges decide questions both of fact and of law, whilst appeal in cassation is restricted to questions of law. Cassation is administered by the Supreme Court *(Hoge Raad)*.[3]

The public nature of court sessions

Court sessions are public unless the law makes an exception. If a judge in a certain case fears for the disturbance of the public order, he (or she) can close the doors of the courtroom and shut the public out. This hardly ever happens. It does occur in criminal cases concerning juveniles or dealing with sex crimes that the doors are shut to protect the juvenile or the victim of the sex crime.

Article 121 of the Constitution *(Grondwet)* provides that judgements have to be pronounced in public. As a consequence, many court decisions are published in various legal magazines. Publication is not done by a public institution, such as the courts themselves or the Ministry of Justice, but by commercial publishers. The publishers are dependent on, for instance, an attorney or a public prosecutor to indicate an interesting judgement. Nowadays, more and more courts publish their judgements on the Internet.[4]

Professionalism

Dutch judges must have a law degree and additional training within the courts (see section 3). There are no juries and almost no laymen involved in administering justice. Nevertheless, when laymen do participate, it is only in mixed tribunals, led by a professional lawyer functioning as chairman. For instance, the Rent Assessment Committee *(Huurcommissie)*, which deals with disputes concerning the renting of houses, consists of a representative of the tenants as well as a representative of the landlords and the chairman is a lawyer (see section 5).

---

3   Cassation originated from the similar French institution.
4. The easiest way to find important judgements is to surf the site: http://www.rechtspraak.nl (Dutch only).

1.2 Informal justice

There is often a more *informal* way of resolving legal conflicts. In these informal procedures, most of the above-mentioned principles do not play a decisive role in the form of the procedure. The arbitrator in such procedures is not necessarily a member of the judicature, the procedure is less strict and the judgement is only enforceable after the formal procedure has been followed too.

Sometimes, the legislature creates such an informal procedure to resolve a conflict, when there is a difference in power between the parties, such as between a landlord and a tenant, or between a private individual and a public institution. The less powerful party has a much better opportunity to present his or her objections if the procedure is less formal. An example is the Rent Assessment Committee, mentioned above, and the National Ombudsman (see section 5). There are also areas of law where contracting parties and professional groups create their own alternative to the judicial procedure, by choosing arbitration by an arbitrator with professional knowledge (for instance, the Medical Disciplinary Committee *(Medisch Tuchtcollege)*, which handles complaints about doctors) or with knowledge of the trade (for instance, the various complaints commissions dealing with consumer complaints, see section 5).

2 The judiciary

2.1 The judicial organization

The courts
The judicial system was designed in the 19th century. The Judicial Organization Act dates from 1827 and has been frequently changed since. The last fundamental changes took place in various steps between 1990 and 2001: the organization of the courts and their jurisdiction has been restructured.

The courts that make up the judiciary are the District Court *(arrondissements-rechtbank)*, the Court of Appeal *(gerechtshof)* and the Supreme Court *(Hoge Raad)*. The country is divided into five areas of jurisdiction *(ressorten)*, each with one court of appeal in the main city of the *ressort*. The five Courts of Appeal are located in Amsterdam, Den Haag, Arnhem, Leeuwarden and Den Bosch. The five *ressorts* are divided into nineteen districts *(arrondissementen)*. In every *arrondissement*, a District Court *(arrondissementsrechtbank)* has jurisdiction.[5] The Supreme Court *(Hoge Raad)* has its seat in Den Haag.[6]

The courts are subdivided into divisions: the district court into a civil, an administrative, a criminal and a local division *(kantonsector)*; the Court of Appeal in a civil, a criminal and a fiscal division. The Supreme Court is divided into four

---

5. *Ressort* and *arrondissement* are French words only used in Dutch to indicate the division of the country into districts in which a specific court has jurisdiction.
6. This city, also known as The Hague, is not the capital of the Netherlands, which is Amsterdam, but it is the seat of Government.

divisions: a civil, a criminal and a fiscal one and a division for complaints about judges. The administrative judiciary has a slightly different organization than the civil and the criminal judiciary (see paragraph 2.4).

Every court has its own secretariat *(griffie)* which consists of lawyers and office clerks. The lawyers are the registrars *(griffiers)* who assist the judge by making the minutes of the court sessions and by writing drafts of the judgements in simple cases.

Council for the Judiciary *(Raad voor de rechtspraak)*

On 1 January 2002, the Council for the Judiciary *(Raad voor de rechtspraak)* was established. In many European countries, there is an equivalent of this Council, which represents and supports the judiciary as a whole in matters of finance and policy. In broad outlines, there are two reasons to establish such a Council. The first motive is to enhance the public's confidence in the judiciary and in its authority. The second is to encourage the efficiency of the courts, which was the main reason why the Council was established in the Netherlands. The Council consists of five members who are nominated by the Minister of Justice and appointed by Royal Decree for six years. The members of the Council are experienced judges. The Council negotiates with the Minister of Justice about the budget for all the courts, it assists the court management, it supervises the financial policy of each court, and it tries to increase efficiency and to improve computerization. The Council functions as a spokesperson for the courts and promotes their interests.

This Council is a controversial novelty. Parliament, lawyers and the public feared for the independence of the courts and still fear that the focus on the quality of management and efficiency will be to the detriment of legal quality, that is, the quality of the courts' decisions. Opponents resigned themselves to the establishment of the Council because the Minister assured that the Council would only be engaged in management and not in administering justice itself, nor in the selection of judges.

Public Prosecution Service *(Openbaar Ministerie)*

The Public Prosecution Service *(Openbaar Ministerie)* is a subdivision of the judiciary. During a trial, the Public Prosecutor stands next to the table where the judges sit. This position is indicative of the role of the prosecutor representing the state in the criminal process (see paragraph 2.4). The main tasks of the Public Prosecution are in the field of criminal law:
– to supervise investigations and inquiries that are carried out by the police;
– to take the decision whether or not to prosecute and on what charges;
– to act on behalf of the state during the trial and prove that the accused committed the crime (it is not for the accused to prove his innocence);
– to execute penal sentences.

2.2   Jurisdiction

The courts hear civil, criminal and administrative cases. In most cases, the District Court is the first instance court, except in administrative matters, when the procedure is slightly different. As mentioned in section 2.1, the District Court is

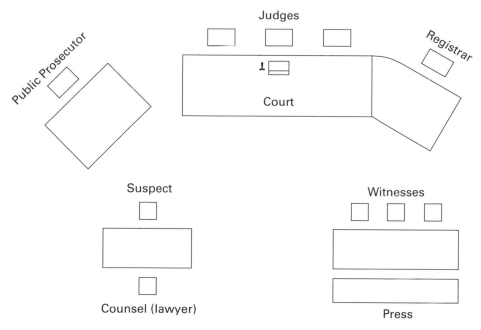

Figure 2 - The Court Room: Criminal Division of the District Court

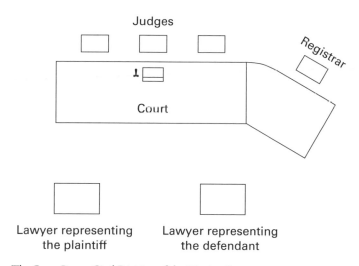

Figure 3 - The Court Room: Civil Division of the District Court

divided into divisions, among others the local division *(kantonsector)*. Until recently, this local division was a separate court, which was highly accessible. In the recent restructuring of the judicial organization, the 62 local courts were integrated into the nineteen district courts, but only at the administrative level, which means that the informal characteristics of these local courts have been preserved. So, in the district courts, two different kinds of legal proceedings exist side by side. In the local section, the single judge *(kantonrechter)* hears small civil claims; these are claims of less than € 5000 and all claims regarding labour law and rent law. In criminal cases, the jurisdiction of the local devision is restricted to (minor) offences such as traffic offences, poaching, noise nuisance, public drunkenness and all the offences described in the third book of the Criminal Code *(Wetboek van Strafrecht)*.[7]

In the district court, the first instance judge usually sits alone as well. Only if the single judge finds the case too complicated, will he (or she) refer it to a full panel of three judges. The jurisdiction of the district court is general; this means that whenever the law does not indicate a particular court, the district court has jurisdiction. Dependent upon the subject matter, civil law, criminal law or administrative law, one of the three corresponding divisions deals with the case.

In general, there is an appeal instance after every first instance court. There are some exceptions to this rule: for instance, no appeal is possible for civil claims smaller than € 1750. In most cases the Court of Appeal *(gerechtshof)* is the appeal court. This court sits with three Justices *(raadsheren)*. In appeal, the appeal court once more decides on points of fact and of law; in other words, the lawsuit is reviewed completely.

A full panel of the Supreme Court consists of five Lords Justices, but a panel of three deals with most cases. In cassation, the Supreme Court does not decide on the facts of the case: it accepts the facts as the lower courts have ascertained them. The main function of cassation is to guarantee uniformity in the interpretation of the law. If a decision of a lower court is subject to cassation, the Court considers whether the decision violates any rules of procedure or a rule of law.[8] The Supreme Court can confirm the judgement or set it aside. In the latter event, there are three options: (i) the Supreme Court nullifies the decision and refers it back to the same court which decided on the case; (ii) it nullifies the decision and sends it to another court of appeal; (iii) it overrules the decision and passes judgement itself.

> Supreme Court: 3 or 5 Lords Justices
>
> 5 Courts of Appeal: 3 or 5 Justices
>
> 19 District Courts: 1 or 3 Judges

Figure 4

---

7. The jurisdiction of the *kantonsector* in criminal cases is set out in article 382 of the Code of Criminal Procedure and in civil cases in article 93 of the Code of Civil Procedure.
8. Until 1963, article 99 Judiciary Organisation Act stated that the Supreme Court was allowed to examine whether the judgement of a lower court violated any statutory legal provisions. Since 1919, the Supreme Court had tried to extend its jurisdiction and in 1963, article 99 was amended to enable the Supreme Court to examine if a judgement violates the law (not restricted to statutory law).

2.3   Civil and criminal procedure[9]

Consider an example. Jan drives his scooter and crashes into the back of Karin's car. There is a lot of damage. Even worse, Jan is unconscious and lies bleeding in the street; Karin has badly hurt her neck. Bystanders call the ambulance and the police. A few hours later, Jan is released from hospital. The doctors have closed Jan's wounds with stitches and let him sleep off his drunkenness. Karin has left the hospital with a brace on her neck because of whiplash.

Karin's car has sustained a great deal of damage. The garage estimates the material damage to the car at an amount of € 5000 and she wants to file a personal injury claim. However, Jan is not insured and offers to repair her car with a friend. Karin does not accept this offer. She wants payment of all her claims but Jan does not have that kind of money. So Karin seeks legal advice and wants to take her claims to court.

In cases before the civil division of the District Court, the assistance of a lawyer representing the litigants in the proceedings is compulsory. So, Karin turns to a law firm in her neighbourhood. Her lawyer tries to settle the case but his efforts are not rewarded. To start the legal proceedings, the lawyer sends a writ of summons to Jan, stating Karin's complaint and the nature of the compensation she claims (the statement of claim) and when he has to appear in court. This claim falls within the jurisdiction of the civil division of the District Court. Neither Jan nor Karin have to appear in person, because the pleadings are mostly in writing. Jan also has to turn to a lawyer who will answer the summons (statement of defence) within a certain time limit determined by the court. If the judge has questions or thinks it is possible to settle the dispute, he (or she) invites the parties for a hearing *(comparitie)*. After that, there is a second round of written pleadings (a replication on Karin's side again and a duplication on Jan's side). The judge passes judgement on the basis of the file.

If either of the parties is not satisfied, each of them can appeal to the Court of Appeal. The whole process repeats itself, but now in a higher court. If legal questions remain after the judgement of the Court of Appeal, it is possible to approach the Supreme Court to nullify or overrule the decision.

But in this case, there is more. Jan has committed several criminal (traffic) offences: drunk driving, driving without insurance and careless driving. The police have made a report of the offences. On the basis of this report and the evidence the police have gathered, the Public Prosecutor decides whether the offences are serious enough to prosecute Jan. The Public Prosecutor has a great deal of discretion on whether or not to prosecute. There is no obligation to prosecute; it has to be in the public interest to do so. If there is no reason to keep Jan in detention because he is no danger to society and there is no risk he will obstruct the investigations of the police, a summons orders him to appear in the District Court. If Jan is smart, he will

---

9. The judicial procedures are regulated in several statutes:
    – criminal proceedings in the Code of Criminal Procedure *(Wetboek van Strafvordering)*;
    – civil proceedings in the Code of Civil Procedure *(Wetboek van Burgerlijke Rechtsvordering)*;
    – administrative proceedings in the General Administrative Law Act *(Algemene wet bestuursrecht)*.

turn to a lawyer to advise him and represent him in court, but this is not compulsory in criminal cases.

In criminal proceedings, unlike civil proceedings, the trial itself is the focus.[10] During the trial, all evidence is presented and discussed by the prosecution as well as the defence. After this, the court takes six weeks to reach its decision. Both parties, Jan as well as the Public Prosecutor, can lodge an appeal with the Appeal Court. If legal questions remain after the decision in appeal, both the suspect and the Public Prosecutor can approach the Supreme Court to nullify or overrule the last decision.

As you may have noticed, Karin has not been involved in the criminal procedure. This is because the victim plays no significant part in a criminal process. The prosecution defends the public interest and not an individual victim of crime.

2.4   Administrative judiciary

The administrative judiciary has a slightly different organization than the civil and the criminal judiciary. In a modern society, the role of the government is, to a large extent, that of providing services to the citizens. If the latter need actions from administrative agencies, they file a petition. The answer from an administrative body to the petition has an individual (referring to a particular person) and concrete (referring to a particular object) character and is called an administrative order *(beschikking)*.[11] If the order is not satisfactory, a complaint procedure – described in the General Administrative Law Act *(Algemene wet bestuursrecht)* – is available. After a complaint, the administrative body that issued the order has to reconsider it: this is called administrative revision. If the objections are rejected, it is possible to turn to the administrative division of the District Court for judicial review. Both parties, the citizen as well as the administration, can appeal to the Judicial Division of the Council of State *(Afdeling Bestuursrechtspraak van de Raad van State)*. This is the last instance: after this appeal, cassation to the Supreme Court is not available. So, in the administrative justice system, just as in civil and criminal proceedings, three instances are involved. In civil and criminal proceedings, these three instances involved are all courts, but in administrative proceedings one of the three is an administrative agency; the three instances in administrative proceedings are administrative revision, judicial review and appeal.

10. This is based on the immediacy principle in criminal law: the proceedings have to be conducted in the presence of the accused. See also Chapter 6, section 3.
11. Thus, an administrative order is distinct from regulations made by the administration, which are general and abstract.

2.5   European courts

Two European courts have great influence on Dutch law.

a.   The Court of Justice of the European Community (The European Court of Justice)
The European Court was established by the EC Treaty and sits in Luxembourg. The main function of the Court of Justice is to ensure that Community law is interpreted and applied in the same way in each Member State. Its decision on the interpretation of EU law is final. When a national court has to apply EU law and has doubts about the right application of a provision, it can ask the European Court to explain the European law: the preliminary ruling. Since 1989, the court has been divided into two instances: The Court of First Instance and the (original) European Court. The Court of First Instance gives rulings on particular cases, such as cases relating to unfair competition between businesses and specific actions of individual citizens of the Member States.
Since 1995, the European Union has also had a European Ombudsman. He investigates complaints about EU institutions that are not under the jurisdiction of the European Court.

b.   The European Court of Human Rights
After World War II, many European states were convinced that such a disaster should never happen again and established the Council of Europe, which now has forty Member States. The main task of the Council is the development, maintenance and enforcement of the fundamental rights that are enumerated in the European Convention on Human Rights. For this purpose, the European Court of Human Rights rules in individual cases as the final court of human rights issues. Its seat is in Strasbourg (France). In 1998, the way the court operated was made more efficient in order to get rid of the long delays in cases – sometimes, the proceedings lasted more than six years.

   Dutchmen often think the Dutch legal system respects human rights, but there have been several instances in family law, criminal law, and administrative law in which the ECHR found breaches of the Convention. An (arbitrary) example is the case of *Berrehab v. The Netherlands*,[12] in which the Court held that the deportation of Berrehab was a violation of the right protected by article 8: the respect for family life. Berrehab, a Moroccan national, had married a Dutch woman while residing in the Netherlands. Their child was born two years later, some days after the divorce. For four years, Berrehab contributed to the child's support and saw his daughter four times a week. The Dutch government refused to extend his permission to remain in the Netherlands and deported him. Although the deportation had a legitimate aim: 'the economic well-being of the country', it conflicted with the right to respect for family life.

---

12. ECHR 21 June 1988 (No. 138), 11 E.H.R.R. 322.

2.6 Case law as a source of law

Judges, according to the myth, do not make law, but they only interpret existing law because only the Parliament creates law. This theoretical position corresponds to the division of governmental powers: according to Montesquieu, the judge should function as 'la bouche de la loi' (as the voice of the statute). In fact, the lawmaking power is more or less a shared power. Although – as in all civil law systems – the Dutch legislature has the legal power to create law, this power is no longer exclusive. Legislatures, which nowadays are called upon to establish the framework of the legal order, do so by formulating commands and creating rules of law. Courts are not authorized to use this method. Nevertheless, the judiciary makes rules too: there is a complicated synergy between both powers. The legislature has never been able and will never been able to construct a comprehensive set of rules anticipating all possible legal disputes. When human relationships change daily, legal relationships cannot be expressed in a static form. There will always be new developments which requires a system that is capable of adaptation. The role of the judiciary is to adapt law to social reality. The legislature can change the judge-made law if it has resulted in a rule the legislature does not approve of, or it can affirm the judge-made rule by codifying it if it does approve.

There are many examples of this synergy between legislature and judiciary. The most famous one is the issue of euthanasia. Medical developments in the last ten years have made it possible to postpone death, but this does not always involve an acceptable quality of life for the patient. Doctors looking for a remedy have explored the possibilities to stop further treatment, or to help to end an unbearable life. The Criminal Code forbade this kind of medical help and doctors were prosecuted for acts which the majority of the Dutch public approved of. The legislature was unable to change the law because Parliament could not reach an agreement. So, very cautiously, the judiciary started to formulate conditions for impunity for the doctor who stopped treatment or helped to end intolerable suffering. In 2001, the Criminal Code was changed and the *Wet toetsing levensbeëindiging op verzoek* (The Termination of Life on Request and Assisted Suicide Act) formulated the necessary precautions doctors have to take when performing euthanasia or assisted suicide.

Legal provisions are always general rules and they need interpretation before they can be used. So judges always need to be creative to some extent when they interpret existing legal rules. If the Supreme Court decides in such a case, it establishes an interpretation of a rule for future cases. Lawyers have to ask whether a new case is comparable to the case the Supreme Court has decided and what the formulated rule means for this new case. There is no 'binding precedent rule' but a system that resembles it. A lower court has to consider statutory law, the relevant decisions of the Supreme Court, and other sources of law, and last but not least, social values. How the judge considers all these sources is his own responsibility; there is no legal hierarchy in the sources of law – except for certain rules of a treaty.[13] However, he

---

13. Article 94 of the Constitution states that statute law that conflicts with the self-executing rules of a treaty will not be applied.

knows that each of his decisions can be overruled in appeal and cassation. Each time, a judge should try to pass a judgement that respects the legal system, survives appeal and is acceptable to the general public.

3 The judge

The Dutch judge is a professional judge. Every Dutch lawyer *(jurist)* is trained at university and has a master's degree in law; they bear the title of Master in the sense of expert *(meester*, abbreviated as *mr.).*[14] On 19 June 1999, the European Ministers of Education signed the Bologna Declaration. In order to create a European area of higher education, they agreed on the adoption of a higher education system (i) of easily comparable degrees and (ii) based on two main cycles. The first cycle, lasting a minimum of three years, is awarded with the Bachelor's degree. This gives access to the second cycle that should lead to the Master's or doctorate degree. This Declaration has changed Dutch academic education. Since September 2002, all universities offer bachelor programmes and in September 2004, they should offer Master's programmes. At the moment, it is not sure whether the Master's degree in law will be awarded with the title Master of Arts (MA) or Master of Laws (LLM).

The symbol of Justice is a blindfolded lady with a pair of scales in one hand and a sword in the other. This image reveals what we demand of judges: the scales suggest professionalism, the blindfold integrity and the sword decisiveness. Professionalism means knowledge of the law, analytical power, a sense of context, the ability to listen, clarity of expression, persuasiveness and empathy. With all these various demands to fulfil, it is not surprising that intensive training is given to judges. After graduation, lawyers can apply for an in-service training for judges and public prosecutors that takes six years. There is a second way to become a judge. After at least six years of law practice, a lawyer can apply for a position as judge. The recruitment policy aims at half the judges to be recruited from among experienced outsiders. The selection procedure contains an assessment, psychological tests and three interviews, each time with different members of the selection committee consisting of lawyers with all kinds of social experience. A third way to become a judge is to be a deputy judge *(rechter plaatsvervanger)* who has a regular law job elsewhere and works as a judge on an irregular, part-time basis. Deputy judges have the same powers in hearing and deciding cases as regular judges. Now and then, the impartiality of the deputy judge is questioned. How impartial is a solicitor in his role as a deputy judge when he administers justice in the case of a client of his own law firm? How impartial is a company lawyer in his role as a substitute judge when he administers justice in a case of his rival in business? Owing to these critical questions, many courts do not employ solicitors from law firms in the same district.

At the smaller district courts, judges do occasionally work in two divisions simultaneously, e.g. the criminal and the civil divisions. If a judge sits only in a

---

14. Mw. mr. T. de Jong is a woman who is a lawyer. *Mw.* is the abbreviation of *mevrouw* meaning Mrs. or Miss, and *mr.* stands for *meester.*

specific division, as is the case at most courts, he can do so for a number of years. He then generally has to move ('circulate') to a different division of the court.

The Crown nominates judges and justices for life by Royal Decree. For the nomination of the Lords Justices of the Supreme Court, another procedure is applicable. Parliament chooses three candidates out of six recommended by the Supreme Court itself. The Crown nominates one of the three candidates chosen by Parliament. In the 19th century, 75% of the Lords Justices were judges or prosecutors before nomination. Since World War II, the share of former judges and prosecutors has decreased to about 50% in favour of an increase in academics. The change in composition reflects the changing role of the Supreme Court. In the 19th century, the Supreme Court was the highest court in individual cases supervising the application of the laws by the lower courts, whereas nowadays the Court's case law is also seen as another source of law development in addition to parliamentary legislation.[15]

4   Legal aid

Litigants can expose themselves to substantial financial risks. The outcome of the litigation is unsure and the loser takes it all: after all, he will have to foot the bill of the other party's costs in addition to his own. Although in the local division of the District Court *(kantonsector)* a party can represent itself during a trial, in all the other civil and criminal proceedings the representation by a lawyer is compulsory or essential. The accessibility of the courts therefore depends on the extent to which a party can afford the services of a lawyer, the hourly rate of a commercial lawyer – in 2003 – being approximately € 200. In the Netherlands, lawyers are not allowed to take a case on a 'no cure, no pay' basis.

In 1970, the alarm bell rang: a substantial part of the Dutch population could not afford legal assistance and, as a result, were deprived of legal advice and of the court they were entitled to. Legal aid was introduced. Since then, it has been possible for people with a low income to get free legal advice and to take legal action with the help of a lawyer who is largely paid by the government. The impecunious litigant himself has to contribute between € 64 (for a family with an income below € 1130 a month) and € 551 (for a family with an income below € 2067 a month).[16] On a yearly basis, 2,5 to 3 million people call upon legal aid.

The government is currently trying to abolish legal aid – since the caseload of the courts is still growing – and replace it with free legal information, but of course legal information will never been able to replace legal aid. That is why people who cannot afford commercial legal advice will now need to take out a commercial legal assistance assurance. So after 40 years, it is questionable again whether everyone will get the legal advice they need.

---

15. Freek Bruinsma, *Dutch Law in Action*, Nijmegen: Ars Aequi Libri 2000, p. 31.
16. These are the figures for 2003. The Minister of Justice has proposed to increase the contribution in 2004 with 50%.

5   Informal justice

At the beginning of this chapter, I wrote that Dutch law provides a formal way to solve a legal conflict, but also many more or less informal ways. In this section, some examples of the latter will be discussed.

National Ombudsman

If there is a complaint about a government act that is neither an administrative order nor an act of legislation, it may be that the *Nationale Ombudsman* (National Ombudsman) is authorized to investigate and advise. The *Ombudsman* investigates the complaint and decides whether the governmental body has acted reasonably. His report informs the petitioner, the accused and Parliament of his conclusions.

Rent Assessment Committee

The Rent Assessment Committee *(Huurcommissie)* is an autonomous organization. There are 59 local Committees, with one central secretariat that is part of the Ministry of Housing, Spatial Planning and the Environment. Each committee consists of a representative for the tenants and one for the landlords; the chairman is a lawyer appointed by the Crown for a fixed period of six years. The tenant is able to apply to the Rent Assessment Committee in cases of overdue maintenance and defects to the dwelling and in cases of a disagreement about the level of the rent. The procedure is very simple: the tenant has to fill out a form and has to pay a fee of € 12,50 and then he will be summoned to appear for a hearing. The landlord has to refund the fee to the tenant if the complaint is upheld.

Complaints commissions

In many branches of industry, complaints commissions deal with consumer complaints. For instance the banking business, the travel agencies, the carpet industry and the laundry sector all have an internal procedure and a commission to deal with complaints. In the Netherlands, the activities of the complaints commissions are characterized as quasi adjudication *(quasi-rechtspraak)*. The commission usually consists of a representative of the particular branch of industry, a delegate of a consumer organization and a neutral lawyer acting as chairman. Although the proceedings are often in writing and the plaintiff has to pay a fee that will be returned to him if the complaint is found to be justified, the procedure is free from formalities. The result of the procedure is a binding advice in the form of a settlement contract *(vaststellingsovereenkomst)*. Nevertheless, if the opponent does not follow the advice, the plaintiff should start a civil action; on the basis of the binding advice, it will be easier to prove his claim. Many institutions, even semi-state controlled companies such as the juvenile social service or the blood transfusion service, have internal boards for complaints. This type of dispute resolution is an important extra-judicial way of solving the smaller legal conflicts.

Mediation

Mediation *(bemiddeling)* is a new form of dispute resolution. The ultimate goal of mediation is to realize a 'win/win' situation that benefits both parties. Mediation is an outstanding way of resolving a conflict between parties with a lasting relation. Modern mediation techniques have improved and been systematised thanks to American research. Mediation has changed into a professional activity: the mediator knows how to stimulate the parties to respect each other's interests. In 1993, the Netherlands Mediation Institute *(Nederlands Mediation Instituut, NMI)* was formally established as an umbrella organization with the main purpose of stimulating and promoting the practice and quality of mediation.

The Dutch government is interested in mediation because it expects that mediation may contribute to reducing the workload of the courts, shortening the length of court proceedings and improving access to the courts. The government started a project to discover whether court-annexed mediation is desirable. In this project, mediation is provided as an extra service during civil court procedures. At the hearing, the judge handling the case may refer the parties to a mediator. If such mediation is unsuccessful, the court procedure is resumed. The judge is not informed of the negotiations during the mediation after the court case is resumed. The mediation procedure is free of charge for the parties. The mediator, however, receives a fixed fee that is paid by the Ministry of Justice. If the project proves the usefulness of mediation, legislation will follow.[17]

17. Annie de Roo & Rob Jagtenberg, 'Mediation in the Netherlands: past-present-future', *Electronic Journal of Comparative Law* 2002, vol. 6.4.

Part II

Constitutional Law

4 Inhabiting Legality

How the Dutch keep reconstructing their 'Rechtsstaat'

Willem Witteveen

1 Legality as an edifice

Legality, the rule of law and the constitutional state are words evoking a family of concepts. They are suggestive of a 'government of measures, not of men'; of a normative framework supportive of 'democracy'; of a political system in which 'basic human rights' are respected and protected. This cluster of related concepts is characteristic of all western democracies. It has taken a slow process, from the late Middle Ages to today, to achieve its particular contemporary forms. There are different emphases, however. Legality focuses on legislation as the primary instrument to administer a complex society. The rule of law is associated primarily with impartial and independent judges. The constitutional state is said to operate by the rules of the constitution and its functionaries accordingly follow an ethic that does not allow them to yield to the temptations of corruption. The family of concepts forms a normative background of notions generally accepted by most people in the cultures adhering to the ideals in question. The various emphases provided by different conceptions of the ideals are of importance too, however. There can be marked differences between political systems that either focus on legality (like Germany) or on the rule of law (as in the United Kingdom) or on constitutionalism (like the United States).

The Dutch use the word *rechtsstaat* to refer to the whole family of concepts and, accordingly, there are overtones of legality, rule of law and constitutionalism to be discerned in it. In debates and controversies, the *rechtsstaat* at times is taken in the sense of legality: reference is made to the legal forms of the administrative state. At other times, what is taken to be the crucial component of the *rechtsstaat* is the court system: outside of political influence, controlling the legality of the acts of the administration. The idea of constitutionalism is never far away either, as is shown by the readiness to bring into play a large number of human rights, guaranteed by the Dutch constitution and a number of international treaties enjoying a similar legal status.

The Dutch understanding of their *rechtsstaat* is historically constituted but it is also highly adaptable to new demands and circumstances. This makes it hard to say precisely of what it consists. A metaphor can perhaps best capture the importance the *rechtsstaat* has for the Dutch. Their *rechtsstaat* is like a house they live in, an old house as can be found on an Amsterdam canal, with a foundation and several storeys which have been added to the main building in the course of the centuries. The Dutch inhabit legality, they treat it as an edifice, a structure used for practical purposes of living together. Accordingly, they also do not hesitate to keep on reconstructing the edifice as needs require it, not caring overmuch about stylistic consistency. Again, as can be seen in many Dutch cities, historical buildings are often renovated and made usable for purposes unthinkable to their original owners (such as an internet café housed in a building used originally by a rich, patrician family).

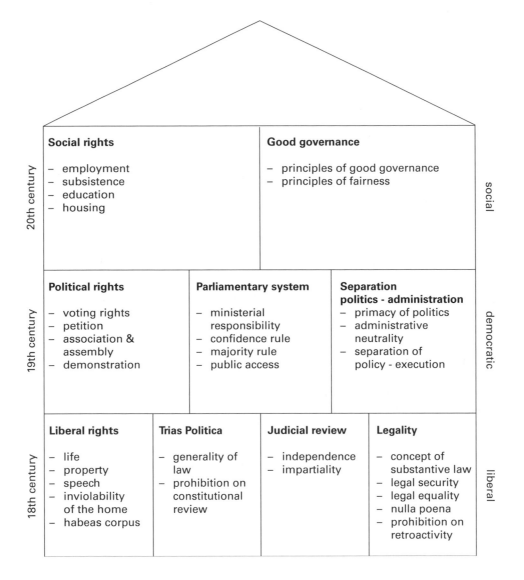

Figure 5 - The edifice of the constitutional state

The foundations of the Dutch *rechtsstaat* are old; they go back to medieval times. They consist of ideas and concepts derived from the ancient legal tradition and the republican heritage that pre-dates the modern Dutch constitutional state (established in 1814). The ground floor of the building of the *rechtsstaat* is built in the liberal style, manifesting the major 18th century ideas and institutions of classical legality (such as a catalogue of liberal human rights and the Trias Politica). The first floor, devoted to the 19th century, contains a number of period rooms in the democratic style (showing, among other exhibits, a wide collection of political rights and an early version of the parliamentary system). The top floor, drawn up during the 20th century, shows the social face of the *rechtsstaat*, as manifested in the addition of social rights and in a set of principles of good governance. The attic above these three floors of the edifice, is momentarily under construction; it is still not entirely clear in what style the new additions will be executed, but very likely the Dutch *rechtsstaat* of the future will adapt to the emerging information society by developing a new digital style.

While the challenges of the new century prompt intense rebuilding activities, this does not mean that the older storeys and period rooms are a safe haven. Rather, all the elements of the *rechtsstaat* are at times under discussion and revisions of even strongly established ones (such as the electoral system, using proportional representation) can be undertaken. Construction work is clearly not only done at the top of the house but on all floors and even in the foundations. We will now introduce you to the characteristics of the edifice and some themes and problems pertaining to it by inviting you for a tour of the building. As a preliminary, we visit the foundations, the traditions supporting the house of the *rechtsstaat*. It is possible to skip this part of the guided tour and rejoin the group at ground floor level where the basic liberal ideals of legality are found.

2 Foundations: the legal tradition and the republican heritage

2.1 The legal tradition

The oldest part of the foundations goes back to the late Middle Ages; it consists of concepts and practices derived from the legal tradition as it developed in Western Europe surrounding the body of Roman law *(corpus juris romani)* and canon law (the law of the Church of Rome). Upon the 11th century rediscovery of the 6th century Roman law system of emperor Justinian, in the newly emerging universities, a tradition of law developed which left its imprint on all aspects of social life, including the art and practices of governance. For one thing, the legal tradition fostered the emergence of a class of legal specialists, such as notaries, lawyers and university professors, who developed among themselves a legal science (conducted in Latin, the international language of the day). The knowledge of law became a professional concern and the body of knowledge itself was supposed to be part of the body of the law itself, evolving organically with new rounds of discussion about the interpretation of the canonical Roman law texts between legal specialists. In this way, the law became a relatively autonomous undertaking, containing texts, ideas and practices which were to a certain extent independent of other activities (such as governing). The major legal institutions (such as courts) were manned by the legal professionals and so became part of this relatively autonomous 'sphere' of law as well.

The *corpus juris*, as it was called, literally means that the law has an organic structure, that it is a body evolving, growing, adapting over time to new challenges. This is the background of the authoritativeness of legal pronouncements. Harold Berman sketches the genesis of the legal tradition and states that, as a result of its relative autonomy and its historicity (being old and able to adapt to changing circumstances), the law gradually became able to pose limitations on political authorities.

> 'The historicity of law is linked with the concept of its supremacy over the political authorities. The developing body of law (...) is conceived to be binding upon the state itself. Although it remained for the American Revolution to contribute the word "constitutionalism", nevertheless, since the twelfth century in all countries of the West, even under absolute monarchies, it has been widely said and often accepted that in some important respects law transcends politics. The monarch, it is argued, may make law, but he may not make it arbitrarily, and until he has remade it – lawfully – he is bound by it.'[1]

In this quotation, not only is constitutionalism mentioned explicitly, but we can also recognize one of the important tenets of legality: that there is a legal competence to make laws and the authorized law-making institution is bound by the rules governing the proper use of this competence; laws made in disrespect of these rules are *ultra vires*, invalid. Of course, the autonomy of law and its authority with political actors wielding real power was still rather limited and often precarious. Learned jurists could be hired to underwrite claims to power, for instance, and, as a result, a battle of interpretations regarding the valid rules and precepts ensued, in which the political authorities could find sufficient justification to do as they pleased.

According to Berman, it is the development of canon law, the law of the Church of Rome, which reinforced the nascent ideal of the rule of the law. In 1075, Pope Gregorius VII through his bull *Dictatus Papae* claimed that the Church had full and exclusive authority in all religious matters (broadly defined as pertaining to all aspects of human life between birth and death). This meant a protracted war between the Pope and the German Emperor, who had a similar claim to supreme authority. In this so-called investiture struggle, which the Church won in 1122, the Church, rather paradoxically, became the first recognisably modern state organization. Berman points out that at the end of the investiture struggle, the Church possessed an independent, hierarchically organized public authority; its leader had the right to make laws; there was an administrative organization applying these laws to the community of the faithful; there was even a court system within the church resolving conflicts about the application of its law. The Church effectively fulfilled legislative, executive and judicial functions and developed its own system of law, canon law. It taxed its members and it had, through the ritual of baptism, a

---

1. Harold J. Berman, *Law and Revolution. The Formation of the Western Legal Tradition*, Cambridge Mass.: Harvard University Press 1983, p. 9.

certified method to create membership, entailing rights and obligations. The Church was not fully victorious, however. Alongside the jurisdiction of canon law, there came to exist other jurisdictions, notionally subordinate perhaps but in practice relatively autonomous. There was secular law in many varieties: the law of the Emperor, of princes, of city-states; feudal law regulating the relationships between lords and vassals; but also functional law such as the system of mercantile law developed by the trading cities along the European coasts in their Hanseatic league.

The full picture is complex and we need not draw it fully, to see that legal pluralism became the reality in post-medieval Europe. The plurality of legal orders had two important consequences for the freedom of its subjects. The power of one jurisdiction was limited by the power of other jurisdictions. Civil freedom became enlarged through this competition of jurisdictions. When one legal system was deemed too oppressive, people could emigrate into another one. Another consequence of legal pluralism was that the potential for conflicts between the different legal orders increased. To the legal professionals increasingly fell the task of defining and guarding the boundaries between the jurisdictions. The law aspired to find peaceful resolutions to conflicting power claims otherwise easily leading to violence and war. Constitutionalism followed this developmental logic of the legal tradition.

The story of the legal tradition and its contributions to constitutionalism and the rule of law is quite a general one, it is a story pertaining to all Western countries. It forms a foundational layer of concepts (such as the concepts of liberty and authorization) and practices (such as the practice of obligatory legislative consultation or the practice of binding legal advice) which can be mobilized when individual liberty is under threat or when political authorities know no bounds. The Netherlands are no exception.

2.2 The republican heritage

The republican heritage is a more recent and more local element in the foundations of the edifice of legality inhabited by the Dutch. The Dutch republic came into being during the war of independence against the Spanish monarchy (1568-1648). The Dutch state was effectively independent from about 1600 onwards, until the French occupation by Napoleon in 1795. It was called the Republic of the Seven United Provinces and under this significant name it exhibited some remarkable characteristics:
- It was a loose confederacy, in which the participating provinces jealously guarded their political and economic autonomy and found it hard to cooperate in central institutions, of which there were few (the Estates General, the republican Parliament, was in practice a meeting of strictly mandated delegates from the provinces; the Estates General were, not surprisingly, often a monument of indecisiveness).
- It had no central bureaucracy but a limited number of functionaries that were provided by the autonomous provinces.
- It had very tight controls on the army and the fleet, denying these institutions social prominence and political power.

- In the House of Orange, it had its ruling dynasty, but these notables were not monarchs but Stadholders *(Stadhouders)*, executive functionaries of the Republic rather than princes in their own right; only in 1813, would the Dutch monarchy have its beginning.
- The cities, which were economically the most important entities in the provinces, were run by an elite of 'regenten': burghers who were merchants first and politicians second, their rule was in a large measure pragmatic rather than principled.
- There was large religious diversity; while the Dutch Reformed Church in the aftermath of the war with Catholic Spain became the official state church, it did not completely dominate religious life and in practice, the Dutch republic developed into a regime where all religions were tolerated, even though some groups (the Catholics and the Jews) were not allowed to practice their religion openly.
- In keeping with the tolerance practiced by the Dutch, there was also a climate of opinion in which a comparatively large freedom of expression developed; there was no censorship and as a result political books from countries that did have censorship were often printed in Holland.

The contributions of this long period of republicanism to the typically Dutch *rechtsstaat* experience are both profound and diverse and largely subconscious. Qualities of the *rechtsstaat* which are deriving from its republican heritage are among others:
- A preference for decentralization; even in centralized legislation, there are often important provisions allowing for provincial or local regulation and policy-making.
- There is now an extensive welfare state bureaucracy but it is often viewed with suspicion; rules and bureacrats are popularly seen as a 'threat to freedom'.
- Its controls on military power are generalized into a preference for checks and balances, for institutional arrangements limiting action possibilities of all the agencies involved.
- While the Netherlands are now a constitutional monarchy and the Queen is very popular, she does not behave with the royal grandeur of monarchs with a more absolutist heritage; the Dutch monarchy has little effective power and operates under full ministerial responsibility.
- The political culture of the 'regenten' meant a tendency to accommodate interests in a pragmatic way; this tendency towards political compromise involving all relevant parties is at the basis of the contemporary political culture often referred to as the 'poldermodel'; as a result of this compromise mentality, of this search for solutions that are acceptable to almost every interest, political debate is not very confrontational or adversarial and political life is dominated by a technical rationality of decision-making.
- In keeping with the heritage of indecisive parliamentarism, of sharing and contesting and diffusing responsibilities, Dutch political debates go in many rounds and are rarely brought to a definite conclusion; the legislative process

tends to mimic this tendency and to proceed in many incremental stages of amendments to the existing laws.
- The Dutch *rechtsstaat* is characterized by a strong preference for classical human rights, such as religous freedom and freedom of expression; this clearly builds on the republican heritage of tolerance and individual freedom.

3 The 18th century: liberal ideals

On the ground floor of the Dutch edifice of the *rechtsstaat*, we find a number of liberal ideals that were articulated during the 18th century. All over Europe and in the emerging Untited States of America, these liberal ideals were highly controversial, since they clashed with the existing social order of what, in France, was called the *ancien régime*. As a result of the French Revolution of 1789, these ideals were realized up to a point and their appeal spread widely over Europe. The French Revolution began as a moderate democracy but radicalized with the Jacobin Terror. It was institutionalized in the Napoleonic Empire and ended in 1813 with the defeat of Napoleon. A conservative Reaction followed but the restoration of the old order, instituting monarchy again as the dominant political organization principle, was soon followed by new liberal challenges and yet more radical (socialist, anarchist, communist) revolutions. In the Netherlands, the liberal ideals definitively won the day in the Constitution *(Grondwet)* of 1848. Another important influence on the spread of liberal ideals was the American Revolution which produced a Declaration of Independence (1776), proclaiming the ideas of national sovereignty and inalienable human rights. The United States produced a written constitution which would become a model for many countries shifting to the liberal mood. Both the American and the French Revolutions were firmly committed to the liberal ideal of universal human rights, as witness the already mentioned Declaration of Independence and its famous French equivalent, the *Déclaration des Droits de l'Homme et du Citoyen* (1789). In 1798, as part of the French revolutionary movement conquering Old Europe, Dutch revolutionary sympathizers of these liberal ideals proclaimed their own catalogue of human rights in the Constitution of the Batavian People ('Staatsregeling voor het Bataafsche Volk').

The actual realization of the 18th century liberal ideals in the Netherlands only took place in the course of the 19th century. An important vehicle for this was the (written) Dutch Constitution, which was amended a number of times in order to incorporate new versions that had won approval in society and among a governing elite that was on the whole rather more conservative. The Constitution of 1848 is especially of great importance.

On the ground floor of the Dutch *rechtsstaat*, we find four richly decorated period rooms in the liberal style: Liberal Rights, Trias Politica, Judicial Review and Legality. We will briefly sketch their contents, referring to the actual Dutch Constitution for their contemporary formulations.

3.1   Liberal rights

The American Declaration of Independence proclaims that 'all men are created equal' and it mentions 'certain unalienable Rights', such as 'Life, Liberty and the pursuit of Happiness'. The modern Dutch catalogue of liberal rights is more specific, but adheres to the same idea. It has devoted the first half of its First Chapter to a catalogue of these liberal rights, beginning with the principle of equality (and the prohibition of discrimination) in article 1. The other obviously liberal rights in the First Chapter of the Constitution are:
- the freedom of religion (article 6);
- the freedom of expression (article 7);
- the right of privacy (article 10);
- the freedom of life, formulated as the right of personal integrity (article 11);
- the freedom of the home (article 12);
- the right to secrecy of communication (article 13);
- the right of property (article 14);
- the right of personal liberty (article 15);
- the right to be heard by a court *(habeas corpus*, article 17);
- the freedom of education (article 23).

With the exception of article 1 ('All persons in the Netherlands shall be treated equally in equal circumstances. Discrimination on the grounds of religion, belief, political opinion, race, or gender or on any other grounds shall not be permitted'), none of these freedoms is granted in an absolutist fashion. All liberal rights are subject to certain legal limitations, especially when the right in question is used to infringe the rights of others (itself a liberal notion) and when important social objectives such as public order or public health are at stake. When limitations are deemed necessary, they always have to be in accordance with the law. This principle is derived from the rule of law ideal and it finds its clearest expression in a rider added to many liberal rights articles: 'Everyone shall have the right to (...) without prejudice to his responsibility under the law.' When this formula is used, it means that only the highest legislative procedure may be used to legislate a limitation; it has to be done by a formal statute (see also under section 3.4, Legality).

The catalogue of liberal rights that are valid under Dutch law is not limited to the First Chapter of the Dutch Constitution. They can also be found, in slightly different words, in the European Convention on Human Rights (ECHR), which is applicable in the Netherlands. Limitations are also recognized in the ECHR but according to a rather different formula. Here, not only is the limitation to be made by a legislative act (but not necessarily by the highest legislative procedure), it is also bound to certain explicit social goals (such as public health) and it must be 'necessary in a democratic society'. This wider array of grounds defining the limitation of liberal and other human rights is of importance in relation to the possibility of judicial review of the constitutionality of an act limiting a right in the Member States of the ECHR; we will get back to this question later.

3.2 Trias Politica

Under the heading of Trias Politica, three important powers of the state are understood: the legislative, the executive and the judicial power. Liberal ideals concerning the Trias Politica give expression to the normatively proper relationships between these three powers of government which, taken together, comprise the organizational aspect of the rule of law. In a positive vein, the Trias Politica is designed to promote individual liberty. Negatively speaking, the Trias Politica aims at the avoidance of tyranny.

There are, historically speaking, two variants of the Trias Politica, two main schools of thought about the proper way legislation, administration and judging should be organized to safeguard the freedom of the citizens in a democratic state. One is the doctrine of the *separation of powers*, the other the doctrine of the *balance of powers*. Both doctrines can in nucleus already be found in Montesquieu, whose book *The Spirit of the Laws* (of 1748) is at the basis of the Trias Politica. Later, the Federalist Papers, that influential argument shaping the American Constitution, took up Montesquieu's two models, developing especially the idea of balance of powers through the notion of 'checks and balances'. Meanwhile, in Germany, many authors under the influence of Kant preferred a purified version of separation of powers as their image of constitutional liberty. Both doctrines can be found at work in Dutch constitutionalism, so that it is worthwhile to explain them first and then look at their concrete manifestations in Dutch constitutional law.

The separation of powers recognizes three powers of government (legislative, executive and judicial) and conceives of them as three stages in a process of governing. First, there must be laws, accepted by the representatives of the people. Then the administration must shape its policies on the basis of these laws, even when the laws leave them discretion in their task orienting themselves on the principles laid down by the legislative process. The last step is the judicial review of the legality of administration by an independent and impartial judiciary, not over the whole gamut of administrative activity but case by case, on the instigation of a citizen claiming infringement of his or her rights. A strict separation of powers requires that not only are the functions separated but especially the organs fulfilling them and the persons taking part in these functions must be independent of each other. As a result of this strict approach, the separation of powers comes down to a number of constitutional prohibitions:

– The legislator must make general acts and must refrain from taking concrete decisions of governance.
– The legislator may not take decisions of a judicial nature.
– The administrative agencies may not make their own rules.
– The public authorities may not prevent citizens from going to court.
– The judges, in deciding a controversy, may not make new law (that is up to the legislator only).
– The judges may not do more than review the legality of public administration and must especially refrain from pronouncing upon the desirability of public policies.

As this sheer list of prohibitions suggests, the separation of powers is a stern doctrine indeed, creating difficulties for public authorities who want to deal quickly and effectively with a new problem (they must wait until there are adequate rules) or for democratic bodies who are more ambitious than the legislative function allows (they cannot take everything into their own hands). In Dutch constitutional law, all of these prohibitions are sometimes invoked. They have not uniformly found expression in the written law, however, and are sometimes treated as unwritten constitutional norms. A very important written separation of powers norm is found in article 120 of the Constitution, which forbids constitutional review of formal statutes (Acts of Parliament). If the legislative organ enacted a statute abrogating the freedom of a certain religion deemed socially dangerous, for instance, the legislative organ itself should be the judge of the constitutionality of such an act, and, even in clear cases of violation of the constitutional norm, the judges would not be allowed to intervene; they would then, it is feared, take over the legislative function. (An important exception to this state of affairs will be mentioned in section 3.3)

The norms relating to the freedom of the administration to pursue its policy goals are generally much more relaxed than those relating to the judiciary. For one thing, the legislator through Acts of Parliament usually creates considerable scope for administrative law-making, making the administration in actual fact into much more than an executive body.

The balance of powers also takes the three government functions as its starting point, but does not take a temporal and normative succession of functions as the most salient feature. The organs performing the three functions need not be separated so much as made sufficiently independent and motivated to be able to control each other. Through the limitation of one power by the 'balancing' influence of another power, the freedom of the citizens is better safeguarded than through a sharp demarcation of their respective domains. Friction and strife, influence of one power upon another, are necessary to bind public authorities to the rules and to protect the freedom of individuals. The prime example of balance of powers is the American arrangement of checks and balances between Congress and the President. They each have their own powers (of legislation and execution of the laws respectively) and so separation of powers is the starting point, but they can interfere with each other's powers. Congress can make laws, the president can veto these laws (a 'check') and then a two-third majority in Congress can override the veto (a 'balance'). As a result, the powers in the state have to take each other into consideration and in this way supposedly cannot act rashly or tyrannically. The Dutch legislative process producing Acts of Parliament is another example of an arrangement characterized by checks and balances, but differently organized: as participation of the one organ in the functional activities of the other. Acts of Parliament must be made with the participation and consent of both the government (which also has the executive power) and the two houses of Parliament (which also have a number of powers designed to control the executive function). The method differs from the American one but the result is comparable: limited power to make laws.

Balance of powers is a doctrine that does not so much lead to a list of clear prohibitions as to a set of normative guidelines for 'good' governance, designed to combine effective administrative action with optimal citizen freedom. For the legislative function, one of these guidelines stresses the desirability of a wide and fair consultation of social organizations and concerned interests before new legislation is enacted, taking care not to grant one or more of these organizations and interests the chance to dominate this consultation procedure. For the executive function, a guideline that is deemed highly relevant is the maxim to make the government organization both strong and accountable to all those depending upon its well-functioning. The judicial power is enjoined to have a large measure of freedom in the interpretation of the laws, so bringing the existing law in an almost common law-like fashion into harmony with new developments in society, but to refrain from trying to dominate the political process or to interfere with administration policies when this is not absolutely necessary to protect a legally recognized interest of high importance (such as the constitutionally guaranteed liberal rights). As these examples show, the doctrine of balance of powers often does not concern the articulation of the powers themselves so much as their actual use in legal and political practice.

3.3   Judicial review

Something has already been said about this element of the liberal ideal; a glimpse at this room of the edifice of the Dutch *rechtsstaat* could as it were already be had from internal windows in the previous rooms we visited. The reason to mention it separately is that, in judicial review, the idea is manifested of the protection of the laws that is promised to each individual and this idea is an important constitutive element of the liberal approach. Indeed, in the United Kingdom the rule of law is largely taken to refer to the protection the laws offer to individuals and the redress they have to a court of law when the laws do not in fact protect their rights. Under the heading of judicial review, the quality of judicial operations is raised as an issue in its own right. What can citizens expect from their courts under the rule of law?

As a liberal ideal, the protection of the laws afforded by the judiciary was firmly established in the constitutions of the 19th century and the so-called 'organic' laws meant to give effect to constitutional principles. The ideal was largely uncontested, flowing from the tenets of the legal tradition at the basis of constitutional thinking. Its contours are still familiar:
-    The judiciary is supposed to be independent (and immune from political or social influence) (see Chapter 6 of the Constitution, especially article 117, guaranteeing appointment for life).
-    It aims at impartial justice (see the Judiciary Organization Act, dating back to 1827, article 12).
-    It applies and interprets the laws (but it does not proclaim new ones) (see the Law containing general principles for the legislation of the Kingdom of the Netherlands of 1829, especially articles 11, 12 and 13).
-    Trials are conducted in public and the decisions are pronounced in public (article 121 of the Constitution).
-    Judgements need to specify the grounds on which they are based (principle of motivation) (article 121 of the Constitution).

These principles express for the Dutch legal culture (and probably for the whole family of Western legal cultures) what it is to have a court system at all. If the administration of justice systematically violated one or more of these fundamental principles, it would not be accepted as the proper exercise of the judicial function.

But in the 19th century, the protection of the laws through the judiciary was not extended to all categories of disputes. It was limited to civil law and criminal law cases. Conflicts between citizens and the public authorities regulated by administrative law were not generally entrusted to the judiciary. These conflicts were dealt with by a separate system of administrative review, under which it was possible to file complaints with higher public bodies in the governmental hierarchy, culminating in an appeal to the Crown. There were all kinds of exceptions to this system however, with the result that many conflicts could not be brought to an independent higher body at all. In some of these cases, the courts were by a special act entrusted with jurisdiction and sometimes the courts took on such cases under their general power to treat civil cases relating to torts and damages (also those involving public authorities). When government itself became more pervasive in the 20th century, shifting from the limited tasks it performed for public order, defence and public health to the vast array of tasks associated with the welfare state, the limitations of the system of administrative review became apparent. Gradually, a comprehensive system of judicial review of administrative acts emerged. A very important influence in this development was formed by European human rights law. Article 6 of the ECHR, dealing with the judicial function, was interpreted dynamically by the European Court of Human Rights in such a way as to greatly extend the protection of the laws through the judiciary; it also reinforced the fundamental principles of judicial review already acknowledged in Dutch constitutional law. A landmark case was the *Benthem* case (in 1985), establishing that the whole system of administrative review through the Crown was in contravention of article 6 ECHR.

The liberal rights enshrined in the ECHR were not only nor even primarily influential through the case law developed by the European Court. The Dutch courts directly apply the provisions of the ECHR as part of Dutch law and they have been as dynamic or more in their interpretation, making the catalogue of rights into much more than minimal norms common to all European jurisdictions. The right to family life of article 8 has, for instance, been interpreted by the Dutch Supreme Court in combination with the principle of equality to be applicable not only to traditional family forms but also to newly emerging forms of family relationships, such as contractual relationships between unmarried partners. Earlier, we observed that Dutch courts are not allowed to review the constitutionality of formal legislation (under article 120 of the Constitution), so that complaints about statutory regulations in contravention of the liberal rights of Chapter 1 of the Constitution are bound to fail. But these same liberal rights, contained in the ECHR, can be invoked in the courts! This is possible in accordance with article 94 of the Constitution, holding that 'statutory regulations in force within the Kingdom shall not be applicable if such application is in conflict with provisions of treaties that are binding on all persons or of resolutions by international institutions'. Human rights provisions are taken to be 'binding on all persons' and so can be invoked in order to escape from the application of statutory regulations conflicting with them. By the back door, so to speak, the judiciary that was denied constitutional review under the doctrine of separation of powers is assuming a kind of constitutional review under international law that accords much better with the doctrine of the balance of powers.

The extension of the protection of the laws through the judiciary has been so large that, at the beginning of the 21st century, it was widely felt that in principle there is always a court competent and willing to hear a complaint or to settle a controversy. So the room of judicial review is today frequented much more often and its furniture used more intensively than in its liberal heyday.

3.4   Legality

The liberal principle of legality accords a special significance to the legislative process. It conceives of the citizens as free individuals who only have to accept limitations to their liberties when these have been expressly proclaimed by the legislator in laws applying equally to all and approved by the representatives of the people in Parliament. In Dutch constitutional law, the procedural safeguards of this principle of legality are held to materially protect a sphere of freedom for the citizens, while enabling society to regulate itself through the democratic processes pertaining to its government and its Parliament.

There is a hierarchy of legislative agencies. At the top stands the formal statute or Act of Parliament: all products of the legislative process in which the government and the two chambers of Parliament cooperate in order to pass statutes, as described in Chapter 5 of the Constitution. Formal statutes can delegate law-making powers to the government: general administrative orders, published by Royal Decree. It is also possible to delegate further down in the hierarchy to a particular government minister. Provinces and municipalities have law-making powers of their own which must be used in conformity with national legislation. Then, there are various other kinds of regulatory agencies possessing their own subordinate legislative powers; all government bodies also proclaim non-binding directives relating to their tasks and policies and, under some conditions (such as official publication), these are regarded as law as well and can even be applied by the courts.

The hierarchy between legislative instruments takes effect in the demand that all lower regulations must conform to conditions put upon their use by higher ones, especially by formal statutes. While judges are not allowed constitutional review of formal legislation, they can review the constitutionality of lower legislative instruments. Formal legislation is at the top of a vast conglomerate of lower forms of regulations. Seen from the perspective of the citizen or the organization who is supposed to obey the laws, there is virtually no knowing all of the relevant and applicable regulations emanating from the regulatory hierarchy, so that the call for deregulation and simplification of regulation is often heard.

The primacy of the legality principle is brought out by noticing the liberal aims that it purports to serve: protection of basic freedoms, legal certainty, equality under the laws and democratic self-regulation by the people through its representatives.

Legality takes on an especially strong form in criminal law, where the threat to individual liberty is in principle the greatest. The *nulla poena* principle, as it is called, demands a previous statute to declare a certain conduct criminal (see article 1 of the Criminal Code), so that citizens can plan their life in accordance with the known dictates of the criminal law. It is thus not allowed to retrospectively declare certain conduct criminal when the formal statute does not expressly prohibit it; new crimes, for instance those resulting from the emergence of new technologies, are protected until the legislative process has duly taken its course.

The *nulla poena* principle does not only relate to the matter of criminal law but also to its procedural and operational aspects: the investigation, prosecution, trial and punishment of criminal acts have to be in conformity with the rules provided by formal legislation (see article 1 of the Code of Criminal Procedure). It is in practice not easy to adhere to these procedural and operational demands of legality, since in the politically supported 'war on crime' new criminal technology tends to be answered by new investigative technology and the police and the judicial authorities are under great public pressure to use the latest available technical methods, even if such use is not based on valid formal statutory rules.

The prohibition of retroactive laws, very strong for criminal law, is also taken to be a general principle of legislation. Since there can sometimes be strong practical arguments in favour of a retroactive law, aiming to correct mistakes in the law or to achieve greater fairness in the application of the law to various groups, outside of criminal law, the prohibition on retroactivity is not as firmly held. The method of retroactive legislation is often used especially in taxation law, where the government wants to combat clever evasions of tax law and to optimize its income. As a rule, however, it is accepted that retroactivity is to be avoided and especially so when the import of the law is not to benefit but to burden the people or organizations it addresses.

What can be the meaning of legality outside of criminal law? The intentions of the liberal constitution makers in the 19th century were originally to produce codifications of law in three large areas: civil law, criminal law and administrative law. Codifications did indeed ensue relating to civil law (an adaptation of the Code Napoleon in 1838) and to criminal law, but the codification of administrative law turned out to be illusory. There were simply already in the liberal 19th century too many activities in which the government was involved, making a complete codification of all this varied and sometimes conflicting material impossible to achieve. The administration also succesfully resisted this effort, arguing that so many of the actual operations of public bodies had to be local and flexible and timebound and that what was required was 'discretion' rather than fixed rules in order to achieve their aims. What was achieved, however, were a number of separate statutes relating to independent domains of governance, such as land planning, housing and health care. These specialized administrative laws provided some legal certainty to those involved with its matter but at the same time, they ruled mostly for the possibility of delegation of legislative powers to public bodies lower than the formal legislator, at levels of government where the legislative process could be taken up with greater speed. Flexibility and administrative discretion proved on the whole to be stronger motives than the desire for legal certainty and for equality under the laws.

The hold of the principle of legality outside of criminal law is still tenuous. It was, for instance, widely recognized that, in the welfare state, decisions about the withdrawal of government subsidies for individuals and organizations could well be greater infringements of their 'liberty' than the prospect of punishment. However, because the provision of subsidies was a discretionary matter of administrative law, there was no statutory protection for the recipients of subsidies. In response to a number of complaints of this type, there is now a General Administrative Law Act (of 1992) in which procedural rules and demands of proper governance are articulated that apply to all public bodies and that create a measure of legal certainty for those depending on these public bodies. This statute also gives some general rules relating to subsidies.

4 The 19th century: democratic institutions

The first floor of the Dutch edifice of the *rechtsstaat* houses a number of important democratic institutions. Citizen participation in politics and government takes certain institutional forms in the course of the 19th century, as the outcome of intense political and social struggles. With some important modifications, these institutional forms persist into our own time, notwithstanding growing unease with some of them, leading to a call for constitutional and governmental renewal ('democratization') from the 1960s onwards. The rooms on the first floor of the Dutch *rechtsstaat* may show signs of wear and tear but they are full of activity, under the headings of: Political Rights, Parliamentary System and Separation of Politics and Administration.

4.1 Political rights

Liberal rights celebrate individual freedom. They protect the conscience of the individual (freedom of religion), cater to the individual need for expression (freedom of speech), they protect individual life and make possible personalized rights to property. All of these rights have a social dimension as well, since they are meaningless in isolation from other individuals and groups. The social dimension of the liberal rights comes to the fore at a later stage (in the 20th century mostly), just like the emergence of particular social rights not related to liberal ideals. In between, there is also a political dimension of liberal rights to be reckoned with. Religion, protected by state power, can become an important social force and can organize itself to have political influence. Freedom of speech is a most powerful means of expressing unorthodox political ideas with impunity and gaining a following for them. Even the rights to life and personal property are important safeguards for political action, making it safer for individuals to participate in political activities that go against vested interests and that might meet retaliation. The protection the *rechtsstaat* offers for individual freedom is a precondition for attempts to conquer power and perhaps 'change the system'; liberal rights have even been instrumental in revolutions aiming to destroy the liberal state. (However, Dutch political history does not show much evidence of easy power conquests leading to systemic change nor of revolutionary changes in political arrangements; the art of compromise has at all times been more important than practices of agitation and civil strife.)

Freedom of expression can especially be seen as both a liberal and a political right. It is guaranteed in article 7 of the Constitution and in article 10 of the ECHR. In the early stages of its recognition, it needed a helping hand from the Dutch Supreme Court to become politically efficacious. The constitutional provision spoke of the 'making public' of one's thoughts and feelings and it did not literally mention the right not only to print a book or paper but also to distribute it in the streets (as, for instance, part of a political demonstration). Some municipalities passed a local ordinance forbidding just this. The Supreme Court in a landmark case *(Haagse Ventverbod*, 1892) decided that 'making public' included the right to unhampered distribution of thoughts and feelings, in a long line of cases refining this idea into a doctrine allowing some measure of regulation (in the interests of public order, for instance) but making it impossible for municipal authorities to forbid distribution through a suitable medium of expression altogether.

Other political rights are needed to make the freedom to hold political views socially and politically effective. It must be possible to assemble peacefully and to hold a demonstration (see article 9 of the Constitution), to offer a petition to the authorities (see article 5 of the Constitution), and perhaps most importantly, it must be posssible to form one's own associations (see article 8 of the Constitution). In this latter right lies the basis for organizational diversity. Political parties and trade unions, for instance, need a legal form to be legitimately active and the freedom of association protects this fundamental political right. The rider added to the constitutional right is, as with most liberal rights, that by formal statute the right of association may be restricted in the interest of public order. On the basis of this restriction (in which we now recognize the principle of legality), it is possible, and it occasionally happens, that criminal political organizations (with anti-democratic aims) are prohibited.

The most important political right relates to the workings of representative democracy: the right to vote. Citizen participation in public life without the right to vote would not produce a democracy. Article 4 of the Constitution recognizes the right to vote as a right that accrues to every citizen (applying the equality principle) and similarly the right to be elected as a member of representative bodies. As a necessary corollary, there is also the right to be eligible for appointment to public service, protected by article 3 of the Constitution. Behind these now uncontroversial provisions, there lies a protracted history of political struggle over the extension of the franchise. At the time of the liberal Constitution of 1848, the principle of equal electoral participation was already accepted but there were still many restrictions in force. Voters had to be male, they had to have a certain income (measured through their contribution at the tax office). Women and the poor (and many with middle incomes) were excluded. Liberal and conservative governments, in Holland as elsewhere, were afraid that poor and uneducated voters would make the wrong choices, not being able to consider the General Interest, and would deliver the country to revolutionary forces (such as the emerging socialist and anarchist groups) that might tear down all of the established liberal order and would threaten the propertied classes. The solution to this potentially divisive conflict was informed by the conciliatory mores of republicanism: the franchise was extended by small gradual steps, introducing for instance voters who had some schooling, or who showed other signs of social integration, and lowering the wealth or taxation threshold. When religious political parties, working for the emancipation of Catholics and reformed Protestants, joined forces with social-democrats and social liberals, the arguments denying the right to vote to classes of citizens became unacceptable. In 1917, the right to vote was extended to all male citizens, regardless of other qualifications of wealth and education, and in 1922, all female citizens were also awarded the right to vote.

The second half of the 19th century was characterized by social struggle generally between different emancipatory movements confronting the dominant liberal-conservative consensus. The first political party in the Netherlands was the party of the emancipatory movement of reformed Protestants who had always taken second place behind the reigning Protestant orthodoxy. This Anti Revolutionary Party was established in 1879 (the revolution in its title is the French Revolution with its liberal and secular ideology). The reformed Protestants built a strong network of supportive institutions, comprising churches, schools and even a university. Alongside the reformed Protestant network, there also emerged a political party for Catholic voters and in the Catholic regions of the Netherlands (especially the south), a social life of exclusively Catholic organizations step by step took shape. Socialists, anarchists and social-democrats also created political movements and similarly attempted to found their own organizations in all spheres of life. The religious parties fought hard against the educational system with its liberally inspired public schools. The socialist groups struggled to improve the lot of the poor and the laborers. The liberal-conservative consensus did not produce a counterforce of the same intensity or ideological valour. The year 1917 marks the peaceful resolution of these controversies in the Pacification Settlement. There was something in it for all contestants: the religious parties were awarded the constitutional right to create their own schools, to be paid from public means on an equal basis with the public school system. The socialist movement won the general franchise. All parties agreed on a change of the electoral system that would continue the newly marked balance of forces. The district system was discarded and proportional representation introduced.

After the 1917 Pacification Settlement, a unique social system developed in the Netherlands: pillarization. Dutch society was organized along denominational lines. If you were a Catholic, you would spend your whole life in Catholic institutions (church, school, sport club, radio, trade union), voting for the Catholic political party. If you were reformed or Protestant, you would then live your life solely among religious fellows. Alongside these two 'pillars', there was a general pillar of public institutions, adopted by liberals and socialists. As a result, during the heyday of pillarization, there was a kind of social *apartheid* in the Netherlands, where people only knew and interacted with their religious or secular likes. Proportional representation meant that there were virtually no important shifts in the political alignments in Parliament. As a political system, pillarization tended towards elite rule with the elites at the top of the pillars accommodating with each other and governing the country in a culture of political compromise and respect for vested interests.

After 1960, this pillarization culture started to crumble. Growing welfare, increased mobility, the technology of television, decreasing religious ties and the spread of higher education all contributed towards social and political democratization. The system of social apartheid quickly disappeared, the traditional elites lost much of their legitimacy and the political alignments began to be more unstable. Proportional representation is still the established electoral system, however, and this ensures that many different parties have a voice in Parliament and that governments are always coalitions between a number of ideologically distinct political parties. In the new political culture after pillarization, many of the old characteristics can consequently be found.

4.2   Parliamentary system

The Constitution of 1848 brought the Netherlands a parliamentary system of government, in effect limiting the power of the Dutch monarchs of the House of Orange who had ruled the country in an enlightened but authoritarian fashion after the defeat of Napoleon. In its contours, the parliamentary system established in the 19th century is still the same today:
- The Government consists of the King[2] and the Cabinet of Ministers (article 42, section 1 Constitution).
- The Ministers, and not the King, are responsible for acts of government (article 42, section 2 Constitution).
- Parliament, consisting of two chambers, represents the entire people of the Netherlands (article 50 and 51 Constitution).
- The Second Chamber is directly elected by all voters, the First Chamber is indirectly elected through the members of the Provincial States.
- The Second Chamber has the political primacy through its more extensive legislative and controlling powers.
- The Government is accountable for all acts of government to Parliament, especially to the Second Chamber.
- Ministers or the Cabinet of Ministers must resign when they explicitly lose the confidence of a majority in the Second Chamber of Parliament (unwritten confidence rule).
- Each of the Chambers may be dissolved by the Government (article 64 Constitution).

---

2. The term 'King' refers to the constitutional function, which can be fulfilled by either a king or a queen. At present, this is Queen Beatrix.

As this list shows, not all of the rules comprising the parliamentary system are codified in the Constitution. The most important rule of all, the confidence rule stating that no government can stay in office when it has lost the support of the political majority in Parliament, is unwritten to this day, even though it is generally accepted. This reflects a certain ambivalence in the attitudes the Dutch political elites have always shown towards their constitution: yes, it is an important state document but no, it must be used in a pragmatic way, reflecting rather than governing the political norms evolving slowly in the actual practices of politics and governance.

The principle of ministerial responsibility is codified (article 42, section 2) but still governed by unwritten conventions as to its extent. What is clear is that all royal acts and all acts of the ministers themselves are comprised by ministerial responsibility, but it is contested how far ministerial responsibility goes when the acts of civil servants subordinate to the ministers are at stake. Not all acts by civil servants which are rejected by a parliamentary majority reflect back upon the responsible cabinet minister; parliamentary scrutiny is less strict when civil servants have acted outside of their authority or in contravention of ministerial orders. What is, on the other hand, considered to be a grave political sin is for cabinet ministers to misinform Parliament about a controversial incident of policy. All in all, the true extent of the principle of ministerial responsibility cannot be determined by reading the Constitution and has to be established in parliamentary debates.

The parliamentary system depends upon and gives shape to an important principle of constitutionalism, which is perhaps as fundamental as the legality principle itself: publicity. The proceedings of Parliament are open to the public and they are reported upon by the news media and all limitations upon these and other forms of publicity are generally viewed with suspicion. Without the publicity principle, there would be no point to the demand that Parliament represents the entire people of the Netherlands. Internal cabinet discussions are, in contrast, not public but when they lead to results, publicity quickly comes into play. The cabinet and the ministers seek publicity through their publication of policy documents and bills. The Freedom of Information Act opens documents in possession of the government to public scrutiny, within a number of statutory defined limits (such as danger to the safety of the state or encroachment upon the private affairs of individuals). It is hardly possible to overestimate the importance of the publicity principle for the actual functioning of the parliamentary system; indeed, it is a necessary precondition for a *democratic* rule of law.

4.3   Separation of politics and administration

Political rights make the effective organization of citizens into political parties legally possible, opening up the vista of representative democracy. The parliamentary system provides the institutional infrastructure, giving wide scope to government to pursue its policies but placing all governmental activity under parliamentary scrutiny, thus reinforcing the ideal of representative democracy. As a consequence of the prominence of political rights and the parliamentary system, replacing more authoritarian arrangements and making representation a crucial component of politics, the relationship between politicians and civil servants had to be redefined as well.

The doctrine of the separation of politics and administration developed in response to this need. It has three components. The first one is the recognition of the primacy of politics. The administration of the state apparatus must be directed from the political centre. When the political process leads to new directives, for instance in the shape of new legislation, these directions must be followed immediately and administration may not try to circumvent them or to obstruct their execution. In turn, administrative activity derives its legitimacy in society from exactly this idea of the primacy of politics: the citizens can be told that they have to obey government orders and regulation and have to cooperate willingly with its policies because they have, through their representatives in Parliament, had a say in the political process authorizing them. Legality, in the sense of the primacy of politics expressing itself through legislation and regulation, works both ways: limiting governmental activities to an area allowed by the law and enabling government to act with increased authority and effectiveness.

The second component of the separation of politics and administration is the requirement of administrative neutrality. The administration should not only abstain from influencing the political process, it should also be neutral towards citizens and organizations. It should not be a political actor nor an adjunct to societal actors but occupy a neutral, impartial position. This means many things:
– The authorities must themselves scrupulously adhere to the law.
– They must always act in as public a manner as possible, making known their policies beforehand so that the public can orient itself on them.
– They must pursue a balance between all the interests at stake in a given administrative decision.
– They must promote legal certainty and legal equality.
– They must observe procedural fairness.

In the course of the 20th century, these standards of administrative neutrality were given legal shape in the principles of good governance, but long before this, the outlines of the demands following from the ideal of administrative neutrality were clear: to be lawful, impartial and fair.

The third component of the separation of politics and administration is the differentiation between policy and execution. Policy (in an untranslatable Dutch word, *beleid*) is seen as the determination of goals and the finding of suitable means to attain them and of planning procedures facilitating their achievement, all within the authorizations given by formal statute. So, policy is comparable to the political process in being about means and ends, but differs from it in being secondary, subordinate, auxiliary, directed activity (it obeys the demand of the primacy of politics). Policy is necessary because the legislator cannot know beforehand exactly what administrative activities will be needed. Statutes have to grant discretion to deal with the contingencies of administration. Once policy has been determined, in accordance with the statutory requirements, the execution of both policy and the laws can begin. This is seen as a different activity than the activity of deciding on policy, even though knowledge of the execution of policy is needed to update policy (and presumably, to adapt the laws when they are not adequate to the task). Under the heading of the execution of policy, at the end of the 19th and the beginning of the 20th centuries, administration increasingly became a matter of expertise. Insights derived from science (such as economics) were employed in the execution of policy. The cultivation of expert knowledge helped differentiate the domain of execution as a technical domain from policy making or from the democratic political processes at the back of it.

In conclusion of this tour of the democratic floor of the edifice of the *rechtsstaat*, it can be noted that the democratic institutions developed in the 19th century also animate political life in the 20th century. But after the 1960s, they are increasingly seen as inadequate, so that on all fronts demands for change are being articulated. The end of pillarization brought increased demands for more voter influence on political decision-making. The traditional elites were no longer trusted to the same extent. A new political party, D66, campaigned for more direct democracy, calling for a district system, supposedly making a more direct interaction between voters and their representatives possible. It was also sometimes argued that a number of important leadership positions should be open to election, bringing the parliamentary system nearer to a presidential system. In addition, it should be possible to hold referenda about important new laws. While political rights were widely felt to be too constricted and the parliamentary system was experienced as too alienated from what people think and want, the administration came under attack for its technocratic and bureaucratic character, not being responsive enough to new social needs. While the call for democratization came mostly from the left, the attack on bureaucracy was mainly inspired by the political right. All in all, the central tenets of the political system were challenged and became themselves a topic of political controversy. This, on the whole, did not lead to important changes in the democratic institutions developed in the 19th century.

5   The 20th century: social aspirations

The second floor of the Dutch edifice of the *rechtsstaat* houses legally recognized social aspirations. These are on the one hand derived from social aspirations already implicitly recognized on lower levels of the house of the *rechtsstaat*: they bring different interpretations of ideals such as equality and liberty. On the other hand, they represent an almost revolutionary change in the conception of what the state is and what it should aim to achieve. While liberal ideology conceives of the state as minimally as possible, as guarantor of basic freedom and social order, always respecting the market as the main mechanism for exchange and distribution, in the 20th century, a social consensus slowly emerges seeing the state in more ambitious terms: as the guarantor of the liberal values plus the right to lead a decent life, taking responsibility for the provision of a vast array of goods and services that are not automatically supplied by the market and redistributing incomes in order to achieve a measure of social justice. The state should not behave so much, as the saying goes, as a 'nightwatchman' protecting an ordered existence but as a 'caring parent', responding to the needs people individually and in groups are unable to cope with. The liberal state is supplanted by the welfare state. This means a vast growth of governmental activities and of the power bureaucracies have over the lives of people. As a reaction against this drastic change in the ambitions, the scale and the range of governmental activities, new guidelines for judicial review of administration have developed. The rooms to be found on the second floor of the Dutch *rechtsstaat* as a result mirror each other: Social Rights and Good Governance.

5.1   Social rights

Liberal rights protect individual freedom by not interfering with what people think and believe and do, except where these liberties produce harm to others or threaten overarching social aims (such as peace and order). Individuals are independent and autonomous beings, says the liberal axiom, and they must in crucial areas of life be left alone. Prototypical examples of liberal rights are the freedom of religion and the freedom of expression. Social rights also sponsor individual freedom but they do this quite differently: by interfering in the conditions preventing freedom from coming into being. The new supposition is that first some material conditions must be met before the liberties of the spirit can be fully enjoyed. The prototypical social rights are therefore the right to subsistence and the right to a measure of education; these are preconditions for a free and independent life. If liberal freedom can be called negative, requiring government abstention, social freedom is positive, it requires action rather than withdrawal.

Since 1981, the Dutch Constitution contains in its First Chapter a number of social rights:
– the right to work (article 19);
– the right to be provided with the means of subsistence, that is to be entitled to social security benefits (article 20);
– the right to live in a clean environment (article 21);
– the rights to health, housing, social and cultural development and leisure activities (all contained in article 22);
– the right to education and to receive financial support making education feasible (article 23, see also under liberal rights).

It is important to look at the way these rights are worded. They are no grandiose proclamations, promising as it were a Right to Universal Happiness. It is typically stated that the right in question shall be 'the concern of the authorities'. Government agencies are supposed to develop regulation and policies in order to work towards the achievement of the noble social aims, but they are not mandated to do so on pain of being answerable to a court when an individual thinks her social rights are not sufficiently realized. The social rights are declarations of intent rather than enforceable individual rights. There is one very important exception, however, that is the right to subsistence granted in article 20. The Constitution requires an Act of Parliament to make available an individually enforceable right to subsistence; this demand has indeed been realized in the General Subsistence Act *(Algemene Bijstandswet).*

The list of social rights recognized in the Constitution is interesting for another reason as well. It reflects the areas of government policy marked for their bureaucratic interventions in society and so illustrates nicely the shift away from the liberal state towards the welfare state. The functioning of the economy, social security systems, environmental policy, the organization of the health care system, land use planning and housing, even culture politics and the provision of leisure facilities are not mere topics of 'concern to the authorities', they are vast areas of intervention in which persistent problems appear that are never fully solved but displaced and deferred to the future. A welfare state taking responsibility for a broad range of social problems is expensive, it requires a lot of power and can be very bureaucratic. In all three aspects, a clash with liberal rights is possible. The money needed for the welfare state will have to come from taxation and redistribution of income, limiting the right to personal enjoyment of earned income that liberals value so greatly; the powers needed to be an efficient organization can infringe a whole range of civil liberties and the machine-like nature of bureaucracy virtually guarantees that people depending on it are never left alone in their privacy. As a countervailing power, the courts have been mobilized by citizens filing complaints and they have responded with a subtle doctrine of good governance.

5.2   Good governance

The first tentative steps towards a doctrine of good governance were taken in the period of social reconstruction following the Second World War. Rebuilding the country, the administration needed vast powers to intervene in society and direct the reconstruction efforts under way in all sectors of the economy; it also had to take many decisions about the allocation of scarce resources (such as housing facilities) that could not in the circumstances be left to market forces alone. The traditional liberal approach would have favored formal legislation authorising these interventions but the slow and cumbersome nature of the legislative process made this an unworkable option. As a compromise between the ideal of legality and the practical necessities of administration, the autorizations were indeed laid down in formal statutes but in very general terms only, while the regulations actually binding upon the citizens were articulated in legislation futher down the hierarchy. These lower-level regulations would, moreover, provide ample 'discretionary powers' for administration. As a result, the administration was in many areas of governance no longer materially bound by formal statutes. In compensation of this legality deficit, the courts started to develop case by case a new doctrine of good governance, stating a number of principles of due process, fairness and reasonableness that in a democracy upholding the ideals of the rule of law would have to be followed by any government agency worthy of the name.

It started out rather modestly with a theory of *marginal judicial review.* A conceptual distinction was made between those aspects of a governmental decision that were legal and those that were dictated by considerations of policy. The courts promised not to enter into the policy considerations, refusing to judge on the effectiveness of the measures the government agency was taking, but it reserved the right to judge on the legality of these considerations and decisions. It would thus presumably not interfere with the core of governmental activity but only check the margins. The first court cases under this theory of marginal judicial review concerned governmental acts for which a wide discretion had been granted but where no rational policy at all could be discerned, so that the element of reasonableness was totally lacking. The pronouncement was that in this case 'no reasonable human being' could conceivably have come to the decision taken. This was rather stark language but relating to a very limited domain of legality; as soon as some person could be found who could provide reasonable arguments, so it seemed, the courts would not object.

In the course of time, the reasonableness test of good governance underwent a subtle change, however, which greatly increased its practical value. The courts no longer looked for imaginary human beings who could be supposed to conceive of possible reasons justifying a governmental act but they started to distinguish a number of principles of good governance which all reasonable citizens could expect to be observed by their government in all its acts. This effort to develop a system of principles of good governance generated wide support, in the academic world but also among citizen groups, and finally also from the formal legislature who mandated, after the fact, the courts to develop these general principles of good governance further. So, under the umbrella of marginal judicial review, in fact a very thorough and extensive control of the legality of administration could mature.

It is customary to distinguish between formal and material general principles of good governance. The set of formal general principles itself focuses first of all on the qualities of the processes through which the government agency has reached its decision:
- the principle of careful preparation, requiring among others that all relevant aspects of the decision are taken into account;
- the principle of fair play, demanding that citizens are treated without prejudice, receiving equal chances to get a positive answer to their requests (for instance for a government permit to do something);
- the prohibition of wrongful use of procedural options, requiring government agencies to choose such a process of decision as affords most guarantees for reasonableness.

There are also formal general principles relating to the way decisions are argued:
- the principle of correct motivation, demanding arguments that can truly be said to support the decision taken (and so not omitting or distorting relevant arguments);
- the principle of formal legal certainty, requiring a formulation of the decision that is clear and without ambiguities.

The material general principles formulate demands relating to the content of the decision taken:

- the demand of material legal certainty, prompting government agencies to live by their own earlier decisions and forbidding, for instance, retroactive decisions when these are detrimental to the citizens concerned;
- the principle of good faith relating to expectations, stating that when a government agency has acted in such a way as to evoke a justified expectation on the part of citizens, the government agency must make good on its promise;
- the equality principle of governance, requiring equal treatment of persons and cases on the basis of the policy objectives laid down by the government agency and prompting government agencies in their development of policy purposes to seek to distinguish between categories only on the basis of objectively relevant differences;
- the principle of material careful preparation, holding that there must always be a balancing of all the interests pertaining to a policy or a decision and requiring that this balancing process uses only arguments that are fair, impartial and proportional.

Taken together, the formal and the material general principles of good governance have become a vast network of rule-of-law considerations, applicable to all governmental decision processes and their outcomes. The vast power of government bureaucracies is increasingly held up for court inspection as to its legality in this expanded sense. But the system is still officially grounded on the ideal of marginal judicial review, leaving wide discretion to agencies for using political and policy considerations in the conduct of administration. Not surprisingly, a tension is often seen between the encompassing practice of judical review and the marginal judicial review doctrine, with some critics holding that the courts are too actively interfering in the normal democratic processes of public administration and other critics complaining about the reluctance of the courts to really go all the way in protecting the liberal and social rights of the citizens against government intrusions.

6   Why the *rechtsstaat* is permanently under construction

Here ends our guided tour through the edifice of the Dutch *rechtsstaat*. After a brief visit to the foundations where we saw some of the remnants of the legal and the republican traditions, we have on the ground floor of the house of the rechtsstaat visited the stately period rooms of the liberal ideals of the rechtsstaat in their 18th century articulation and have looked upon their gradual realization. We have then climbed to the first floor of the edifice, where the democratic institutions were located which, from the 19th century onwards, have made it possible to practice what was preached. Climbing higher still, we discovered on the second floor the social aspirations that in the 20th century turned the liberal state into the welfare state. We have indeed come far. Looking back on what we have discovered, remembering the many rooms and their different interiors, we do not see the kind of fixity we would expect in a museum where every object is periodized and neatly labelled and located in the correct period room. Instead, it seems that in all the rooms, on all three floors, there is construction work underway and we see many objects belonging to one room or century being transported to other rooms where they also might belong. It is as if the whole edifice of the *rechtsstaat* is simultaneously inhabited by the Dutch people and subject to very thorough revisions.

This indeed is, metaphorically speaking, the true condition of legality in the Netherlands: it is permanently under revision and under reconstruction. Why? Are the Dutch restless innovators, slaves to new modes of thought, open to all kinds of influences and international trends? Or do their ideals and institutions and aspirations constantly fail to provide the direction and the protection expected from constitutional law? There is some truth to both of these suggestions. The Netherlands are no island in the world or in Europe. When international trends and developments mark different conceptions of legality, the Netherlands are bound to follow. An example is the spread of constitutionally guaranteed liberal and social rights after World War II, when the Dutch enthusiastically took up the cause of international protection of human rights. Likewise, the remarkable prominence of judicial control, manifested in the idea of the balance of powers and in the ideals of human rights review and good governance, can be related to international trends in most Western states where judge-made law has on the whole become much more important. It is, on the other hand, also true that in the Netherlands there is often disappointment about the real protection or the real direction provided by constitutional guarantees. The democratic institutions of the parliamentary system are not above criticism, the guarantees offered by the formal process of legislation often do not lead to laws that are generally accepted as expressions of the General Will. The old liberal ideals need to be reassessed in a welfare state and the new social rights do not of themselves produce universal happiness. Tampering with the system of the rule of law is definitely also a result of inbred frustrations caused by a constitutional system that promises more and greater things than it can deliver.

But this is not the whole story. The need to periodically undertake vast reconstruction efforts of the edifice of the *rechtsstaat*, even while the building remains inhabited, is given with the nature of the enterprise. When the related ideals of the rule of law or of legality or of the constitutional state first take hold, there is no neat blueprint available for a building optimizing all of the conflicting demands made under such ideal conceptions. It is at the outset not clear how government can both protect individual freedom and achieve social objectives, what solidarity means in a world of free markets, how legislation can be an expression of what the people want and judges can still independently provide justice in individual cases; it is forever problematic how the ideals have to become translated institutionally. Once preliminary institutionalizations have taken place, the danger manifests itself of a loss of meaning in the actual operations of the new structures and processes. Do the government machines subsidizing housing, education and health really promote the liberties of individuals? The inbuilt tension between the ideal and its manifestation in practices means that reconstruction has to be undertaken, not only in order to cope with new developments and to answer new challenges to the ideals, but also to keep institutions and practices alive to their original purposes. The *rechtsstaat* will never be a fully ordered state or a closed society.

Meanwhile, the dynamics of reconstruction are greatly stimulated by the fact that the world in which the Dutch live is changing all the time. New challenges to the ideals of the *rechtsstaat* and their practical realization are continually under way. An example is the emergence of the information society. According to Bovens, it has four distinguishing features, all of them affecting the edifice of the rechtsstaat:
– deterritorialization, or the tendency to cross borders and disengage activities from specific physical locations, thus undercutting the presumption of sovereignty of the constitutional state over a territory with physical borders;
– turbulence, or the speed and unpredictability of new technologies, threatening the stability of regulations and administrative practices;
– horizontalization, or the replacement of hierarchical power relations by horizontal relations of mutual influence, promoting many different kinds of negotiated arrangements of decision-making and undermining the authority of the state;
– dematerialization, or the increasing importance of information (intangible) rather than other resources for the interactions between citizens and the government and between citizens generally, affecting the way citizenship is defined (citizens are for example no longer equal when some of them have better access to important information).[3]

In sum, in the information society government loses the certainty of many of its traditional methods of governance. At the same time, it has to find new ways of realizing the old liberal ideals, it has to redesign its democratic institutions and shape its social aspirations differently. Bovens argues that the principle of legality will lose much of its meaning in the information society unless it is supplementend by an increase in transparency (of the regulations themselves but also of the policy processes and of policy performances). He predicts a shift towards more horizontal relations within the constitutional state and argues for new information rights as a fourth generation of rights (supplementing the liberal, political and social rights defined earlier in the history of the *rechtsstaat*). All in all, he is in favour of adding a fourth floor to the edifice of the *rechtsstaat*.

It is too soon to be able to say whether the emerging information society will indeed bring such profound changes to the edifice of the *rechtsstaat* as Bovens envisages. But what is certain is that the reconstruction of the *rechtsstaat* will continue. Facing new challenges and contemplating novel mechanisms for the rule of law, driven by frustration about what actually has been achieved as part of the project of the constitutional state, the Dutch will not be content to leave the old structures intact; surely, they want to live in a better house.

---

3. M.A.P. Bovens, *De digitale rechtsstaat*, Alphen aan den Rijn: Samsom 1999.

5 Legislation in the Netherlands

The Communicative Turn[*]

Bart van Klink

1 The powers of the written word

In modern society, legislation is one of the main instruments the government uses to influence people's behaviour. Although empirical research has shown that laws often do not achieve their goals and produce many harmful side-effects,[1] there is still a strong faith in the powers of the written word. In times of crisis, people are inclined to call for more legislation to solve the problem at hand, whereas legislation might as well be part of the problem. Or, the existing laws may seem correct *on paper*, but they may simply not be sufficiently enforced and upheld *in practice*. A catastrophe in recent Dutch history illustrates the point. On New Year's Day 2001, a bar in Volendam burnt down and fourteen people were killed and many people were badly injured. The fire was caused by fireworks that set the Christmas decoration on fire (which was hanging rather low from the ceiling). In reaction to an appeal for stricter rules, the Dutch Minister of Health, Welfare and Sport introduced a law that put a ban on clothes that easily catch fire within a second. Although most of the clothes nowadays already conform to this standard, research showed that the Volendam fire occurred not only because the rules were not strict enough, but above all because there had not been proper safety inspections in bars and because the responsible authorities had not coordinated their activities properly.[2]

In this chapter, it will be shown how laws are made in the Netherlands and how the Dutch government tries to cope with the different kinds of problems legislation can cause. Firstly, the process of legislation – which starts with the political decision to make law and ends with the Act entering into force – is described (section 2). Secondly, the policy that the government developed in order to improve the effectiveness as well as the lawfulness of legislation is dealt with (section 3). Thirdly, some new forms of regulation are discussed that are supposed to solve, at least partially, many of the problems that are connected with traditional, so-called instrumental legislation (section 4). As will become clear, part of the solution is sought, both in legal practice and in legal theory, in making law more flexible and

---

[*] The author thanks Sanne Taekema for her useful comments on the first draft of this chapter. Laetitia Laman and Rob van Gestel helped me in finding the appropriate literature. Moreover, I would like to thank Hildegard Penn for her thorough (and merciless!) correction of my English.
1. See, e.g., A. Allott, *The Limits of Law*, London: Butterworths 1980.
2. To be sure, there were some serious deficiencies in the existing legislation, but the main problems occurred in the enforcement practice (see further section 3.2).

more responsive to the wishes and the needs of citizens. In the final section, this 'communicative turn' will be evaluated briefly and some speculations about its future will be presented (section 5).

2 The process of legislation

2.1 Making law through Acts of Parliament: nine phases

Before a set of rules can be called a 'law' officially, quite some time passes during which many people have to do a lot of work. This section describes the Dutch process of legislation for bills, which are usually proposed by the government and have to be accepted by both government and Parliament. The passing of other kinds of legislation (such as regulations originating from the government or a minister only) follows different, less extensive, procedures, which will not be discussed here. The way in which the Dutch Constitution may be amended and European Community regulations are implemented in Dutch legislation will be described briefly.

A bill passes through several phases, from its preparation to the official publication of the Act in the *Staatsblad* (Bulletin of Acts and Orders).[3] The process of legislation is embodied partly in written laws (the Constitution, the 1962 Act on the Council of State and several procedural regulations), in policy documents such as the *Aanwijzingen voor de regelgeving* (Recommendations for Regulations) and the *Draaiboek voor de wetgeving* (Scenario for Legislation),[4] and partly given shape in actual practice. Below, nine phases will be described.

A Phase of initiative
In the phase of initiative, a competent authority – in most cases an individual minister or the government as a whole, occasionally the Second Chamber of Parliament[5] – takes the decision to start preparations for new legislation or the amendment of existing legislation. This decision can be made for several reasons: because political parties agreed to do so in their negotiations to form a coalition government, because pressure groups or organizations in society ask for new legislation, because of EC (or other international) obligations, because an urgent problem emerges that calls for immediate legislative action, because policy-making officials take the initiative, and so on. Ideally, the initial phase results in a project plan for the development of the legislation, to which the responsible authority has agreed.

---

3. These phases are described in P. Eijlander & W. Voermans, *Wetgevingsleer*, Deventer: W.E.J. Tjeenk Willink 1999, chapter 12.
4. Published as *Aanwijzingen voor de regelgeving*, Den Haag: Sdu 1998, and *Draaiboek voor de wetgeving. Systematische beschrijving van de procedure*, Ministerie van Justitie, directie Wetgeving, Den Haag: Sdu 1996.
5. A recent example is the proposal to penalise stalking, which is now codified in the Dutch Penal Code. Because the Second Chamber seldom make uses of its right to initiate legislation, the process of legislation will in the following be described for bills that are proposed by (a member of) the government.

B Departmental preparations

After it has been decided that new legislation has to be made or existing legislation should be amended, preparations are started within a ministry. If the legislation deals with a complex and important subject matter (such as the amendment of the Dutch Civil Code), preparations are carried out mostly according to a pre-established plan. This means that a permanent group of officials, a so-called task force, prepares the draft text of the law and the accompanying explanatory memorandum. In the explanatory memorandum, the general aims of the law are stated and an explanation is given per article. Preferably, the task force that is responsible for the preparation consists of policy-making officials or experts in the given field, legislative officials and persons who are acquainted with the execution and enforcement of the law. Experts from outside the ministry concerned can be added to the team or can be asked for advice. On some occasions, a so-called draft bill *(voorontwerp)* is made in order to stimulate public debate on the matter. The outcomes of the debate are incorporated in the eventual text of the bill. Although this procedure may seem time consuming, it often increases the political support for the bill. Draft bills are mostly made public and have to be discussed in the Cabinet only if the draft bill is expected to have significant political or financial consequences, if it touches on the position of the Cabinet or on the policy of other departments, if it has not been possible to reach an agreement beforehand or if the draft bill is a report of an advisory board from outside the ministry concerned.

The departmental preparations not only consist in writing texts, but also in the collection of materials, the consultation of experts and further planning. Gradually, in close co-operation with the officials concerned, general policy agreements are transformed into more concrete, legal rules. At the end of this phase, a bill is presented to the responsible official, who decides whether the bill can be presented to other ministries for consultation.

C Interdepartmental consultations

It is important that bills are presented to other ministries for consultation, primarily because it improves the quality of the legislation. In other departments, there may be knowledge and experience about certain aspects of the bill, with which the bill can be improved. Secondly, such consultations increase the political support for the bill and prevent that other members of the government be surprised when it is discussed in the Cabinet. However, sometimes problems arise out of the interdepartmental organization. To begin with, the necessary consultation of and cooperation with other departments take a lot of time. Besides, the coordination is not always perfect, as the *Securitel* case showed in 1996.[6] Because of a lack of coordination, the Dutch

---

6. C-194/94, *CIA Security v. Signalson and Securitel*, ECR [1996] I-2201. In response to the Securitel case, the Dutch government decided in 1998 that in each department the quality of the legislation organization and the process of legislation should be investigated periodically. For that reason, the Review Committee on Legislation was appointed. The final report of this Committee, called *Van wetten weten* ('Knowing about Laws' – the pun gets lost in translation, fortunately), was published in April 2002.

government omitted to inform the European Commission in the proper way about new technical regulations, so these regulations were considered 'not applicable' by the European Court of Justice. To tackle these problems, some authors advised to set up a central and independent directorate for legislation.

It depends on the subject matter which other ministries are consulted. In any case, the Ministry of Justice is involved. The Ministry of Justice judges whether the bill complies with constitutional, European and international rules and standards, and with the Rule of Law. In this evaluation, the requirements of good legislation have an important place: lawfulness, feasibility and enforceability, effectiveness and efficiency, subsidiarity and proportionality.[7] The Ministry of Justice will also be consulted if the bill has a bearing on civil law, penal law and/or the general part of the administrative law. The Ministry of Economic Affairs looks into the financial consequences of the Bill and the Ministry of the Interior considers its effects for lower bodies. If a department is heavily involved in the preparation of a bill, it sometimes co-signs the bill with the ministry that initiated the process of legislation.

D Advice and deliberation

In order to improve the communicative quality of the legislative process, qualified advisory boards and organizations are asked for advice and are involved in deliberations about the bill. By consulting people from the 'world outside', the responsible authority is able to check the support in society for a bill and to benefit from their knowledge and experience. Moreover, it helps to close the gap between the law in the book (the legal text) and the law in action (the way in which the legal text is put into practice). What departments have produced in their ivory towers, often appears not to work in real life. It is hoped that by consulting representatives of all those involved beforehand the law can be better upheld. However, the responsible authority is not obliged to ask for advice, but it *can* do so. An exception is constituted by the Council of State, which *always* has to be consulted about bills.[8] Advisory boards and organizations can give advice without a prior request. For example, the Dutch Social and Economic Council or SER *(Sociaal-Economische Raad)* gives advice to the government, either solicited or unsolicited, on social and economic issues. The SER checks, among other things, whether a bill promotes a balanced economic growth and sustainable development, the largest possible labour participation and a fair distribution of incomes.[9] As a rule, advice given is published.

E Decision of the Cabinet

Next, the bill is discussed by the Cabinet. If all ministers agree, the Cabinet takes the decision that the bill is sent to the Council of State for advice. This decision implies that the responsible minister is authorized to present the bill to the Second Chamber of Parliament, unless the Council of State severely criticizes the bill or the bill is

---

7. These requirements will be discussed in more detail in section 3.
8. See further under F.
9. See www.ser.nl.

amended substantially after the advice given by the Council of State. The Cabinet may also decide that the bill will be shelved, that further deliberation between the responsible authorities has to take place, that the responsible minister will deliberate with one or more colleagues involved and that, if an agreement is reached, he will be authorized to ask the Council of State for advice, or that it agrees with sending the bill to the Council of State, together with a remark that the bill will be amended on certain points. A bill on which the Cabinet has agreed is not publicly accessible. However, usually, the minister primarily responsible will publish a press report in which the main lines of the bill are stated.

F Advice from the Council of State

The Council of State has to give its opinion about bills, drafts for orders in council (*algemene maatregelen van bestuur*) and proposals to approve treaties. The Council of State is the last and most authoritative advisor of the government in legislative matters. Besides, a section of the Council of State is an appeal court in matters of administrative law, a combination of functions which has given rise to the criticism that the Council disturbs the balance of power.[10] Advice by the Council is, in the first place, intended for the minister(s) or other members of the government who introduce the bill. Indirectly, the advice is addressed to the members of Parliament and all those involved in the process of legislation. It is possible to appeal to the advice during the deliberation in Parliament. As it is published, the advice of the Council is accessible to the public. On average, the Council needs five months to draw up its advice. After the advice has been given, in the department a so-called further report (*nader rapport*) is made in which the responsible authority gives its reaction to the advice. Depending on the content of the advice and possible prior arrangements, the (amended) bill, the advice and the further report will be discussed in the Cabinet. In this phase, amendments in the text of the bill are generally only small, because the Council of State is not in a position to advise about them. If the amendments are more drastic, they have to be sent to the Council for advice.

Together with the introduction of the bill in the Second Chamber, the advice of the Council of State and the accompanying further report are published. The Council of State judges the bill according to standards of good legislation. The Council checks primarily whether the arguments that are given for the choices made, are sound. These arguments can be found, in particular, in the explanatory memorandum that accompanies the bill. In addition, the Council pays attention to the correct use of regulation, conformity with European and international law, with the Constitution and principles of law, consistency with other, connected legislation and the technical qualities of the bill. The advice results in a judgement in which the Council addresses the question whether the bill can be sent to the Second Chamber or not. In the best case, the Council agrees with the bill and advises to send the bill to the Second

---

10. This seems to follow from the decision of the European Court of Human Rights in the *Procola* case, 28 September 1995, *Pub. ECHR*, Series A, vol. 326.

Chamber. In the worst case, the Council advises not to send it (which is really a disgrace for the responsible authority). In 1999, the Council of State criticized severely a bill on labour and care because, among other things, the framework it set was considered to be too vague. As a consequence, the Cabinet had to reconsider the bill. There was no political support for changing the bill itself, but to the explanatory memorandum and the further report extensive argumentations were added.[11] After consultation of the Council of State, the bill is ready for presentation in Parliament.

G Presentation of the bill in the Second Chamber

The Dutch Parliament is divided into two separate houses: the Second Chamber *(Tweede Kamer)* and the First Chamber *(Eerste Kamer)*. In principle, both houses fulfil the same function: both are part of the legislature, both have been granted parliamentary rights, such as the right of (parliamentary) enquiry, the right of interpellation and the right to question. Together they constitute the States General or Netherlands Parliament *(Staten-Generaal)*. The States General are supposed to represent the entire Dutch population, according to article 50 of the Dutch Constitution. Political primacy is located within the Second Chamber. The Second Chamber consists of 150 members, who are elected directly by the people in elections every fourth year, while the 75 members of the First Chamber have no direct, but an 'indirect' democratic mandate. They are elected by the Provincial States, whose members are chosen directly by the people in elections every fourth year. The First Chamber likes to think of itself as a *chambre de réflexion* (chamber of reconsideration) that guards against unconstitutional or otherwise bad legislation. It is composed of members whose main occupation is outside Parliament, while membership of the Second Chamber is a full-time job. According to some legal scholars, the Second Chamber does not take its duty to supervise the quality of legislation seriously enough. It is accused of falling victim to the current fads of public opinion. It is supposed to pay too little attention to the requirements stated in the *Recommendations for Regulations* and to the commentaries of the Council of State. However justified the criticism often may seem, it does fail to appreciate the political character of this institution. It is not there to make the best legislation possible, but first and foremost to defend specific interests and to please the electorate.

A bill is first sent to the Second Chamber, because of the latter's political primacy. In the process of legislation, the Second Chamber has two special rights that the First Chamber does not have: the right to propose new legislation and the right to amend bills.

As soon as a bill reaches the Second Chamber, a standing committee, consisting of members of the Chamber, is charged with preparatory research. The committee

---

11. The *Kaderwet Arbeid en Zorg* (Framework Act Labour and Care) came into force on 1 December 2001 (see *Stb.* 2001, 567). This example is borrowed from P. Eijlander & W. Voermans *(Evaluatie regeerakkoord 1998 vanuit wetgevingsperspectief,* Tilburg: Schoordijk Instituut, Universiteit van Tilburg 2002, p. 47-50).

delivers a report on the bill, which consists of the written comments on the bill provided by the various parliamentary groups within the committee. The authority concerned responds with a memorandum of reply. Sometimes, the committee and the government produce more than one report and memorandum. If there are no comments, a blank report is delivered. In the course of the preliminary research, the committee can at any time decide to deliberate with the government, both orally and in writing. Moreover, it makes inquiries by, e.g., paying working visits, consulting experts and arranging public hearings. The government has the competence to amend the bill, as long as the Second Chamber has not accepted the bill. Such amendments are embodied in a ministerial memorandum of amendment *(nota van wijziging)*, to which an explanation is added. On far-reaching amendments, the Council of State is consulted if the Cabinet so decides. Like the government, the Second Chamber is entitled to propose amendments. The right to amend bills is one of the most significant powers of the Second Chamber. Usually, the amendments of the Second Chamber are introduced later on in the process, just before or during the plenary discussion. The Council of State is not consulted on these amendments. The authority concerned can adopt an amendment from the Second Chamber. In that case, the amendment is part of the bill.

After the parliamentary investigations have been completed, a process which may take years, the plenary discussion of the bill starts. The discussion in the Second Chamber takes place in two phases. In the first phase, the bill is debated as a whole. Members of the Second Chamber are allowed to ask questions about the bill, which the minister concerned subsequently answers. In the second phase, the separate articles are discussed. Members of the Second Chamber deliver a reply *(repliek)* and the minister offers his rejoinder *(dupliek)*. During the plenary discussion, members of the Second Chamber as well as of the government can propose changes to the bill. When the discussion is closed, the Second Chamber turns to deciding on the bill and on the amendments (if there are any). There is a vote per article. As soon as a decision is made on all articles and the preamble of the bill, the Chamber takes the final decision on the bill as a whole. The official concerned has the competence to give his opinion on the amendments and on the possible rejection of the bill. For example, he may discourage an amendment or declare it unacceptable. It has far-reaching consequences if the official states that a possible rejection of the bill is unacceptable; if the Second Chamber nevertheless rejects the bill, the official concerned – in most cases the minister or the state secretary under whose authority the bill was drafted, but sometimes the government as a whole – may decide to resign. However, if a bill does not seem to have sufficient support in the Second Chamber, the official will withdraw the bill in most cases. If the bill is accepted, it will be prepared for presentation in the First Chamber.

H Presentation of the bill in the First Chamber
In comparison with the Second Chamber, the procedure in the First Chamber is less complicated and therefore takes less time, as a rule, because the First Chamber has no right to amend bills, nor does it have the right to initiate legislation, which the

Second Chamber has. That is, it has no right to propose new legislation. As soon as a bill is introduced in the First Chamber, the government cannot amend it anymore. Like in the Second Chamber, a standing committee is charged with preparatory research. During the research, several documents (an interim report, a memorandum of reply or a statement with reference to the government report, the committee's final report) can be exchanged. Subsequently, there is a plenary discussion of the bill in the First Chamber, on a Tuesday, the only day in the week on which the First Chamber meets. Members of the First Chamber simply have the choice either to accept the bill or to reject it. Therefore, they vote exclusively on the bill as a whole. If, during the discussion in the First Chamber, it becomes clear that the majority in the First Chamber will not accept the bill without amendments, the government can submit a proposal of amendment to the Second Chamber. This exceptional document, which constitutes in fact a right to amendment in disguise, is called an amending Act *(novelle)*. Alternatively, the government can decide to withdraw the bill altogether. Usually, the First Chamber is reluctant to reject a bill, because the Second Chamber has the political primacy. In the rare case that the First Chamber rejects a bill that has been passed by the Second Chamber, Dutch constitutional law does not have any arrangement for resolving this conflict. Therefore, some authors have proposed a conflict ruling that gives the Second Chamber the final say.[12]

As mentioned before, the 75 members of the First Chamber have no direct mandate, in contrast to the Second Chamber, whose 150 members are elected directly by the people in elections every fourth year. Some legal scholars have argued that the members of the First Chamber should also be elected directly instead of by members of the Provincial States, while others have argued for an entire abolition of this – what they consider as – old-fashioned institute or 'old people's home for retired politicians'. The discussion about its status was rekindled after 18 May 1999, when the First Chamber rejected – by only one vote! – a bill which proposed to add to the Constitution a corrective legislative referendum.[13] This remarkable episode in recent Dutch political history is called 'the night of Wiegel', after the liberal senator whose vote was held responsible for the rejection of the bill.[14] Although the outcome may not always seem pleasant, many people feel that the reflection the First Chamber provides is not a luxury we can do without in these busy times.

---

12. Kortmann & Bovend'Eert ('The Netherlands', in: *International Encyclopedia of Laws. Constitutional Law*, Suppl. 35, January 2000, The Hague: Kluwer Law International 1992-... at p. 88).
13. A corrective legislative referendum is an opinion poll among all citizens of a country (or a particular group of citizens) about a bill, on which the citizens can only vote 'yes' or 'no'; the only other possibilities are not voting or returning a blank vote. Under certain conditions (e.g., a sufficient number of people have voted in the referendum), the government has the duty to submit to the will of the people.
14. Which is, of course, nonsense from a logical point of view, because one vote *in itself* can never constitute a majority; only a *sum* of votes can.

1 Signing the act and publication

After the acceptance of a bill by the First Chamber, only a number of formal actions have to be carried out in order to enact the bill. An Act of Parliament has to receive the royal assent from the Dutch Queen. She signs the original version of the Act, which is already signed by the presidents of the Second Chamber and the First Chamber and the *slotformulier* (final document) of the law. Subsequently, the Act is sent to the primarily responsible ministry in order to be countersigned. The countersigning authorities sign twice. Finally, the law is published in the *Staatsblad* (Bulletin of Acts and Orders) together with the date as of which the Act is to come into force (which must be later than the date of publication in order to prevent retroactive legislation). As soon as the Act has reached the *Staatsblad* and has entered into force, the legislator's job is formally completed. However, it has to be checked whether the Act is complied with. Does the law in the books correspond with law in practice? Nowadays, many Acts contain provisions in which the duty to evaluate that particular Act, once or periodically, is codified (the so-called *evaluatiebepalingen* or evaluation provisions). The duty to supervise has to be carried out by the legislator, in particular the department(s) involved. Depending on the results of the evaluation, the legislator can decide to start the legislative process all over again. In this sense, the process of legislation is an ongoing, cyclical process.

In figure 6, an overview is given of the process of legislation in the Netherlands.

2.2 Amending the Constitution

In the Dutch Constitution, fundamental rights, such as equality, freedom of religion, freedom of speech, the right to vote or to stand for election, are incorporated. Furthermore, the Constitution consists of provisions concerning the organization of the state. The most important organs are mentioned (for instance, the government, Parliament and the Council of State), together with their competence. As such, the Constitution provides the legal foundation of our society. The present Constitution dates back to 1815; it has been amended many times since. The last time the Constitution was amended was in 1983.

The procedure for amending the Constitution is more complicated than the procedure for Acts of Parliament as described above. Article 137 of the Dutch Constitution demands that a proposal for amendment be discussed twice in the Second Chamber and the First Chamber. During the first hearing, the procedure is the same as for 'ordinary' statutes. After the preparation of the amendment(s), the proposal is sent to the Second Chamber and to the First Chamber for approval (in that order). If the proposal is accepted by both, Parliament has to be dissolved and general elections have to be held. The new government has to present the proposal for amending the Constitution again in the Second Chamber and the First Chamber, where it will be discussed by the newly elected members. During this second discussion, both only have the choice of either accepting the proposal or rejecting it; amendments to the proposal are not allowed. Moreover, in order to

111

A Phase of initiative	B Departmental preparations	C Interdepartmental consultations
A minister, a state secretary or the government decides that preparations for new legislation are to start.	The bill is drafted by a ministry, together with an explanatory memorandum.	The bill is presented to other departments for consultation.
D Advice and deliberation	E Decision of the Cabinet	F Advice from the Council of State
Organizations in society may be asked for advice.	The Cabinet discusses the bill and decides whether the bill can be sent to the Council of State.	The Council of State gives its advice on the bill.
G Presentation of the bill in the Second Chamber	H Presentation of the bill in the First Chamber	I Signing the Act and publication
A standing committee studies and delivers a report on the bill; the Second Chamber secretaries may amend the bill; first there is a vote on every article of the bill and then there is a vote on the bill as a whole.	A standing committee studies and delivers a report on the bill; the First Chamber discusses the bill and votes on it; formally, the First Chamber has no right to amend the bill.	For the bill to be enacted, it is to be signed by the Queen and the ministers and/or state secretary involved; finally, the law is published in the *Staatsblad*.

Figure 6 - The process of legislation in the Netherlands

accept the proposal, a so-called 'qualified majority' is required, that is, two-third of the votes that are cast. If the proposal gets approval both times, the Constitution is amended.

Although the Constitution does not have the same 'holy' status it has, for example, in the United States, it is thought to be a good thing that the Constitution cannot be changed as easily as 'normal' legislation since it contains our basic values and arrangements. In sum, three important 'safety valves' are built into this system. Firstly, the proposal is discussed twice in the government and in Parliament. Secondly, the citizens are consulted between the two discussions by means of general elections. Finally, a proposal can only be accepted in the second discussion by a qualified, two-thirds majority. Some authors, however, have argued that the second safety valve – consultation of the citizens – has little meaning because in actual practice constitutional amendments are 'taken along' with the ordinary, periodical elections. In that case, the amendment become only one of the many other possible focal points during the election campaign.[15]

In the Netherlands, the judge does not have the competency to test Acts of Parliament against the standards of the Constitution.[16] The legislature – that is, members of the government and Parliament – is considered to be able to judge whether a bill complies with constitutional provisions or not. Several Dutch scholars have expressed their doubts on this point and have argued that judges in general or some special legal institution should have the right of constitutional review.[17] However, it is still assumed that such a right contravenes the separation of powers doctrine: a small and non-elected group of judges should not have the possibility to overrule the will of the people, as expressed in law by the government and the States General. Since judges already have the competence to review Acts of Parliament against the standards of higher European legislation, in which almost the same values are embodied as in the Dutch Constitution, there does not exist a strict separation of powers. It would therefore be more consistent – as some authors argue – to grant judges the right of constitutional review. That would also improve the Constitution's status as an important source of law.

2.3 The implementation of EC decisions

Of course, the Dutch legal order does not exist in splendid isolation. The importance of international law has increased over the years and it increasingly influences the substance of Dutch legislation. As stated in article 93 of our Constitution, legal rules from an international origin – for example, provisions of treaties or resolutions by international institutions – penetrate directly into our legal order, in so far as they contain provisions that may be binding on all persons 'by virtue of their contents'. This is the so-called moderately monistic system, according to which the rules of international law do not have to be converted to national law in order to be binding (as is the case in a dualistic system), but are binding directly under certain conditions (that is why the system is called '*moderately* monistic'). Citizens can derive rights from this international law, government agencies have to comply with it and the Dutch judge must apply it as part of the positive law. Article 94 of the Dutch Constitution even states that regulations which spring from treaties and resolutions

---

15. W.E. Bakema, 'Het parlement als institutie', in: TH.L. Bellekom et al. (ed.), *Inleiding staatkunde*, Leiden: Samsom 1991, p. 249-274.
16. A judge has the competence to test lower legislation, such as regulations by a minister, against the standards of the Constitution.
17. See, e.g., B. van Roermund (ed.), *Constitutional Review/Verfassungsgerichtbarkeit/Constitutionele toetsing. Theoretical and Comparative Perspectives*, Deventer: Kluwer Law and Taxation Publishers 1993.

by international institutions and which are binding on all persons have precedence over national statutory regulations in cases of conflict. If a matter is regulated by international law that has priority over national law, the Dutch legislature only has the possibility to supply the international law with supporting rules. Often, international law demands legislative action from the national government as well. This means that the national legislature has a duty to make rules of its own, for example, to improve the working conditions in its country.

In many areas (for example, economic affairs, traffic, agriculture and fishery), EC law is nowadays the most important source of international law in the Dutch legal order.[18] EC law can be conceived as the law that springs from the treaties establishing European integration, such as the Treaty on European Union,[19] the EEC Treaty (in which the European Member States decided to cooperate more closely in economic affairs)[20] and the law that is created by official institutions of the European Union (such as the European Commission). The Dutch legal order is an integral part of the EC legal order that is involved increasingly in policy- and law-making. Because of the rise of EC law, the legislature in the Member States has less room for national regulation and is, instead, more occupied with the implementation and realization of European law. Independent of the system of reception in a country (as stated above, in the Netherlands there is a moderately monistic system), EC law has so-called direct applicability within the legal domain of the Member States; its applicability thus does not depend on conversion into national legislation. This is an important difference between EC law and most other types of international law. In ordinary treaties between sovereign states, a number of binding agreements are laid down, whereas in EC treaties a whole new legal order is created, whereby the Member States have conferred certain powers to a supranational body and, as a result, have lost (part of) their sovereignty.

Besides direct applicability, EC law in many cases has direct effect as well. To have direct effect means that European directions are directly, without interference from a member state, applicable to the citizens of the Community. The national judge can also apply EC directions that are meant to have direct effect (which is not always the case). Moreover, to have direct effect means that citizens can appeal to EC directions, not only against a member state, but also against each other. There is one exception:

---

18. 'EC' stands for 'European Community'. Although there are in fact three European communities, established through three different treaties, it is more common to speak of the European Community as a general category. The Maastricht Treaty established the European Union as an even more general category in order to indicate that the Member States aim at cooperation, not only in economic and internal affairs and in matters of justice (the first and second pillar of European cooperation), but also with regard to foreign and safety policy (the third pillar). Within the European Community, directives and regulations are promulgated, whereas the European Union produces 'soft law', that is agreements between Member States.
19. Treaty on European Union, [1992], OJ C 24, or, in short, the Maastricht Treaty, named after the Dutch city in which the negotiations on the treaty took place.
20. Treaty establishing the European Economic Community, 25 March 1957, *Trb.* 1957, 91.

individuals cannot appeal to a directly binding clause from a directive against some other individual. EC directives lack direct effect in many cases: directives are aimed at the Member States, to force them to obtain a certain result, by means of their own choice. The Member States are allowed to convert the directives in the way they want, as long as implementation is exhaustive and sufficiently precise. Provisions from EC regulations have direct effect if they contain general obligations for citizens. Such provisions do not need to be converted into national legislation since the EC law already has direct applicability. To prevent that the same clause is promulgated twice, both in the EC and in the national law, it is not allowed to copy the provision.

The distinction between direct applicability and direct effect is quite confusing, especially because of the concepts used. In short, direct applicability addresses the question whether an international norm is internal national law at all, whereas direct effect refers to the individual's possibility to invoke the norm. Direct applicability is a condition for direct effect: it has to be established first that a norm is applicable in a country, before it can be invoked by an individual.

Member States are not to limit themselves to simply tolerating the existence of EC law; they have a duty to ensure its realization. This duty springs from the principle of loyalty to the Community, which is laid down in, for example, the European Community Treaty. From a legal point of view, it means that the national laws have to be amended to conform to EC law. The process of amending national law in conformity with EC law is called the 'implementation' of European Community law. The Dutch *Recommendations for Regulations* define implementation as 'the execution of a binding decision of the Council of the European Union, of the European Parliament and the Council jointly, or of the Commission of the European Communities, in national law, by means of the proclamation of generally binding directives.'[21] According to the Dutch Minister of Justice, implementation in this sense consists of four elements, in so far as it concerns the legislator:
1. codification of the rights and duties that are guaranteed in the EC decisions;
2. amendment of national regulations that are not compatible with those decisions;
3. creation of the necessary structure for execution and enforcement;
4. notification to the Commission about (drafts for) implementation regulations.

Various types of measures and instruments can be used for the implementation of EC decisions. Besides legal measures, such as rules and administrative decisions, often actual measures are taken. EC law makes demands as regards the form and means of implementation (for example, the measures taken must be knowable and foreseeable). Moreover, certain demands follow from Dutch constitutional law. The implementation must fit the system of our Constitution, which means, among other things, that the principle of the primacy of the legislator must be upheld. The principle states that, when implementation takes place not only in Acts of Parliament

---

21. My translation.

but also in other regulations, the Act should contain the main elements, such as its scope, the structural elements and the most important stable norms of the regulation at hand. In order to save time, especially in the case of EC directives, the government does not always make use of Acts of Parliament, but chooses more flexible forms of implementation instead, for example delegation clauses in a government or ministerial regulation. EC law does not provide procedures that determine how Member States must implement EC decisions. In the Netherlands, there is no special legislative procedure for the implementation of EC decisions. The procedure which has to be followed, depends on the type of implementation chosen. If an EC decision is implemented through an Act of Parliament, the legislature has to follow the constitutional procedure as described above.[22] In sum, the process of implementation of European regulations does not differ from the national process of legislation, because European regulations are implemented *by means of* the national process of legislation in the Netherlands.

3   Legislation policy

3.1   *Regulatory crisis in the welfare state*

On paper, the process of making law seems to be quite thorough and well organised: a bill has to pass several phases, in which many competent officials, organizations inside and outside the government and citizens contribute to the quality of the legislation. The parliamentary organization provides a refined system of checks and balances, which has to guarantee that not only the interests of the majority and the well-to-do are served but also those of less fortunate minority groups in society. However, in reality, all is not gold that glitters. From the beginning of the eighties of the last century, more and more complaints arose about the quality of the law, not only in academic circles and among citizens but also within government itself. It became common to speak, quite dramatically, of a 'regulatory crisis'.[23] The welfare state, which was built up after the World War II, had led to an explosion of legislation. Besides fulfilling its traditional tasks – maintaining order and arbitration in conflicts –, the state wanted to intervene more actively in society in order to achieve social change. The so-called instrumental function of legislation was put in the front: it was more important *that* legislation reached certain policy goals (like the establishment of a social security system) than *how* it did this and what effects and side- effects it caused.[24] That many laws were not as effective as could be expected

---

22. For further information on EC law and its implementation, see, e.g., V.J.J.M. Bekkers et al., *Brussel en Nederland: tegenliggers, spookrijders of reisgenoten?*, Zwolle: W.E.J. Tjeenk Willinke 1993; J.M. Bonnes, *De uitvoering van EG-verordeningen in Nederland* (diss. Tilburg), Zwolle: W.E.J. Tjeenk Willink 1994, L.F.M. Besselink, *An Open Constitution and European Integration. The Kingdom of the Netherlands*, SEW 1996, nr. 6, p. 192-206 and Eijlander & Voermans 1999 (chapters 5 and 11, see note 4).
23. Eijlander & Voermans (1999, p. 146, see note 4).
24. The next section will elaborate on the subject of instrumentalism.

and produced rather harmful side-effects, was ignored or simply not observed. Politicians were accused of falling victim to the illusion that society can be transformed in a desired direction by sheer state intervention. Moreover, as some legal scholars argued, legislation did no longer provide enough protection against those in power. The 'intrinsic value' of law was neglected.[25] The complaints bore on two kinds of problems: too much legislation ('overregulation') and too much qualitatively poor legislation.

Overregulation has many negative consequences for society. An influential report by the Geelhoed Committee mentions five of such consequences:[26]

1. Governmental regulations are not geared to each other sufficiently, with the result that they cause confusion and disturbance in society.
2. Governmental regulations that aim at correcting and influencing social practice can disturb its self-regulating function.
3. Such regulations are not transparent or well ordered, and therefore they are no reliable compass for decision-making in society. As a result, citizens try to evade and get round the legal rules.
4. Governmental regulations that were originally promulgated to support results of decision-making in society, lead to calls for further interventions. As a result, activities that were carried out mostly in the private sphere were transported to the public sphere (as is shown in matters of welfare).
5. State interventions which are based on governmental regulations, have effects opposite to the ones intended, either because the presumptions on which the state policy is based are outdated or because the decision-making in the public sphere cannot keep pace with developments in the private sphere.

Overregulation may lead to problems in the execution and enforcement of legal rules and therefore to a lack of effectiveness and efficiency. Legal rules are not generally accepted by the citizens and no longer function as guidelines for their actions.

Another kind of problem is the lack of quality of many regulations. This means that many regulations contradict higher regulations (such as the Constitution and treaty provisions) or fundamental legal principles (equality, legal certainty, clarity and so on). This not only applies to regulations by lower authorities, but also to Acts of Parliament, which comes about in – what is meant to be – a careful and thorough process. A notorious case is the *Harmonisatiewet* 1988 (Harmonisation Act), by means of which the Dutch government wanted to cut down expenses on student grants and loans. The Act was challenged even up till the Dutch Supreme Court. In the so-called *Harmonisation Act* decision of 1989, the Supreme Court stated that, although it was not competent to carry out constitutional review, certain provisions

---

25. C.J.M. Schuyt, *Op zoek naar het hart van de verzorgingsstaat*, Leiden: Stenfert Kroese Uitgevers 1991, p. 194-201.
26. *Commissie Vermindering en vereenvoudiging van overheidsregelingen* (Committee on the simplification and reduction of government regulations) (1983/1984: 16; my translation).

of the Act went against justified expectations of some of the students and therefore the principle of legal certainty was violated.[27] After this decision, the government decided to amend the Harmonisation Act in favour of the students who were excluded by the former Act. However, the lacking quality of legislation in terms of the Rule of Law and its large amount are still important matters of concern.

To tackle both kinds of problems, the Dutch government developed a legislation quality policy (*wetgevingskwaliteitsbeleid*). To begin with, the government intends to propose lesser bills. Instead of relying on legislation, less time-consuming and sometimes more effective means of problem-solving have to be investigated first.[28] Subsequently, if it has been established that legislation is necessary as well as possible, attention should be paid to the quality of statutory regulation. In several policy documents, the Dutch government has developed so-called quality criteria (*kwaliteitscriteria*), which every government action has to meet.

3.2   Quality criteria

The quality criteria for legislation are formulated, for the first time explicitly and extensively, in the policy document *Legislation in Perspective* (*Zicht op wetgeving*) from 1991.[29] In this document, six requirements are described. These criteria assist the legislature in answering the question of whether legislation is really necessary and, if so, in determining the substance of the bill at hand. Moreover, these criteria are part of a later evaluation of the Act.

A   Lawfulness and the realization of the principles of justice
Lining up with the natural law tradition, the Dutch government claims firmly: 'As a matter of course, laws should be consistent with justice.' This premise is considered to be the most essential quality criterion for legislation. However indisputable this claim may seem, controversies will inevitably arise in interpreting and concretising the general concept of justice. The government remains almost silent on this point. In the policy document *Legislation in Perspective*, only two examples of principles of justice are given: the protection of vulnerable interests and legal security. Subsequently, the government states that laws should be in conformity not only with principles of justice, but also with international and Community law and with the Dutch Constitution. More attention should be paid to a correct level of legislation, the allocation and delegation of powers, entry into force and transitory law. Finally, the national legislature should take care of a timely, proper and full implementation of the numerous EC regulations.

---

27. HR 14 April 1989, *NJB* 1989, p. 469.
28. This will be the topic of section 4.
29. *Legislation in Perspective. A Policy Plan for the Further Development and Implementation of the General Legislative Policy, Aimed at the Constitutional and Administrative Quality of Government Policy*, The Hague: Netherlands Ministry of Justice 1991 (translation of *Zicht op wetgeving*). See especially section 2.2 of the policy document.

B Effectiveness and efficiency

It goes without saying that the law should, 'at least to a significant extent', lead to the achievement of the aims of the legislator. In addition, the law should achieve its targets without leading to 'unnecessary inefficiency in society or the government'. As the government notices, the criteria of effectiveness and efficiency are sometimes lost sight of in practice, during the various phases of the legislative process. Unwanted negative side-effects of regulations are neglected. It follows from these criteria that the objectives forming the basis of the law are formulated clearly and comprehensively before the law is drafted. These aims must be formulated as concretely as possible. In the explanatory memorandum, a summary of the aims of the legislator should be given in a 'lucid and comprehensible fashion'. Moreover, an extensive information campaign and careful monitoring during the implementation of the law are required.

C Subsidiarity and proportionality

A fundamental criterion in all exercise of power, according to the Dutch government, is that 'no drastic interventions should be undertaken by the government unnecessarily'. This criterion is deduced from the principles of subsidiarity and proportionality. At the national level,[30] the principle of subsidiarity holds that, where possible, responsibility should be left or entrusted to local authorities and social organizations. The central government should, as far as possible, confine itself to creating necessary preconditions, establishing minimum requirements, supporting social processes and guarding against unwelcome and inadequate results. Instead of intervening directly and unilaterally in society, policies should be made more in interaction with society. The Dutch government admits that its possibilities to control are limited, in a practical sense and also as a matter of principle. Therefore, new forms of government regulation, in which the government only supports people and organizations in making law, should be promoted. Self-regulation, albeit within a legal framework, becomes the new legislative fashion.[31]

Attention to the self-regulatory capacity of people and organizations arises not only from the principle of subsidiarity, but also from the principle of proportionality. The principle of proportionality requires a reasonable ratio between the benefits and costs that may be ensuing from the law. This principle is applied by the EC Court of Justice and is codified in the General Administrative Law Act (Algemene wet bestuurs-recht), article 3:4. As an example, one can think of a tax law that disadvantages certain citizens in society without giving them sufficient compensation.

D Feasibility and enforceability

In order to reach their goals, laws should be feasible and enforceable. Otherwise, the laws run the risk of becoming 'symbols, mere words'. Enforceability is the possibility

---

30. The principle of subsidiarity is also of importance in the division of tasks between the European Community and its Member States.
31. This notion will be discussed in section 4.2, under H.

to force compliance with legal regulations, both with the help of legal responses to non-compliance and by taking actual measures. This requires that the executive machinery has enough capacity and expertise and that the executive bodies cooperate with each other. Feasibility, which is not defined in the policy document, is closely related to enforceability and refers to the executive's general capacity to execute the law. The government argues that feasibility and enforceability are too often considered in isolation at the end of the process of legislation, while they should be taken into account at the very beginning of policy development and in later phases of the process. After it has been established that a law is both feasible and enforceable, it must ascertained that this is done in an efficient way: the costs arising for the administrative and judicial authorities must be restricted as much as possible.

E Coordination

Because of inadequate coordination between the rules within a legal system, the legal system becomes inconsistent and friction among lower legislative orders, implementation and enforcement authorities, citizens and courts ensue. Moreover, the principle of legal certainty is harmed. As the government notices, coordination is necessary in at least two categories: to begin with, if rules and regulations relate to different issues, but strongly influence one another. In such a case, the coordination or integration of these rules and regulations can prove a remedy. Subsequently, coordination is desirable if there is an unnecessary or unwelcome diversity in rules and the practice concerning the same or related topics, for instance due to the separate development of policy and legislation in different or even the same policy area. This diversity can be effectively reduced by harmonisation. An example is the Dutch General Administrative Law Act, which combines rules from many different prior administrative laws and court decisions.

F Simplicity, clarity and accessibility

Finally, the government attaches great importance to the simplicity, clarity and accessibility of laws. The citizens as well as the administrative bodies and courts should be able to understand clearly the meaning of the law. Special attention should be paid to the formulation of legal provisions and to the structure and design of the law. Sometimes, the subject matter asks for a detailed and complex regulation, but where possible, obscurity should be avoided. According to the government, many rules are still 'sadly inadequate', measured by this criterion. Therefore, there is a good deal of work to do.

As can be inferred from the report of the Polak/Versteden Committee,[32] several of these quality criteria were violated in the case of the Volendam fire, mentioned in section 1. To begin with, the applicable legislation went against the requirement of

---

32. *De cafébrand in Volendam: Een ramp om van te leren. Rapport van de commissie ingesteld door de commissaris van de Koningin in de provincie Noord-Holland (The fire in the Volendam bar. A Catastrophy to Learn from. Report from the Committee Appointed by the Queen's Commissioner in the Province of North Holland)*, 26 March 2001.

clarity. In 1993, a new Fire Safety Regulation *(Brandbeveiligingsverordening)* was promulgated which stated, among other things, that licenses that were granted during the old regime had to be considered as licences under the new regulation. This phrasing was far from clear, because the old regulation, at least with respect to arrangements, did not work with licenses *stricto sensu*, but only with announcements *(meldingen)*, which were followed up by a declaration of permission. According to the committee, this kind of negligence can cause problems with the application of the law and therefore threatens to contravene the requirement of effectiveness too. Subsequently, in 1994 a new Construction Regulation *(Bouwverordening)* was promulgated, which at once – with a stroke of a pen and without more ado – created or perpetuated on a large scale an unlawful situation: almost all arrangements and edifices that fell under the old regulation (approximately 200-250 arrangements altogether) were in operation illegally from the moment that the amended Construction Regulation came into force, because they were not allowed to be in operation without a license. An appropriate temporary regulation was not drawn up. This runs counter to the criterion of legal security. Not enough attention was paid to the enforcement and application of the law during the legislative process, which goes against the criterion of feasibility and enforceability. Attention should have been paid, the committee argues, to the enforcement policy, to the quantity as well as the qualification of the civil servants available and to the allocation of tasks within the civil service *(ambtelijke organisatie)* and its divisions (among which the local and regional fire brigade). This was needed especially because in the past almost no declarations of permission or licences were granted and the general allocation of tasks did not make it clear who was responsible for the enforcement of the law. In the Fire Safety Regulation, inspection was not regulated properly: no civil servants were instructed to inspect the observance of the regulation. To make it even worse, the city council of Edam-Volendam failed to execute and apply the existing regulations, especially with respect to the granting of licences. In the 1990s, the city council ignored proposals and signals from fire brigade authorities, civil servants and the mayor, and did not take the enforcement of the rules in hand, knowingly and willingly, according to the committee.[33]

As a result of these deficiencies in the law as well as in its enforcement, the fire in a Volendam bar on New Year's Day 2001, in which many people were killed or badly injured, could not be prevented. This shows that compliance with the quality criteria in the legislative process is not only a theoretical exercise. Only proper legislation can provide a solid basis for the ordering of society.

The six basic quality criteria that are described in *Legislation in Perspective* are further developed and refined in other policy documents, especially in the *Recommendations for Regulations (Aanwijzingen voor de regelgeving)*. As part of the so-called *Operatie*

---

33. In its report the Polak/Versteden committee points to many more flaws in the execution practice, but I have confined myself mostly to deficiencies in the existing legislation.

Marktwerking, Deregulering en Wetgevingskwaliteit (Competition, Deregulation and Legislation Quality Campaign), several kinds of projects have been initiated that are connected with the government's legislation quality policy: projects aimed at reducing the number of regulations that are unnecessarily burdening for its addressees; projects that promote the free market and open competition; projects that improve the quality and transparency of rules and regulations, and, at last, projects that provide a framework for handling a specific problem according to the goals of the overall operation.[34] In the same line of thought, legal scholars have developed so-called principles of proper legislation.[35] Since these principles to a large extent overlap the quality criteria of the government, they will not be discussed here.

4   New forms of regulation

4.1   Exit instrumentalism

Another solution to the regulatory crisis is sought in government policy as well as in academic literature, in new forms of regulation that provide an alternative to legislation in general or to legislation through Acts of Parliament and instrumentalist legislation in particular. If a problem in society emerges, the government should not immediately think of new legislation (of whatever type), but should consider other, less drastic and more interactive means of problem solving. A widely shared view holds that, in the welfare state, the government uses legislation more and more as an instrument to solve problems in society. Laws no longer reflect generally accepted norms and values, but are primarily a means to social change desired by the majority in Parliament. The legislature is supposed to be more oriented towards modification – that is, changing of the current ways of thinking and behaving – than towards codification, or the embedding of generally accepted norms and values in legal rules.[36] As a result, legislation nowadays hardly fulfils its classical function, namely protecting citizens against unlawful intrusions on their freedom by other citizens and by the state itself.

A so-called instrumentalist view on legislation lies at the root of this legislative practice. Instrumentalism originates from legal realism, a movement in legal theory

---

34. The minister of Economic Affairs has sent two letters about this operation to the Parliament. Moreover, every year a report on its results is published in the called *Jaarberichten (Annual Reports)*. Information in English can be found on the Internet site of the Ministry of Economic Affairs: http://www.ez.nl/.

35. See, e.g., I.C. van der Vlies *Het wetsbegrip en de beginselen van behoorlijke regelgeving (het legaliteitsbeginsel)*, Den Haag: VUGA 1984, and I.C. van der Vlies, *Handboek wetgeving*, Zwolle: W.E.J. Tjeenk Willink 1987.

36. According to T. Koopmans ('De rol van de wetgever', in: *Honderd jaar rechtsleven. Jubileumboek Nederlandse Juristen Vereniging*, Zwolle: W.E.J. Tjeenk Willink 1970, at p. 223). As Van der Vlies (1984, p. 78-79, see note 36) notices correctly, this distinction is actually untenable: laws are always more or less modifying (otherwise there would be no need to promulgate them). Since the Dutch doctrine is still haunted by this distinction, it is mentioned here.

that bloomed in the first half of the 20th century in the United States and Scandinavia. Legal scholars associated with this movement include Jerome Frank, Roscoe Pound and Karl Olivecrona. To put it briefly, they tried to turn law and jurisprudence – with the help of the social sciences – into a tool for the emancipation of the poor and the underprivileged. Some of the central premises that are attributed to the instrumentalist view on legislation are:[37]

1. Law is neutral with respect to the goal pursued. Legal instruments are judged only on their capacity to reach targets that are externally formulated. Law does not have an intrinsic value; it does not contain any goals of its own (such as legal security).

2. Law is subordinate to values selected by politics. To begin with, representatives of the people determine the goals that are to be pursued. Subsequently, the means to that end are selected. Politics is superior to law and can dispose of it at its own discretion.

3. Law is a means of control. The control takes place by means of the law from a central point of view outside and above society.

4. Law is focused on its consequences. If legislation is judged, the main question is not: 'Does it fit within the existing legal system?', but 'Is it effective?' A law is effective if the externally determined goals are realized.

5. Science is the 'workplace' for the law. Like every other instrument, law requires maintenance. The research needed for the maintenance of the law is done by the social sciences. By means of empirical data, the social sciences can determine whether the law still functions properly as an instrument or if reparation is required.

In the second half of the 20th century, the instrumentalist view on legislation has been sharply criticized, especially by legal scholars who combined empirical insights from legal sociology and other social sciences with normative suppositions of natural law theory. In the Netherlands, the work of Lon L. Fuller has had and still has a great impact on the way of thinking about legislation and the role of the legislator in society.[38] Fuller turned the premises of instrumentalism almost upside down:[39]

1. Law has an intrinsic value, that is, a value that is worth in itself to be pursued and preserved. Therefore, the means chosen are not value free.

2. Law should not always be subordinated to political majority decisions. As an institution within society, law can conflict with politics.

3. If the legislature seeks to regulate social relationships, the intrinsic qualities of social interactions will have to be taken into account. Only in those cases in which the aims of the people involved differ too much, general rules or

---

37. Schuyt (1991, p. 192-194, see note 26).
38. Lon L. Fuller, *The Morality of Law*, Yale University Press: New Haven 1969 is the canonical text. In W.J. Witteveen & W. van der Burg (eds.), *Rediscovering Fuller. Essays on Implicit Law and Institutional Design*, Amsterdam: Amsterdam University Press 1999, the reception of Fuller's work in the Netherlands is demonstrated.
39. Schuyt 1991, see note 26.

procedures are needed. Otherwise, wherever it is possible to appeal to voluntary cooperation, law must not be used as an instrument of social control. Ideally, law grows out of social interaction ('emergent law') and not the other way round.

4. The consequences of law cannot be judged without taking into consideration the aims pursued and other values. A judgement of the effects of legislation with respect to its aims is not a value-free activity. Fuller rejects thinking in terms of means and ends. In their application, means already contain many value determinations and ends refer continually to other ends.

5. Empirical research cannot decide what law and justice are, for example by simply referring to majority opinions. This has to be done in argumentative practices, in which – according to Fuller – some arguments will prove to be better and more correct than others. Jurisprudence and legal practice neglect their specific tasks and duties in society if they do not engage in these normative argumentations.

In short, law should not be treated as merely an instrument to influence other people's behaviour from a central point of view outside and above society; it has to be regarded as a system of action with an intrinsic value that is given shape in actual practice, in cooperation with all involved, including citizens. This view on legislation can be called 'interactionist', because it conceives legislation as the product of a 'partnership' between legal and political authorities (the legislature, the administration, the judge) on the one hand, and 'ordinary' people on the other hand.[40] Law should grow out of social interactions instead of political majority decisions only.

The interactionist view of legislation has gained popularity among several Dutch legal scholars.[41] It also influences the practice of policy- and law-making in the Netherlands. In *Legislation in Perspective*, the Dutch government explicitly recognized that it is not the only or even the main source of law: 'It is starting to become more widely recognised that the responsibility of the authorities does not per

---

40. The notion is borrowed from W.J. Witteveen *(De geordende wereld van het recht*, Amsterdam: Amsterdam University Press 2001, p. 61-62).

41. See, e.g., W. van der Burg ('The Expressive and the Communicative Functions of Law, Especially with Regard to Moral Issues', *Law and Philosophy* 2001, nr. 1, p. 31-59), J. van Schooten-van der Meer *(Regelvorming in de rechtsstaat. Een onderoek naar de legitimering van en de werking van het moderne recht en de alternatieve reguleringsvormen* (diss. Twente), Enschede: Twente University Press 1997), C.J.M. Schuyt *(Ongeregeld heden. Naar een theorie van wetgeving in de verzorgingsstaat* (oratie Leiden), Alpen aan den Rijn: Samsom 1982 and Schuyt 1991: chapter 17, see note 26), H. Stout *(De betekenissen van de wet. Theoretisch-kritische beschouwingen over het principe van wetmatigheid van bestuur* (diss. Amsterdam UvA), W.E.J. Tjeenk Willink: Zwolle 1994) and W.J. Witteveen ('Significant, Symbolic and Symphonic Laws. Communication through Legislation', in: H. van Schooten (ed.), *Semiotics and Legislation*, Liverpool: Deborah Charles Publications 1999, p. 27-90). Another, more radical instance of interactionism is the self-regulation approach initiated by the German legal scholar Teubner, whose ideas are adopted by, for instance, A.G. Veldman *(Effectuering van sociaal-economisch recht volgens de chaos-theorie. Beleidsinstrumentering en rechtshandhaving van (supra)nationaal gelijke-behandelingsrecht* (diss. Utrecht), Zwolle: W.E.J. Tjeenk Willink 1995). See further section 4.2, under G.

definition imply that government bodies must always make all the rules and see to their implementation. The legislator can sometimes suffice with providing a framework and checking the outcome afterward.' However, the question arises, if the legislator retreats, who is going to make law?

4.2 Interactionism enters

Implicitly or explicitly building on interactionist premises, new forms of regulation have emerged in the Netherlands that are supposed to provide an alternative to legislation in general or to legislation through Acts of Parliament and instrumentalist legislation in particular. Eight of these forms of regulation are discussed here, together with examples from Dutch law.[42]

A Delegation

In case of delegation, the legislator instructs a lower authority to elaborate certain rules.[43] To that end, rule-making powers are transferred from the legislator to the lower authority, which executes these powers in its own name and on its own responsibility. Sometimes, an Act of Parliament permits that a lower authority, for example the government, transfer its rule-making powers to an even lower authority, for example a minister, i.e. sub-delegation. The Dutch legislature – government and Parliament together – has delegated the competence to elaborate rules on road traffic to the government. The government in turn sub-delegated the competence to elaborate rules on the design of the parking disc. The legislature did not consider it to be efficient to prescribe itself the design of the parking disc. It lacks the knowledge required and, even more, the time to bother itself about these legislative details. The same goes for the government. The Dutch Ministry of Transport, Public Works and Water Management, on the other hand, has enough expertise for making the design. Moreover, a regulation by a minister is easier framed and introduced than an Act of Parliament or a government regulation. Delegation of rule-making power is mostly a case of efficiency.

B Independent administrative bodies

Most of the administrative bodies are described in the Dutch Constitution. Some of them do not have a constitutional basis and they are therefore called 'independent administrative bodies' (zelfstandige bestuursorganen). Independent administrative bodies have various tasks. For example, there are bodies in the field of supervision, such as the Dutch Media Authority (Commissariaat voor de Media). The Dutch Media Authority takes care that the provisions from the Dutch Media Act are complied with. The Dutch Media Act is meant to guarantee the quality of radio and

---

42. This section is based on W.J. Witteveen & B. van Klink (De sociale rechtsstaat voorbij. Twee ontwerpen voor het huis van de rechtsstaat, voorstudie voor de Wetenschappelijke Raad voor het Regeringsbeleid, Den Haag: Sdu 2002, p. 158-160).
43. J.M. de Meij & I.C. van der Vlies, Inleiding tot het staatsrecht en het bestuursrecht, Deventer: W.E.J. Tjeenk Willink 2000, p. 18.

television programs in the Netherlands. The programs of the public broadcasting organizations should not be commercial and should provide a picture of what is going on in society. All sorts of groups have to have access to the public broadcasting organizations. The Dutch Media Authority checks whether the public tasks are fulfilled properly, whether commercial interests do no get the upper hand, and whether the community's money is spent well. A distinctive feature of independent administrative bodies is that the minister's responsibility for their actions is limited. Formally, independent administrative bodies were not subordinated to the minister. The Dutch Media Authority takes its decisions independently from the Ministry of Education, Culture and Sciences, it has to account for them to the minister. The extent to which a minister can exert his influence is determined in the rules governing the foundation of an independent administrative body. As a rule, the minister only has the competence to appoint board members or to annul a body's decision.

C Policy rules (beleidsregels)

In article 1:4 of the Dutch General Administrative Law Act, a policy rule is defined as a general rule about a balancing of interests, the determination of facts or the interpretation of legal provision. A policy rule is not an generally binding prescription *(algemeen verbindend voorschrift)*, but it is a decision by an administrative body within the framework of its competency. Policy rules are thus rules that the administration sets itself in order to fill in vague statutory terms or limit its discretion. The open texture of the law becomes more closed. Especially in the fields of immigration law and tax law, policy rules are often used. The competency to use policy rules is laid down in article 4:81 of the Dutch General Administrative Law Act. This article states that an administrative body can draw up policy rules with respect to its competence, that is exercised under its responsibility or that it has delegated. Moreover, the competence to draw up policy rules can follow from a statutory provision.

D Policy contracts (beleidsovereenkomsten)

A policy contract is an agreement *(verbintenis)* according to civil law between an administrative body and a citizen, in which provisions from public law are included.[44] Like policy rules, policy contracts fill in the space public law leaves open. The administration is only allowed to make use of this instrument in so far as the framework of public law is left intact.[45] The difference between policy rules and policy contracts is that provisions from policy contracts do not apply generally; they only apply to the parties in the contract. Policy contracts are often used when real estate is sold. In that case, the government can include provisions in the contract of sale, for instance, about the intended use of the ground.

---

44. C.P.J. Goorden, *Algemeen Bestuursrecht Compact*, Den Haag: VUGA 1997, p. 149.
45. According to the Dutch Supreme Court (26 January 1990, *NJ* 1991, 393).

E   Covenants (convenanten)

Covenants resemble policy contracts. Covenants are also agreements between an administrative body and some other party, in which provisions of public law are embodied.[46] The covenant party can be either a citizen or another administrative agency. Like policy contracts, covenants fill in the space that the law leaves the administration. The difference between policy contracts and covenants is that covenants are not as easily enforceable if a case goes to civil court. Covenants are agreements with less engagement and therefore they are sometimes called 'pseudo-agreements'.[47] Most of the convenants in the Netherlands bear upon the environment. Within the framework of the so-called target groups policy (doel-groepenbeleid), Dutch public authorities deliberate with target groups about the execution of national policy plans concerning the environment. Global environmental targets that are stated in these plans have to be translated into concrete and realizable aims. Agreements on the elaboration and implementation of the global environmental targets are, for the target group industry, embodied in environmental covenants, called 'declarations of intent'. Subsequently, these declarations of intent have to be elaborated for individual companies, because the declarations contain environmental aims for the whole sector and not for individual companies that take part in the covenant. In a covenant, a company can, for example, bind itself to draft an energy saving plan.[48] Another example is the gentlemen's agreement the Dutch Minister of Health, Welfare and Sport made with the industry about the reduction of phosphates in washing-preparations.

F   Communicative legislation

Instrumental legislation is a kind of autonomous, authoritarian control: the ruler gives commands to the ruled, which ought to be obeyed unconditionally. The substantive provisions are written in a concrete and unambiguous language and are backed up, in case of non-compliance, by severe sanctions. By contrast, communicative legislation is based on a less hierarchical and more interactive approach.[49] The legislator introduces fairly general norms whose content is to be further determined by the members of the interpretive community, consisting of legal and political authorities as well as ordinary citizens. Moreover, structures for deliberation are created which stimulate the communication between the executive, the judiciary and the addressees of the law. The rationale that underlies this approach is that in certain matters persuasion is a more effective instrument than punishment.

---

46. Eijlander & Voermans (1999, p. 75, see note 4) and Goorden (1997, p. 150, see note 45).
47. Van Schooten-van der Meer (1997, see note 42).
48. J.A.E. van der Jagt, 'Convenanten en bedrijfsplannen als toetsingskader bij (milieu)vergunning-verlening', Jurisprudentie Bestuursrecht plus 2002, p. 2-16.
49. The notion of 'communicative legislation' is introduced in B. van Klink, De wet als symbool. Over wettelijke communicatie en de Wet gelijke behandeling van mannen en vrouwen bij de arbeid (diss. Tilburg), Deventer: W.E.J. Tjeenk Willink 1998. W.J. Witteveen & B. van Klink, 'Why Is Soft Law Really Law?', RegelMaat/Journal for Legislative Studies 1999, nr. 3, p. 126-140) offer an introduction to the communicative approach to legislation in English.

As a consequence, law becomes essentially responsive: it is able to react flexibly (which does not mean uncritically) to changed opinions concerning law and justice in society. Instead of sending one-way messages, the legislator engages himself in a dialogue with members of society.

An example of communicative legislation is the Equal Opportunities Act *(Wet gelijke behandeling van mannen en vrouwen bij de arbeid)*.[50] This Act does not contain severe sanctions on the violation of its provisions, but offers possible victims of discrimination the possibility to appeal to the Equal Treatment Commission *(Commissie gelijke behandeling)*. Although this Commission issues decisions that are not binding in a legal sense, it appears that they are often complied with and, moreover, they stimulate debate on the shop floor and make employers more sensitive to matters of equality. Moreover, in the decisions of the Commission the abstract ideal of equality and the standards of the law are concretised for specific problem situations.

G Self-regulation

In the case of self-regulation, the norm addressees make their own norms, which they are expected to comply with. There are many different types of self-regulation.[51] On the one hand, there are types of private conflict resolution and certification in which the government does not play any role, as is the case with the *Nederlands Normalisatie-instituut* (Netherlands Standardization Institute) or NEN. One of the main aims of the NEN is to promote the drafting of Dutch norms and to participate actively in the drafting of European or global norms, whenever national interests are at stake, for example in environmental issues.[52] On the other hand, the legislator sometimes prescribes self-regulation and provides a legal framework for the norms to be drawn up. If these norms are violated, sanctions are imposed. An example of this kind of strongly conditioned self-regulation is the disciplinary law of the professions (such as the legal profession). When the Dutch government in *Legislation in Perspective* speaks of 'self-regulation',[53] it refers to the strongly conditioned type of self-regulation: 'It is necessary to strike a proper balance between government regulation, as an expression of government responsibility, and self-regulation by the people and by social organisations: legally structured and conditioned self-regulation.' It is thus freedom within sometimes more, sometimes less strong limits.

This form of regulation – whether it is really new is a matter of debate – has been inspired by the work of Gunther Teubner, a German legal scholar.[54] Building on

---

50. Van Klink (1998, chapter 8, see note 50).
51. Eijlander & Voermans (1999, p. 70-74, see note 4).
52. See www.nen.nl.
53. See section 4.1.
54. See, for instance, G. Teubner, *Dilemmas of Law in the Welfare State*, Berlin: De Gruyter 1986. A theoretical reflection on Teubner's influence on the legislative practice in the Netherlands can be found in N.J.H. Huls & H.D. Stout (red.), *Reflecties op reflexief recht*, Zwolle: W.E.J. Tjeenk Willink 1992.

insights from biology and Luhmann's system theory, Teubner describes society as a collection of self-referential subsystems (such as economy, politics and religion) that have their own language, with specific codes. Although these subsystems are able to understand each other's languages (in that sense, they are 'cognitively open'), they can only act on this understanding after the terms of the 'foreign' language have been translated into the familiar terms of their own language (in that sense, they are 'performatively closed'). According to Teubner, messages from the legislator can only penetrate a specific subsystem if they are translated into terms that make sense within that system. To improve the effectiveness of the law, it is important that members of a subsystem make their own rules in their own language. The only task left for the legislator is to facilitate and stimulate the self-regulative potentials in society.

H Privatisation
Privatisation is the transfer of a specific task from the public to the private sphere.[55] After the task has been transferred, it is part of civil law instead of public law. The government will especially be inclined to privatization if it expects that the market can better fulfil this task than it can do itself. In the Netherlands, the exploitation of the postal service and the railway was privatized for that reason. However, it does not always turn out well. Recently, the privatization of the Dutch railway was criticised heavily because of the railway's bad performance and therefore the government decided to reverse privatization partially.

5   The communicative turn

In the above, it was shown that the Dutch government, in response to its weakened authority as well as to its decreasing effectiveness, has tried in the last twenty years to make the legislative process more interactive and responsive to the people's wishes and needs. To begin with, it developed quality criteria that ought to improve the lawfulness, feasibility, enforceability, transparency of the law, and so on. These and other requirements were elaborated into concrete guidelines for legislative bodies that are laid down in the *Recommendations for Regulation*. Subsequently, the government has discovered new forms of regulation (or rediscovered old ones, as some might say), such as delegation, communicative legislation, policy rules and contracts, covenants and self-regulation. These forms of regulation have in common that the legislator does not, or to a lesser extent, present himself any longer as the all-determining ruler who gives, from a point of view above and outside society, commands to the ruled. Instead, he presents general norms that have to be concretized and realized within a partnership between legal authorities and ordinary people. Or, he even lets the people themselves make up their own rules, within or without a legal framework.

---

55. Van Schooten-van der Meer (1997, see note 42).

How appealing it may appear, the communicative turn has given rise to debate in recent years, both in academic circles and in (the whole of) society. Legal scholars have claimed that some of the new interactionist types of regulation that the Dutch government promoted do not differ radically from old-fashioned, authoritarian types of regulation and in fact constitute instrumentalism in disguise. For instance, communicative legislation is believed to be still founded on the premise that people's way of thinking and behaving can be and must be changed according to pre-established official norms. Only the means chosen to that end are different and more subtle, for example, when the legislator provides information in order to influence an unwelcome attitude. Instead of following a command-and-control scheme, it now adopts a communicate-and-control scheme.[56] The same can be said about self-regulation: the Dutch government does not transfer wholly its competence to make rules to the people, but often provides a more or less strict and binding legal framework within which the rules have to be made. If these rules are not made or the rules that are made are not satisfactory, the government often threatens the parties involved to promulgate law of its own.

Connected to this criticism, other scholars have claimed, on a more principal level, that the instrumental function is an integral part of legislation in general.[57] However much communication the legislator engages in, inevitably there will be a time when a unilateral and inherently controversial decision has to be made in favour of one particular (interpretation or application of a) rule. This means that some values are included in a legal order, while others are excluded (for the time being). An all-encompassing decision, which includes all possible values and which satisfies all people involved, is impossible from a logical point of view and unworkable in practice. For example, one cannot welcome illegal people to a country and ban them at the same time. The communicative turn can try to postpone this moment of decision or even try to hide it, but ultimately it has to cut the knot. Otherwise, there would be no law.

Moreover, in jurisprudence the criticism is uttered that many of the new interactionist types of regulation are not so much the solution to the regulatory crisis as part of the problem itself.[58] In the communicative approach, the democratically elected Parliament has a lesser role to play in the process of rule-making, or even no

---

56. According to M. Hertogh (in: B. van Klink & W.J. Witteveen (red.), *De overtuigende wetgever*, Den Haag: Boom Juridische uitgevers 2000, p. 45-60). However, Hertogh fails to appreciate that, in the case of communicative legislation, the legislator does *not* presuppose a fixed conception of the value he wants to promote (such as equality) and of the rules that follow from that value. That precisely has to be worked out in a communicative process between legal and political authorities, on the one hand, and citizens, on the other hand.

57. See H. Lindahl (in: B. van Klink & W.J. Witteveen (eds.), *De overtuigende wetgever*, Den Haag: Boom Juridische uitgevers 2000, p. 173-188). Van Klink subscribes to this view in Witteveen & Van Klink (2002, p. 203-217, see note 43).

58. See, e.g., Van Schooten (1997, chapter 5, see note 42).

role at all in some cases of self-regulation. Inevitably, problems of control and representation arise. It is, for example, not always clear who has to account for the rules that are made by way of self-regulation and to whom. Who do the people involved in self-regulation represent? And who protects vulnerable interests that are not represented, and who takes care, in the struggle for particular goods, of the common good? Other requirements of the traditional Rule of Law are harmed as well – so it is claimed – such as legal security (people cannot be expected to know the content of the law anymore) and legality (encroachments on fundamental rights have no legal basis anymore or only a weak legal basis).

In society in general, there seems to exist great discontent with (what is perceived as) the 'soft' or hesitant attitude of the Dutch government with respect to issues such as security, education, health care, transport, and immigration policy. Moreover, the Dutch policy of *gedogen* (officially approved non-enforcement of legal rules), especially with regard to drug crimes, was criticized heavily. In the 2002 elections, the government parties – a so-called 'purple' coalition with a social-democratic, a social-liberal and a liberal party – lost dramatically, while parties that claim to preserve norms and values (a Christian-democratic party) or to improve the government's ability to solve problems in society (a populist party in the footsteps of its late leader, Pim Fortuyn) won overwhelmingly. A substantive part of the Dutch population seems to be tired of communicating and negotiating about legislation; it wants to see hard and tangible results: less crime, fewer traffic jams, fewer illegal people, more nurses and no more waiting-lists in hospitals, more teachers in schools, and so on. Actions instead of words. A new right-wing government has been formed with the winning Christian-democratic party, together with the social-liberal party and the liberal party from the previous government, that has promised to restore law and order.

Because of these developments, it seems likely that the nature of the legislative process and the approach to legislation will change in the following years in the Netherlands. However, a complete return to the old command-and-control scheme of legislation – if it has ever been or can be adopted fully[59] – is not conceivable. In their long history, the Dutch have proved to be too stubborn to subject themselves uncritically and unconditionally to rules made elsewhere. The general feeling seems to be: rules are all right, as long as the annoying ones apply to other people.

---

59. In order to be effective, law not only has to have an instrumental function (as Lindahl demonstrates), but it has to have a communicative function as well. Otherwise, compliance with the law would rest only on force, which is not possible in the long run.

Part III

Criminal Law

6 The Basics of Dutch Criminal Law*

Peter J.P. Tak

1 Introduction

The Dutch criminal justice system has long been noted for its mildness. In support of this view, reference was usually made to the low prison rate in the Netherlands compared to other European countries. In the 1970s, the prison rate was around 20 per 100,000. At present, it tends to be around 90 per 100,000. For many, this increase is shocking. That feeling is understandable when one only looks at the figures. However, reality differs considerably from the picture emerging from the statistics.

The low prison rate in the 1970s and the early 1980s was partly cosmetic because in practice there was a considerable difference between actual prison capacity and the need for capacity, giving rise to 'waiting lists'. In the Netherlands, offenders who are not in pre-trial detention when they stand trial and are sentenced to imprisonment do not serve their prison-sentence immediately after the court session, but are put on a waiting list and called to serve their sentence as soon as there is capacity.

In the early 1990s, the largest ever prison construction program started. Between 1994 and 1996, 14 new prisons were opened and at present prison capacity is around 12,800 cells. Over the last decade, the prison rate more than doubled. The Netherlands had one of the fastest growing prison populations in the world. This increase in prison capacity was partly due to more severe sentences. Although the crime rate has increased substantially, the number of prison sentences, in relation to the increased crime, has remained relatively stable. The average prison sentence, however, has become much longer. In 1970, almost 13,000 (partly) unsuspended prison sentences were imposed with a total of 2,100 detention years. Thirty years later, the number of prison sentences merely doubled but the number of detention years increased to 16,000.

The other reason for increase in prison capacity was a new policy influenced by serious criticisms on the delayed implementation of prison sentences. A remarkable feature of present day criminal law enforcement in the Netherlands is that only a small percentage of all crimes that are registered by the police are actually tried by a criminal court. While the number of registered crimes increased almost fivefold between 1970 and 2002, the number of cases tried in court only doubled.

Proper law-enforcement and administration of criminal justice has become an issue of growing concern. Registered crime has increased sixfold since 1970, but the

---

* This chapter is based on the book: P.J.P. Tak, *The Dutch Criminal Justice System*, WODC-reeks Onderzoek en Beleid nr. 205, Den Haag: Boom Juridische uitgevers 2003.

clearance rate gradually went down to around 14% at present. This is mainly due to a lack of investigation capacity. The increase of the police force and judicial officers did not keep pace with the increase in crime. In relation to the volume of crime, the per capita level of expenditure to control crime is low in comparison with neighbouring countries. The number of public prosecutors and the size of the judiciary is relatively small as well, which leads to a rather slow pace of criminal justice.

2   The Dutch Criminal Code

The history of the present Dutch Criminal Code starts in 1811, when the Kingdom of the Netherlands was incorporated into the French Empire and the Penal Code for the Kingdom of Holland, in force since 1809, was replaced by the French Napoleonic Code Pénal. After the restoration of independence in 1813, the French code was kept in force provisionally, but it contained some important changes. The sanctions system was reformed considerably, for instance by abolishing deportation and lifelong forced labour.

The 1813 Dutch Constitution stipulated that the main body of substantive and procedural criminal law was to be regulated in codes. During the 19th century, a number of draft criminal codes were proposed, but the lack of parliamentary unanimity on the sanctions system and the prison system prevented adoption of any of these drafts. However, important revisions of the Criminal Code did take place, in particular regarding sanctions. The range of sentences was reduced to various forms of prison sentences, fines, suspension of certain rights and forfeiture of certain goods. Corporal punishment was abolished in 1856, as was the death penalty in 1870. Fine default detention was introduced in 1864. In fact, the ideas of the classical school of criminal law, prevalent in the French Code Pénal, gradually were replaced by modern ideas which lead to more humane sanction and prison systems.

In 1870, a penal law reform committee was established that drafted a criminal code which, together with an extensive explanatory memorandum, was submitted to Parliament in 1879 by Modderman in his capacity of Minister of Justice. The Code (Wetboek van Strafrecht) was adopted in 1881, but came into force in 1886, because a number of Acts had to be reformed and new prisons based on the cellular prison system had to be build first.

Since 1886, the Criminal Code (CC) has been reformed considerably. New criminal provisions have been added, for example on discrimination, intrusion of privacy, environmental pollution, illegal computer activities, commercial surrogate motherhood, stalking and virtual child porn. Other offences, such as adultery or homosexual acts between an adult and a juvenile of over 16 years of age have been decriminalized. Termination of pregnancy (induced abortion) and termination of life on request and assistance in suicide (euthanasia) are not punishable anymore, provided that certain legal requirements are met.

Compared to the French Penal Code, the Dutch Criminal Code is characterized by its simplicity, practicality, faith in the judiciary, adherence to egalitarian principles, absence of specific religious influences, and recognition of an autonomous 'legal consciousness'. Its simplicity, for instance, is still illustrated by the legal definitions of criminal offences, the division of criminal offences in either crimes or infractions, and its sanctions system with only four principal sentences: imprisonment, detention, task penalty and fine. Its faith in the judiciary is evident from the absence of specific minimum sentences for serious offences and the wide discretionary power in sentencing. The Dutch Criminal Code does not contain distinctions and definitions of a dogmatic nature. Neither definitions on various forms of culpability or causation, nor definitions on defenses are found in the Code. The Criminal Code is a very practicable one, leaving the development of criminal law doctrine to courts in general and the Supreme Court in particular.

3   The Dutch Code of Criminal Procedure

In the Netherlands, the Napoleonic *Code d'instruction criminelle* was applied until 1838 with some modifications. For example, the French jury system has never been adopted in the Netherlands. The Dutch Code of Criminal Procedure, which came into force in 1838, was not really a new code, but rather a translation of the French Code. The 1838 Code was characterized by strong inquisitorial elements. The suspect was the object of a secret and written investigation procedure without any rights. The numerous attempts to reform the Code of 1838 and to restrict the inquisitorial elements failed, until the present Code of Criminal Procedure *(Wetboek van Strafvordering)* was enacted in 1926.

In the Explanatory Memorandum of the Code of Criminal Procedure (CCP), the code is characterized as 'being moderately accusatorial'. In comparison to the 1838 Code, the new code gave the offender more procedural rights to influence the course of justice. At an early stage in the investigative phase, the offender obtained the right to be assisted by his counsel with whom he can have free oral and written communication. In the pre-trial phase, the offender also acquired the right to remain silent when interrogated. He, furthermore, got the right to be informed about the results of the investigations by the police or the examining judge and to interfere in these investigations, albeit with restrictions. In order to prevent abuse of the procedural rights by the offender, these rights could be restricted 'in the interest of the investigations' by the public prosecutor or the examining judge. Such restrictions, however, can be reviewed by higher judicial authorities.

According to the Code, the emphasis of the criminal procedure lies in the court trial where immediacy is the leading principle.[1] At the court-trial, as a rule, evidence must be produced on the basis of this principle. In 1926, however, the Supreme Court ruled that a *testimonium de auditu*, hearsay evidence, is admissible. Other exceptions to the immediacy principle, such as the use of statements of anonymous witnesses as means of evidence, were later also ruled to be admissible, provided there is other (circumstantial) evidence. Under the influence of decisions by the European

---

1. The principle of immediacy means that a case, including the presentation of evidence, interrogation of witnesses, et cetera, should be conducted orally, in the presence of the accused.

Court of Human Rights, the immediacy principle gradually began to play an important role again in the Dutch criminal procedure. Today, the adversarial character of the court trial is increasingly stressed.

The Dutch Code of Criminal Procedure has been reformed considerably over the last few years. In the past, the Code was regularly supplemented and changed, but the current revisions are of such a nature that the question has already been raised whether it is time for a comprehensive law reform. However, a full law reform in which the general principles of the criminal procedure are reconsidered does not seem necessary or desired. The CCP establishes a balanced allocation of powers and rights to parties in a criminal court procedure. There is no need for a re-allocation of competence. The recent law reforms did not result in a substantially different position of the parties in court, nor in an essential shift in competence. A full revision is also not desired because, from the perspective of the operational situation in the administration of criminal justice, there are many objections. At present, pressure on criminal justice officers is too high to work with a completely new Code. The latter would have the result that the administration of criminal justice would overheat.

This was also the point of view of the Minister of Justice, as expressed in a memorandum to Parliament, in which he extensively dealt with the present state of the Code of Criminal Procedure law reform.

'No' to an integral law reform does not mean that the Code is not involved in a permanent process of reform. Since 1990, over 85 law reforms with important alterations and extensions of the Code took place. There are a number of important reasons for major changes: the age of the Code, technological progress, the impact of international human rights instruments, and the 1996 Parliamentary Enquiry on police investigation methods.

3.1 Main reasons for procedural law reforms

1. The age of the Code

The Code dates from 1926 and reflects a careful consideration of interests and competences of the classic courtroom participants, the suspect and his defence counsel, the police and the prosecution service.

However, the legal position of witnesses and victims was not elaborated at all, or very insufficiently so. Civil compensation *(action civile)* in criminal proceedings was unknown. Furthermore, private prosecution by victims is impossible because, according to Dutch law, the prosecution service is vested with an absolute prosecution monopoly. Thus, the victim of a criminal offence had been allotted a very modest place in the Code.

Ever since the 1993 Criminal Injuries Compensation Act, the victim's position has been considerably strengthened. He or his heirs can now institute a lawsuit to claim civil compensation in criminal proceedings.

The legal position of the witness has also changed. The phenomenon of the threatened witness, who refuses to meet his legal obligation to testify for fear of retaliatory measures, has been recognized. Since the 1993 Threatened Witness Act, a witness protection scheme exists.

2. *Technological progress*

New technological developments enabled the use of advanced technical means of coercion in the fight against organized and serious crime. In this respect, two changes may be indicated. First, the 1993 DNA Act introduced the possibility, in case of serious suspicion of a crime which carries a statutory imprisonment of eight years or more, to take blood for a DNA test for identification without the suspect's approval but by order of the examining judge. Since 2001, on a public prosecutor's order, a buccal mouth swab for a DNA test may be taken from the suspect of a crime which carries a statutory imprisonment of four years or more. Second, the 1993 Computer Crime Act introduced the possibility to intercept all forms of telecommunications and the possibility to intercept all forms of communications by means of long-distance target microphones.

3. *The impact of international human rights instruments*

The third cause of recent changes is the need to meet the demands stemming from international human rights instruments concerning persons accused of crimes and of persons deprived of liberty, in as far as these instruments are directly applicable under Dutch law.

The Netherlands has no constitutional court and article 120 of the Dutch Constitution explicitly prohibits constitutional judicial review of Acts of Parliament (statutes) by courts: 'The constitutionality of Acts of Parliament and treaties shall not be reviewed by courts.' However, the Dutch Constitution obliges courts to review all domestic legislation, including Acts of Parliament, with regard to their compatibility with directly applicable provisions of international treaties to which the Netherlands is a contracting party, such as the European Convention for the Protection of Human Rights and Fundamental Freedoms of 4 November 1950.[2]

Standards on the application of directly applicable provisions of the Convention elaborated in case law by the European Court of Human Rights (ECHR) in Strasbourg must also be applied by Dutch courts. This is not only the case with regard to ECHR decisions ruled against the Netherlands, but also with regard to decisions ruled against other Member States of the Council of Europe, in as far as these decisions contain standards regarding the provisions of the Convention. This means that apart from decisions against the Netherlands, other decisions of the court also have an impact on Dutch criminal procedural legislation and trial practice.

The European Court on Human Rights' decisions in the *Cubber* and *Hauschildt* cases (26 October 1984, A 86 and 24 May 1989, A 154) have resulted in reform of the criminal procedure for juveniles. The *Kruslin and Huvig* case (24 April 1990, A 176) necessitated new procedural provisions for the interception of (telephone) communications, the *Kostovski* case (20 November 1989, A 166) led to the introduction of legislation on anonymous witnesses, and the *Kamasinski*

---

2. See also Chapter 4.

case (19 December 1989, A 168) formed the reference for new legislation on interpretation and translation help during the criminal procedure, while the *Brogan* case (29 November 1988, A 145 B) has resulted in advanced control of the lawfulness of police custody.

In 2000, the position of suspects has been improved in line with the equality of arms principle as expressed in article 6 of the Convention. They now have the right to request the examining judge to carry out further investigations of a specific nature, the so-called mini-investigation (articles 36a-36e CCP).

4. *The recent crisis in police investigations*

In 1996, the Parliamentary Enquiry Committee on police investigations came to the conclusion that the Netherlands was suffering a crisis in police investigations. No legal standards for police investigations methods existed. Neither the courts nor the prosecution service performed its role of supervisor of the police sufficiently conscientiously, so the police could operate outside the authority and control of the prosecutor in charge. Quite often, undercover policing methods were used that were in conflict with the rules of law in a democratic state. The report of the Committee caused a profound shock to those responsible for the supervision of the Dutch police. In 2000, it led to far-ranging legislation on investigative powers and special investigative methods.[3]

4   The Prosecution Service

4.1   *Organization of the Prosecution Service*

The prosecution service is a nation-wide organization of prosecutors. It is organized hierarchically. At the top is the Board of prosecutors-general. The service functions under the responsibility of the Minister of Justice, but it is not an agency of the Ministry of Justice. The service is part of the judiciary. The prosecution service is organized in two layers, corresponding to courts of first instance and courts of appeal.[4]

In addition, there is a national prosecution office located in Rotterdam, which is not linked to a particular district court. This office supervises the national crime squad (LRT). The national crime squad mainly investigates international crimes like human trafficking, terrorism, money-laundering and fraud. The national prosecution office prosecutes cases investigated by this unit. Furthermore, the national prosecution office develops the investigation and prosecution policy with regard to (international) organized crime. An operational task of the office is the coordination and handling of foreign requests for legal assistance.

There is no hierarchical relation between prosecution services of the courts of first instance and the prosecution services of the courts of appeal. Both are subordinated

---

3. Such as observation and tailing, police infiltration, running informers, interception of communication by technical means, covert entry, pseudo-purchase and pro-active investigation (articles 126g-126u CCP).
4. See Chapter 3.

to the Board of prosecutors-general. The board directs the prosecution service as one organization. The prosecution service is headed by a Board of three to five prosecutors-general *(College van procureurs-generaal)*. The Crown appoints the chairman of the Board. The Board has its office *(parket-generaal)* in The Hague. The Board of prosecutors-general may give instructions to the members of the prosecution service concerning their tasks and powers in relation to the administration of criminal justice and other statutory powers, e.g. supervision of the police. Such an instruction may be of a general criminal policy nature or of a specific nature. Prosecutors are legally bound by these instructions. The highest authority over the investigation and prosecution rests with the Board. The Board ultimately supervises the implementation of a proper prosecution policy by the prosecution service and a proper investigation policy by the police. The Board meets on a regular basis with the Minister of Justice.

The Board of prosecutors-general is advised by a number of advisory bodies, consisting of public prosecutors and high police officers. One of these bodies is the serious crime committee, which functions as policy-making body concerning organized crime and which filters recommendations about organized crime control. The advisory bodies initiate the issuing of national prosecution guidelines.

4.2 Main duties and powers of the service

The main task of the prosecution service is to administer, by means of criminal law, the legal order. The prosecution service plays a pivotal role in the administration of criminal justice. The decisions made by the public prosecutor involve profound consequences for the offender, and repeated refusals to prosecute certain crimes may also lead to a decline in the detection and investigation of offences by the police. In turn, the charges laid against the accused largely delineate the adjudicatory functions of the courts.

It is no exaggeration to say that the Dutch prosecution service has enormous powers, at least in dealing with criminal cases. It has a monopoly over prosecutions and employs the expediency principle in this connection. Furthermore, it makes use of its hierarchical structure to pursue a coordinated policy. In this way, the prosecution service is able to determine systematically what cases should be brought to trial and what sentences the courts should be asked to impose.

Since the introduction of the present Code of Criminal Procedure in 1926, the decision to institute criminal proceedings has been reserved exclusively to the prosecution service. Approximately one-half of the crimes, which reach the public prosecutor's office through the intermediary of the police, are not brought to trial, but are disposed of by the prosecution service itself. Usually, this involves a decision not to prosecute through a dismissal due to technicalities, or through a dismissal due to the exercises of the expediency principle, or by a settlement out of court by means of a transaction.[5]

---

5. See also section 6.3.

If the prosecution service decides to refer a matter to a criminal court, suspects in simple, less serious kinds of crimes will generally be summoned by the public prosecutor exclusively on the basis of the information obtained in the police investigation. In cases of a more complicated nature and serious crime, the public prosecutor may apply to the examining judge for a preliminary judicial investigation. When the preliminary investigation, conducted either by the police or by the examining judge, is completed, it is once again the public prosecutor who must decide whether or not to prosecute or to continue the prosecution. If the suspect is notified by the public prosecutor that no charges will be brought (either conditionally or otherwise), the case is terminated, unless fresh incriminating evidence is subsequently discovered.

4.3   Political accountability

The prosecution service is not an independent body, meaning that the Minister of Justice is politically accountable for the policy of the prosecution service and can be held to account in Parliament for intervening or failing to intervene in this policy. He can be questioned by Parliament both for the prosecution policy at large and for individual prosecutorial decisions. This political accountability is one of the core elements of the Dutch *Rechtsstaat*.

The Minister of Justice is hence involved in the formulation of prosecution policy at large. There are regular contacts between the Minister and the Board of prosecutors-general in this respect. The Board of prosecutors-general is responsible for the proper realization of the prosecution policy, as agreed with the Minister of Justice. The Board issues instructions in this respect. The Minister may be involved in decision-making in individual cases as well. He may be consulted by individual prosecutors in cases where the prosecutorial decision may have an impact on the general prosecution policy, or where his political accountability is at stake. The final responsibility rests with the Minister of Justice.

Article 127 of the Judiciary Organization Act (JOA) therefore vests the Minister of Justice with the power to give general or specific instructions on the exercise of tasks and powers of the prosecution service. The Minister may give instructions concerning investigation and prosecution in individual cases as well. Before the Minister can issue such an instruction, the Board of prosecutors-general has to be consulted. The instruction must be reasoned and issued in written form. Officials of the prosecution service are required to follow those instructions. As a rule, such an instruction has to be added to the files, together with the views of the Board of prosecutors-general in order to give the court full information. Parliament has to be notified of a ministerial instruction not to prosecute or not to investigate a criminal offence and of the view of the Board. The need for democratic control increased over the last decades as the prosecution service acquired more adjudicatory powers and only a restricted number of criminal cases were brought to trial.

Although the power of the Minister of Justice to issue instructions under article 127 JOA is unrestricted, the Minister will rarely exercise this power. In most cases, consultation with the Board of prosecutors-general will have the effect that the Board will issue such an instruction. Only in rare cases where the Board disagrees with the opinion of the Minister, is he likely to use this power.

The Minister cannot give orders to the Procureur-General and the Advocates-General of the Supreme Court, who hold an independent position. Otherwise, a conflict of interest might occur between their powers and those of the Minister of Justice.

5 Issues of criminal law

5.1 Definition of criminal offence

The Criminal Code does not give a definition of the concept of a criminal offence. It deals with the conditions that have to be met before an offender can be punished and provides statutory definitions of punishable conduct. The statutory definition of an offence contains the constituent elements of the criminal offence. The constituent elements must be summed up by the public prosecutor in his charge and the presence of these elements must be proven by facts presented by the prosecution service before a court may sentence the offender. When a constituent element is missing in the charge, a discharge *(ontslag van rechtsvervolging)* must follow.

When the public prosecutor cannot prove by evidence that the charge is matched by the facts, an acquittal *(vrijspraak)* must follow.

In practice an offender whose conduct falls within the statutory definition of an offence is criminally liable. In the charge, the absence of defences does not have to be summed up. Substantive criminal law presumes that in most cases defences will not apply. If there are indications that a defence may apply – mainly the offender will raise his defence – the court has to ascertain whether the defence applies. If so, the court has to discharge the accused.

The statutory elements of a criminal offence play an important role in substantive criminal law, in view of the principle of legality.

The principle of legality is established in the Criminal Code. Article 1 reads: 'No conduct constitutes a criminal offence unless previously statutorily defined in criminal statutes.' A similar provision is laid down in the Constitution (article 16).

The legality principle is a guarantee against the arbitrary administration of criminal justice and offers a high degree of legal certainty. The principle guarantees that only the legislature may define criminal offences. The principle guarantees, moreover, that no court may create new criminal offences by analogous interpretation of criminal law provisions. The principle furthermore guarantees that new criminal law provisions may not be retroactive. The prohibition of retroactivity is not applied if a new criminal provision replaces an old one and the re-definition of the criminal offence is to the advantage of the offender or the reduction of the maximum sentence to be imposed is the result of a change of the legislators' views on the punishability of the offence. In these cases, the most favorable provision must be applied. The principle of legality, furthermore, requires that only penalties specified by statutes may be imposed.

5.2 Classification of offences

All criminal offences are classified as either crimes or infractions. There is no clear and conclusive qualitative criterion (such as *mala in se* versus *mala prohibita)*. The division is used for all criminal law statutes. The legislature decides whether an offence constitutes a crime or an infraction.

The classification of offences is decisive for the question by what judge the criminal offence must be tried: crimes (as a rule) are tried by the police judge or full bench of the district court (criminal division), whereas infractions are tried by the local division of the district court (article 382 CCP). The classification is relevant because an attempt to commit an infraction, or complicity as an accessory to an infraction, does not trigger criminal liability.

Minor traffic offences do not constitute a criminal offence but an administrative offence, to be administered through an administrative procedure without direct access to a court. Such an administrative offence is administered by the police through an administrative fine. The maximum fine is € 340. The police officer's decision to impose an administrative fine is final if, within a certain period of time, no appeal is filed with the prosecution service. In the latter case, the public prosecutor has to re-examine the case and can revoke the police officer's decision. When the public prosecutor reaffirms the administrative fine, one may appeal to the local division of the district court who acts as an administrative judge. The court of appeal in Leeuwarden functions as the highest administrative appellate court in respect of administrative offences.

5.3 Minimum age for criminal responsibility

The minimum age for criminal responsibility is 12 years. Children under the age of 12 cannot be prosecuted for criminal offences, but Civil Code measures, such as a referral to a juvenile treatment center, may be applied.

To juveniles between 12 and 16 years of age, juvenile criminal law is applicable. To juveniles aged between 16 and 18, in principle juvenile criminal law is applied as well, but the juvenile court may apply adult criminal law when it finds grounds to do so by reasons of the gravity of the offence, the character of the offender, or the circumstances in which the offence was committed. For the same reasons, to adults aged between 18 and 21 juvenile criminal law may be applied instead of adult criminal law. The statutory age of adulthood is 18 years. There is no statutory maximum age for criminal responsibility, although old age may be taken into consideration by the public prosecutor when deciding whether or not to prosecute a crime.

5.4 Causation

Although, according to many statutory definitions of offences, the causing of harm of a particular kind constitutes a criminal offence – see e.g. the statutory definition of murder – the Criminal Code does not define the circumstances under which an act may be perceived as the cause of a result.

The criterion for causation is developed in the Supreme Court's case law. Initially, the Court used the reasonable foreseeability of the result as the criterion for causation.

Today, the Court applies the criterion of reasonable imputability in its case law. The foreseeability of the result is still an important factor, as is the factor that no other act may predominantly have influenced the result.

5.5   Mental elements

The statutory definition of crimes as a rule contains a mental element (e.g. intent or negligence).[6] This mental element must be present in order to trigger criminal liability and must be proven by the public prosecutor before the court may sentence the offender. If there is no evidence that the mental element is present, the accused must be acquitted. The concept of strict liability is unknown in Dutch criminal law.

When the mental element is not part of the statutory definition of the criminal offence, which is as a rule the case for infractions, the mental element is presumed to be present, unless there are indications to the contrary. The absence of the mental element in such a case leads to a discharge due to the absence of criminal liability.

It is a key principle of Dutch substantive criminal law that there is no criminal liability without culpability or blameworthiness *(geen straf zonder schuld)*.

5.6   Culpability

Two forms of culpability are distinguished: intent *(opzet)* and negligence *(schuld)*.

Intent includes acting willingly and knowingly, as well as acting in the awareness of a high degree of probability. Intent may be present in the form of a *dolus eventualis*, which is the case where the offender willingly and knowingly accepts a considerable chance that a certain result may ensue. The *dolus eventualis*-doctrine is quite often applied in court practice.

Negligence includes both conscious and unconscious negligence. The former is present when the offender is aware of a considerable and unjustifiable risk that the element exists or will result from the act, but thinks on unreasonable grounds that the risk will not materialize. Unconscious negligence is present when the offender was not aware of the risk, but should have been aware of it (carelessness or thoughtlessness).

---

6.   See for example the definitions of the following two crimes: Intentional homicide (article 287 CC): Anyone who intentionally takes the life of another person is guilty of homicide and liable to a term of imprisonment not exceeding fifteen years or a fine of € 45,000; Murder (article 289 CC): Anyone who intentionally and with premeditation takes the life of another person is guilty of murder and liable to life imprisonment or a term of imprisonment not exceeding twenty years of imprisonment or a fine of € 45,000.

5.7   Justification and excuse

The Criminal Code contains a number of provisions establishing defences. In addition to these statutory defenses, there are two non-statutory defences, which have been developed in the case law of the Supreme Court.

The Criminal Code does not distinguish between justification and excuse. In both cases, according to the Criminal Code, the offender is not criminally liable. The distinction between justification and excuse is made in criminal law doctrine.

At present, the prevailing view is that justifications concern the lawfulness of the act whereas excuses concern the blameworthiness. If grounds for justification are present, the violation of the law does not constitute a criminal offence. If grounds for excuse are present, the violation of the law constitutes a criminal offence, but the offender cannot be blamed for having committed the offence. All defences may be invoked with respect to all offences; no single offence is excluded.

Justification defences:

1. *Necessity (noodtoestand)*
   Article 40 of the Criminal Code reads: Anyone who commits an offence as a result of a force he could not be expected to resist is not criminally liable. On the basis of the history of the Code, the Supreme Court ruled that this article includes necessity.
   Necessity is a situation in which a person has to choose between conflicting duties. 'If the person in such a situation obeys the most important one and violates the criminal law by doing so, his act is justified' according to the Supreme Court. In this formulation, the principles of subsidiarity and proportionality are expressed.

2. *Self-defense (noodweer)*
   Article 41 of the Criminal Code reads: Anyone who commits an offence where this is necessary in the defence of his person or the person of another, his or another person's integrity or property against immediate unlawful attack is not criminally liable. As a rule, one may not take justice in one's own hands, but in the case of an immediate unlawful attack one may repel force by force, provided that there is no other convenient or reasonable mode of escape (subsidiarity). The amount of force must be reasonable (proportionality). In assessing whether the force was reasonable, the criminal court may take the personal characteristics of the offender into consideration.

3. *Public duty and official orders (wettelijk voorschrift en ambtelijk bevel)*
   Article 42 of the Criminal Code reads: Anyone who commits an offence in carrying out a legal requirement is not criminally liable. Article 43 of the Criminal Code reads: Anyone who commits an offence in carrying out an official order issued by a competent authority is not criminally liable. In both cases, impunity is guaranteed because the person acted on the authority of a governmental body or public officer.

4. *Absence of substantive unlawfulness (afwezigheid van materiële wederrechtelijkheid)*
   This justification defence is developed by the case law of the Supreme Court. In 1933, the Court ruled that, even though unlawfulness is not an element in the statutory definition of the offence (thus unlawfulness does not have to be proved), the offender cannot be convicted where his act does not result in substantive unlawfulness. This is the case when an act (which is in conflict with the law) serves the same interest as is guaranteed by the law. The legal impact of this non-codified justification is limited. After 1933, the Court did not repeat its ruling.

Excuse defences:

1. *Insanity (ontoerekenbaarheid)*
   Article 39 of the Criminal Code reads: Anyone who commits an offence for which he cannot be held responsible by reason of a mental disorder or mental disease is not criminally liable.
   No statutory standards or case law standards are set for determining insanity, but in practice a person is not held responsible for his criminal conduct if at the time of such conduct, as a result of a mental disorder or disease, he lacks substantial capacity either to appreciate the wrongfulness of his conduct, or to bring his conduct into conformity with the requirements of law.
   In assessing whether the offender cannot be held responsible, the court makes use of reports by psychiatrists.

2. *Duress (overmacht)*
   Article 40 of the Criminal Code encompasses both necessity and duress. An offender who acts under the pressure of an external force he could not reasonably resist is excused. The external force may be an unlawful threat from another person or a natural force.
   If someone acts under the pressure of a force caused by his moral conscience, he does not have the defence of duress. In case of duress, the will of the offender is impaired to such a degree that he cannot be blamed for his act.

3. *Excessive self-defence (noodweerexces)*
   Article 41(2) of the Criminal Code reads: Anyone exceeding the limits of necessary defence, where such excess has been the direct result of a strong emotion brought about by the attack, is not criminally liable.
   When the unlawful attack causes strong emotions such as rage, anger, fear or desperation, the person attacked may not react properly by using a reasonable mode of escape. Due to the emotions, he may overreact and use an amount of force that is disproportionate. Due to the strong emotions, the offender's will is impaired so that he cannot be blamed for his act.

4. *Obeying an unlawful order (onbevoegd gegeven ambtelijk bevel)*

   Article 43(2) of the Criminal Code reads: Obeying an official order issued without authority does not remove criminal liability unless the order was assumed by the subordinate in good faith to have been issued with authority and he complied with it in his capacity as subordinate. Good faith may be both subjective and objective. The latter means that there is still a responsibility on the subordinate to be prudent, and in case of doubt to refrain from obeying the order.

5. *Absence of all blameworthiness (afwezigheid van alle schuld)*

   In line with the principle 'no criminal liability without blameworthiness', the excuse of absence of all blameworthiness has been developed in the Supreme Court's case law. It supplements the codified defences. Absence of all blameworthiness may be due to ignorance of facts, or ignorance of law. The ignorance of facts must be reasonable. The offender must have done all he reasonably could do in order not to be ignorant. If the ignorance is due to indolence, frivolity or indifference, there is no absence of all blameworthiness. The ignorance of law functions as a mitigation of the presumption that everyone has to know the law. The ignorance is only excused when the offender has actively sought expert advice on law by a person or agency having such an authority that he could reasonably trust the reliability of the advice, but was misinformed. Misinformation by the police, a notary, a public official of a ministry may lead to excusable ignorance. Misinformation by his counsel does not lead to excusable ignorance of the offender.

5.8   Inchoate offences

Two inchoate offences are to be distinguished:

1. *Attempt*

   An attempt to commit a crime is punishable where the offender manifests his intention by initiating the crime (article 45 CC). In case of attempt, the statutory principal penalty for the crime is reduced by one third. This sentence reduction has two reasons: less danger to society has materialized than by the consummation of the crime and the reduction may be an incentive for the offender not to consummate the crime. The Code does not define where the preparation of a crime ends and the execution of a crime starts. The Supreme Court's case law seems to follow the objective theory: an act which in its outward appearance should be regarded as being directed to the consummation of the crime is an act initiating the crime. There is no attempt if the crime has not been consummated by reason only of circumstances dependent on the offender's will, the so-called voluntary withdrawal (article 46b CC). The offender's motives for not consummating the crime are irrelevant. There are two reasons for the impunity of this voluntary withdrawal: the offender is not as bad as he initially appeared to be, and impunity may be an incentive not to consummate the crime.

2. Preparation

Preparation does not fall within the scope of attempt since there is no initiation of the crime. For the prevention of crimes, it was felt to be unsatisfactory that the police could not arrest offenders preparing serious crimes. In 1994, therefore, the preparation of serious crimes which carry a statutory prison sentence of not less than eight years has been criminalized (article 46 CC). Preparation of such a crime is punishable where the offender intentionally obtains, manufactures, imports, transits, exports or has at his disposal, objects, substances, monies or other instruments of payment, information carriers, concealed spaces of means of transport clearly intended for the commission of such a crime. In the case of preparation, the statutory maximum penalty for the crime is reduced by one half or to ten years when the statutory maximum penalty is life sentence, since no or less danger for society has materialized. There is no preparation where the crime has not been completed only by reason of circumstances dependent on the offender's will (article 46b CC).

5.9 Complicity

Complicity is the involvement in criminal offences as principal or as accessory before and during the fact. Principals are those who commit a criminal offence, either personally or jointly with another, or who cause an innocent person to commit a criminal offence and those who, by means of gifts, promises, abuse of authority, use of violence, threat or deception or providing the opportunity, means or information, intentionally solicit the commission of a crime (article 47 CC).

Accessories to crimes are those who intentionally assist during the commission of a crime and those who provide the opportunity, means or information to commit the crime (article 48 CC). Accessory to infractions is not punishable. In the case of complicity as an accessory, the statutory maximum of the principal penalty is reduced by one third. If the offence carries a life sentence, the accessory may be sentenced to an imprisonment of fifteen years maximum.

5.10 Corporate criminal liability

Criminal liability is not restricted to natural persons. Private or public corporate bodies, like provinces or municipalities, can also be held liable for committing an offence (article 51 CC). The State as public corporate body enjoys criminal immunity. State agencies however, like ministries, fall within the scope of article 51 CC. When a criminal offence has been committed by a corporation, prosecution may be instituted against the corporation and/or against the persons in the corporation who have ordered the commission of the criminal offence and against those in control of such unlawful behaviour. A person is considered to be in control when he is in the position to decide that the act takes place and accepts the actual performance, or when he is in the position to take measures to prevent the act but fails to do so and consciously takes the risk that the prohibited act is performed. Both the person and the corporate body may be sentenced for the offence.

A corporate body commits a criminal offence if the corporation itself or the management is in the position to control the occurrence of the criminal activities and, moreover, if it turns out in the course of the events that these activities had been accepted by the corporate body.

5.11 Double jeopardy

Double jeopardy or successive prosecutions for the same act are prohibited by article 68 Criminal Code, which reads: No person may be prosecuted twice for an act for which a final judgement has been rendered by a (Dutch) court, except in cases of a review decision by the Supreme Court.

The Code itself does not define what is meant by 'an act'. According to the Supreme Court's case law, where one act constitutes more than one criminal offence, each of them can be prosecuted, provided the offences are different in the objective of prohibition and in the nature of the blame that can be imputed to the offender, e.g. a joy-rider who drives dangerously can be prosecuted both for the offence of joy-riding and for the offence of dangerous driving.

5.12 Statute of limitations

Time limits can bar the prosecution of a criminal offence. The rationale for the time limits is related to the reduced societal need to punish the offender and the difficulties in gathering evidence after a long lapse of time. The more serious the offence, the longer the period of limitation is. According to article 70 of the Criminal Code, the statute of limitation ranges from two years for all infractions, to eighteen years for crimes which carry a statutory punishment of life sentence. The time limits are six, twelve and fifteen years for crimes which carry a statutory imprisonment of less than three, less than ten and more than ten years respectively. Exceeding the time limits leads to a dismissal of the case. The time limits for the enforcement of the sentence are one-third longer than the time limits for the prosecution.

At present (2004), a Bill is pending in Parliament to abolish the time limit for murder and to extend the time limit to thirty years for crimes carrying a life sentence and to twenty years for crime carrying a statutory imprisonment of more than ten years.

6 Issues of procedural law

6.1 Pre-trial investigation

A criminal procedure for a court in first instance comprises two phases: the pre-trial investigation phase and the public trial phase.

There are two kinds of pre-trial investigations:
– the investigation by the police under the direction of a public prosecutor; and
– the judicial preliminary investigation by an examining judge.

The criminal procedure is initiated by the pre-trial investigation carried out by the police as soon as the police are informed of a criminal offence. The purpose of the pre-trial investigation is to gather information on the offence and the suspect. A suspect is anyone who may reasonably be suspected of having committed the offence. The police have the right to question any person in relation to the offence, whether or not this person is a suspect. However, no one is obliged to answer questions put by the police.

The police prepare a written record of the questioning of the suspect and other persons and of other relevant findings of facts. The written records are prepared by the police under oath, and may be used as evidence by the court. The police are authorized to carry out coercive measures such as arrest, body search and search of the premises when the legal prerequisites to do so exist.

The Code of Criminal Procedure does not give a systematic description of investigative measures, nor statutory rules for all investigative methods used by the police. Some statutory rules exist concerning the interrogation of the offender by the police and concerning investigative methods of a coercive nature such as the use of DNA tests for the identification of the offender, or the interception of (tele)-communication. Other important investigative methods, such as the interrogation of witnesses or the application of technical means of investigation such as fingerprints, confrontation through the Oslo-method and the use of dogs for a search have recently been given a statutory basis. The admissibility of these investigative methods previously had been based on the Supreme Court's case law.

Under Dutch law, before a criminal investigation may be started and investigative measures applied, there must be a reasonable suspicion that a criminal offence has been committed. In recent years, the police have more and more focused on the gathering of information about networks, groups and individuals especially in order to know what criminal activities were planned, thus before a criminal offence was committed, the so-called pro-active policing. Pro-active policing methods and covert policing methods like surveillance, infiltration and the handling of informants have recently acquired a statutory basis in the Code of Criminal Procedure by the 2000 Special Powers of Investigation Act.

When the police investigation is terminated, the written records are forwarded to the prosecutor for a decision on prosecution.

6.2 Examining judge

The role of the examining judge in the pre-trial phase has been reduced since the 2000 Act on the Revision of the Judicial Investigation. He performs two functions, namely in determining whether a suspect should remain in pre-trial detention for a period of up to ten days and in (further) investigating crime. The examining judge has powers which the police and prosecutor lack. He may order a witness to appear before him and make a witnesses deposition. The examining judge may order a psychiatric examination of the suspect, involvement of expert witness or intimate bodily examination (DNA).

If the public prosecutor finds that the proper investigation of a crime requires the exercise of one of these powers, he must request the examining judge to start a judicial preliminary investigation.

Furthermore, the examining judge plays a role when intrusive measures such as the search of premises against the will of the resident, or the interception of communication by technical means or the opening of intercepted mail have to be used by the police or the public prosecutor. For the use of these intrusive measures, the police and the public prosecutor have to request permission from the examining judge. Before the examining judge may give his permission, he has to check whether the legal prerequisites for these intrusive measures have been met.

During a judicial preliminary investigation, the examining judge carries out further investigations, if necessary with the help of the police. The examining judge may search premises against the will of the resident and may order that computer data are revealed. He may hear a witness under oath who cannot be present at the trial, or who may not be willing to appear at trial because of fears of retaliation by the defendant. In such cases, the defence counsel is notified and he may attend the hearing and put written questions. Only in a limited number of cases that come to trial a judicial preliminary investigation has taken place.

6.3   Prosecutorial decisions

When the police investigation or the judicial preliminary investigation is terminated, the files are forwarded to the prosecutor who has to take a decision. He can decide:
–   to drop the case, i.e. not to prosecute;
–   to settle the case by means of a transaction; or
–   to issue a writ of summons on the offender.

Non-prosecution
The power to prosecute resides exclusively with the prosecution service. No prosecutorial power is granted to private persons or bodies, not even when the prosecution service declines to prosecute. This prosecution monopoly does not require the prosecution service to prosecute every crime brought to its notice. The prosecution service may decide not to prosecute if a prosecution would probably not lead to a conviction, due to lack of evidence, or for technical considerations (technical or procedural waiver).[7]

The prosecution service may also decide not to prosecute under the expediency principle. The expediency principle laid down in article 167 CCP authorizes the

---

7. The grounds for non-prosecution due to technicalities may be:
    • wrongly registered as suspect by the police;
    • insufficient legal evidence for a prosecution;
    • inadmissibility of a prosecution;
    • the court does not have legal competence over the case;
    • the act does not constitute a criminal offence; and
    • the offender is not criminally liable due to a justification or excuse defence.

prosecution service to waive (further) prosecution 'for reasons of public interest'. In appropriate cases, the prosecutor can decide conditionally to suspend prosecution.

Prior to the late 1960s, the discretionary power to waive (further) prosecution was exercised on a very restricted scale. Thereafter, however, a remarkable change in prosecution policy took place. Research on the effects of law enforcement coupled with the limited resources of law enforcement agencies revealed that it was impossible, undesirable and, in some circumstances, even counter-productive to prosecute all offences investigated. Gradually, the discretionary power not to prosecute for policy considerations began to be exercised more widely. To harmonize the utilization of this discretionary power, the top of the prosecution service, the Board of prosecutors-general, issues national prosecution guidelines. Public prosecutors are directed to follow these guidelines except when special circumstances in an individual case are spelled out. Under these guidelines, a public prosecutor could waive prosecution for reasons of public interest if, for example:

- measures other than penal sanctions are preferable, or would be more effective (e.g. disciplinary, administrative or civil measures);
- prosecution would be disproportionate, unjust or ineffective in relation to the nature of the offence (e.g. if the offence caused no harm and it was inexpedient to inflict punishment);
- prosecution would be disproportionate, unjust or ineffective for reasons related to the offender (e.g. his age or health, rehabilitation prospects, first offender);
- prosecution would be contrary to the interests of the state (e.g. for reasons of security, peace and order, or if new applicable legislation has been introduced);
- prosecution would be contrary to the interests of the victim (e.g. compensation has already been paid).

Public prosecutors are not obliged to motivate their decisions not to prosecute due to technicalities or due to policy considerations. They are, however, obliged to categorize their decisions under one of the reasons or grounds for non-prosecution previously mentioned. This categorization is no guarantee for a uniform application of the reasons for non-prosecution. However, it provides information on the prosecution policy pursued in each of the nineteen prosecutorial jurisdictions and provides insight into the difference in these prosecution policies. It is one of the means to harmonize these prosecution policies.

In the early 1980s, the proportion of unconditional waivers on policy considerations was relatively high. Approximately one quarter of all crimes cleared were not further prosecuted for policy reasons. The rationale was that prosecution should not be automatic, but should serve a concrete social objective. Such a high proportion of waivers on policy grounds was seriously criticized. The prosecution service was instructed to reduce the number of unconditional waivers by making more frequent use of conditional waivers, reprimands or transactions. Today, the percentage of unconditional policy waivers has dropped to around 5%. The decrease of the percentage of unconditional waivers did not lead to an increase in number of cases tried by a criminal court. This is because an increasing number of cases was either waived conditionally or settled out of court with a transaction.

Transaction

Transaction can be considered as a form of diversion in which the offender voluntarily pays a sum of money to the Treasury, or fulfils one or more (financial) conditions laid down by the prosecution service in order to avoid further criminal prosecution and a public trial.

The opportunity to settle criminal cases by way of a transaction has long existed. The first opportunity to settle a case financially was created in 1838 for offences which carry no other statutory sentence than a fine. The offender who offers the prosecution service to pay the maximum statutory fine may settle his criminal case by paying (article 74a CC). The second opportunity to settle a case was adopted in 1921. The public prosecutor may, before trial, propose one or more conditions in lieu of criminal proceedings. Prosecution is in effect suspended until such time as the conditions are met, after which the right to prosecute lapses.

However, until 1983, this opportunity to settle a case financially was exclusively reserved for misdemeanors in principle punishable only with a fine. Following the recommendations of the Financial Penalties Committee, the Financial Penalties Act of 1983 expanded the scope of transactions to include crimes which carry a statutory prison sentence of less than six years (article 74 CC). The restriction that transaction is excluded for crimes carrying a statutory prison sentence exceeding six years has a limited impact. The overwhelming majority of crimes carry a statutory prison sentence of less than six years.

The following conditions may be set for a transaction:

a. the payment of a sum of money to the State, the amount being not less than five guilders and not more than the maximum of the statutory fine;
b. renunciation of title to objects that have been seized and that are subject to forfeiture or confiscation;
c. the surrender of objects subject to forfeiture or confiscation, or payment to the State of their assessed value;
d. the payment in full to the State of a sum of money or transfer of objects seized to deprive the accused, in whole or in part, of the estimated gains acquired by means of or derived from the criminal offence, including the saving of costs;
e. full or partial compensation for the damage caused by the criminal offence;
f. the performance of non-remunerated work or taking part in a training course during 120 hours.

Compliance in due time with the conditions set by the prosecution service does not imply that the offender admits that he has committed a criminal offence.

Acceptance of the public prosecutor's offer to settle a case is as a rule beneficial to the offender: he avoids a public trial, the transaction is not registered in the criminal record and he is no longer uncertain about the sentence. On the other hand, by accepting the transaction he gives up the right to be sentenced by an independent court with all associated legal guarantees (article 6 ECHR). The acceptance must be made voluntarily without constraint.

The almost unlimited power given to the prosecution service in 1983 to settle criminal cases by a transaction without the intervention of a court has been strongly criticized. The most important criticism was that the increased transaction opportunities introduced a plea-bargaining system, represented a real breach of the theory of the separation of powers, undermined the legal protection of the accused, favored certain social groups and entrusted the prosecution service with powers which should remain reserved to the judiciary. Furthermore, it was feared that with nearly 90% of all crimes brought within the sphere of the transaction, the public criminal trial, with its safeguards for the accused, would become the exception and not the rule.

Despite this criticism, the introduction of the broadened transaction was a great success. More than one third of all crimes dealt with by the prosecution service are now settled out of court by a transaction. This is in line with the national criminal policy plan, which formulated the target that one third of all prosecuted crimes be settled by way of a transaction. Transactions for crimes seem to be very popular, both for the prosecution service and the offender. They save the prosecution service and the offender time, energy and expenses, and furthermore protect the offender against stigmatization. Quite often, high transaction sums for environmental crimes committed by corporations are accepted in order to avoid negative publicity.

To minimize the risk of arbitrariness and lack of uniformity in the application of transactions, the Board of prosecutors-general has over the years issued guidelines for the common crimes for which transaction is most frequently used, relating to the principles to be taken into consideration regarding transaction and prosecution.

Since 1993, the police may offer transactions for certain categories of crimes. Shoplifting and drunk-driving have been designated as offences for which the police may offer a transaction. The maximum amount of a police transaction for crimes is € 350 (article 74c CC). By contrast, the maximum amount of a prosecutorial transaction for crimes is € 450.000.

The writ of summons
When a criminal case has not been settled out of court, the prosecutor will summon the suspect to appear in court. The summons comprises the charge *(tenlastelegging)* and a list of witnesses to be sub-poenaed. The public prosecutor is truly *dominus litis*, or master of the trial. The trial judge has no control over the content of the charge. The prosecutor may decide to charge the suspect with a less serious offence (e.g. by disregarding aggravating circumstances) despite the existence of sufficient evidence to charge the suspect with a more serious crime, or may limit the charge to some offences committed by the suspect. The court is informed in an informal way about the other offences committed *(voeging ad informandum)*. For the sentence to be imposed, the court may consider these non-charged offences, provided that the suspect does not deny and the offence can be proved. The trial stage begins as soon as the prosecutor has issued a summons.

6.4 Character of the pre-trial phase

The pre-trial phase has a *moderately* inquisitorial character. Specific inquisitorial elements are present when coercive measures such as bodily searches, searches of the premises or telephone interception are applied.

The inquisitorial character is tempered by provisions providing that the offender has the right to be assisted by a defence counsel and the right to communicate with his counsel without supervision. The suspect is furthermore informed of the progress of the investigations in the pre-trial phase, unless this information hampers the proper conduct of the investigation.

6.5 The trial phase

The pre-trial phase ends and the trial-phase begins with the decision to prosecute the case and to summon the offender. The charge is mentioned in the summons *(dagvaarding)* so that the offender can prepare his defence. A court hearing commences with the identification of the accused by the president of the court and the reading of the charge *(tenlastelegging)* by the public prosecutor. The accused is reminded by the court of his right not to answer questions.

The charge is the subject of the court session. It consists of a description of the alleged criminal offence and closely follows the statutory definition of the offence.

The court does not have the power to modify the charge if it deems this necessary. The public prosecutor is vested with the power to do so, since he is master of the trial. This power, however, is very limited. This is due to what is called 'the tyranny of the charge', i.e. the court may only convict the accused on the basis of the charge.

After the reading of the charge, the court examines the accused and the witnesses (either called by the prosecutor or by the defendant or his defence counsel) and the experts. Afterwards, the public prosecutor and the defence counsel may ask additional questions of the accused and the witnesses. Unlike the accused, witnesses are obliged to answer the questions put by the court, the prosecutor and the defence counsel. Cross-examination, however, is unknown under Dutch law. The examination of the accused and the witnesses by the court is usually combined with the reading by the presiding judge of their statements made to the police or the examining judge. Witnesses are examined after having taken the oath. The defendant may not be questioned under oath. He has the right to remain silent, and cannot be obliged to tell the truth and nothing but the truth.

Although the Code of Criminal Procedure embodies the immediacy principle, obliging witnesses to be questioned in court, witnesses are as a rule not questioned, since the Supreme Court accepts hearsay evidence. In fact, criminal court sessions to a large extent deal with written statements of witnesses filed by the police or the examining judge. Their written statements may be used as evidence provided that these have been discussed in court. This restriction of the immediacy principle has the effect that court trials do not take very long if the accused confesses and does not contradict the written statements of the witnesses. It is rare that a trial last more than a couple of hours, even in serious cases.

After the evidence has been presented and discussed, the public prosecutor makes his closing speech *(requisitoir)*. In his closing speech, he gives a summing up of the evidence and recommends what offence the defendant is to be sentenced for and requests the sentence to be imposed. However, the judge is not bound by this request. Finally, the defence counsel addresses the court with his plea. Before the presiding judge closes the trial the last word is given to the accused.

After the close of the session of the court, the court goes in chambers to deliberate the verdict and the sentence. The verdict must be available within two weeks. The verdict is read in a public session of the court. As a rule, it takes more than two weeks to write a verdict and to give a full summing up of the evidence used for the decision on the guilt of the convict. Such extended verdicts normally are only prepared when appeal or appeal in cassation is lodged. A person convicted may not be ordered to pay the costs of the criminal procedure.

6.6   Rules of evidence

An offender can be convicted only when the court through the court trial has gained the conviction from evidence defined by statute that the offender has committed the offence as charged (article 338 CCP). The evidence may not rest upon the testimony of a single witness *(unus testis nullus testis)* and a conviction may never be based solely on the statement of the accused. A guilty plea is unknown.

The court is free in assessing the truthworthiness of the evidence and the quality of the evidence. In the verdict, the court has to state the reasons for convicting the accused. The burden of proof as a rule lies with the public prosecutor. The court may play, however, an active role in gathering evidence during court trial by ordering further investigation. The presumption of innocence is a fundamental principle of the Code of Criminal Procedure.

6.7   Court decisions

In a judgment, the court can take four procedural decisions and four substantive decisions. As procedural decisions, the court can declare the summons null and void, can declare itself not competent to try the case, can dismiss the case and finally can suspend further prosecution (article 348 CCP). The court must declare the summons null and void when it has not been served properly, or when the charge is not properly formulated or not comprehensible. The court can declare itself not competent to try the case when the offence charged has not been committed within its jurisdiction, or when the offence belongs to the jurisdiction of another specialized court, e.g. the juvenile court. The court must dismiss the case when the right to prosecute a case does not exist (anymore), e.g. due to the statute of limitations, due to a settlement of the case through a transaction, or because a requirement for prosecution has not been met. Under some circumstances, the court must suspend further prosecution, e.g. when the defendant is not fit to stand trial.

When the court decides that the summons is valid, that the court is competent to try the case, and that the case is not to be dismissed or the further prosecution has to be suspended, the court has to give a substantive decision, which means a decision on the charged offence.

The court has to decide four questions:
– Are the facts mentioned in the charge proven?
– Do the facts constitute a criminal offence?
– Is the accused criminally liable?
– What sentence shall be imposed (article 350 CCP)?

The accused is to be acquitted when the essential facts charged are not proven by the evidence presented. A discharge of the accused takes place when the facts charged are proven, but do not constitute a criminal offence, or when the offender is not liable due to a justification or excuse defence. A sentence is imposed when the evidence that the accused has committed a criminal offence is beyond reasonable doubt and when the accused is criminally liable for the offence.

The verdict must be reasoned (articles 358 and 359 CCP). The reasoning concerns the question whether the charge is proven, why an explicit defence is denied, or why despite guilt no penalty is imposed. Furthermore, the sentence imposed must be reasoned. A dismissal, a decision on incompetence, a decision to declare the summons null and void, as well as a decision to suspend further prosecution must also be reasoned. An acquittal does not need a reasoning. Special reasoning is required when the court imposes a more serious sentence than requested by the public prosecutor, or when an entrustment order is imposed.

6.8   Trial in absence of the accused

The accused has the right to be present at the court trial, but he is not obliged to appear in court unless the court orders so, which rarely happens. A case may be tried in the absence of the accused, unless he was not summoned properly. As a rule, the summons must be served to the accused in person, or to his representative, at least ten days prior to the court session.

Prior to the 1998 Procedural law reform Act, the accused lost the right to be defended by his defence counsel if he himself was not present during court session. The European Court of Human Rights has decided in the *Lala and Pelladoah* decisions that this was in conflict with article 6 of the European Convention on Human Rights.

Since that Act, an absent accused may have himself defended by his counsel when the latter is explicitly empowered by the accused to do so. In that case, the trial is considered to take place in the presence of the accused (article 279 CCP).

6.9   Character of the trial phase

The trial phase has an accusatorial character. To a large extent there is an equality of arms between the public prosecutor and the defendant who may present evidence in his favour. Since, however, the main purpose of the trial phase is to discover the truth, a purely adversarial system is not followed. For instance, the system of cross-examination is unknown. It is mainly the judge who asks questions during the criminal trial.

6.10   The victim

The term victim does not occur in the Code of Criminal Procedure, nor in any other criminal law statute. The victim has a procedural role only in his capacity of witness, informer or injured party. He has few rights in the pre-trial and trial phase. He has no right to present a criminal charge or to be heard in his capacity of victim on the charge presented by the public prosecutor. The victim does not have the right to counsel, nor the right of appeal.

Due to the changing attitude towards the weak legal position of the victim and in line with the United Nations Declaration on Basic Principles of Justice for Victims of Crime and the Abuse of Power (1985), a number of guidelines have been issued by the prosecution service on how to treat victims. The guidelines oblige police and prosecutors to inform the victim whether the prosecution of the offender will take place and about the possibility of financial compensation from the offender. Furthermore, the legal position of the victim has been substantially improved by the 1993 Criminal Injuries Compensation Act. He now has access to police files and the right to be informed by the public prosecutor on the state of the criminal procedure. Legal implementation of a restricted right to give an oral statement during court trial – the so-called victim impact statement – is presently under discussion. The model of restorative justice is gaining an increasing number of supporters.

6.11   Complaints by the victim against non-prosecution

The Dutch Code of Criminal Procedure grants the right of prosecution exclusively to the prosecution service. The State thus has a full monopoly on prosecution without any restriction. The victim does not have the right to private prosecution.

Anybody with an interest in the prosecution of an offence can file a protest against a decision to waive a case, by lodging a complaint with a court of appeal. The court examines the manner in which the discretionary power was utilized by the public prosecutor. This examination extends both to the legality of the decision (the issue being the proper application of the law) and to the use of discretion (a study of the extent to which this decision is in line with the general prosecution policy). The complainant has the right to be heard by the court, and may be assisted by his counsel. The court of appeal may order the public prosecutor to initiate a prosecution if it finds that the prosecutor has misused his discretionary power. However, in practice the court of appeal seldom orders prosecution. Annually, around 1,200 complaints are filed.

6.12   Civil claims in criminal trials

Since 1993, the victim can join the proceedings in his capacity of injured party and can claim full financial compensation from the offender to be decided on by the criminal court in connection with criminal proceedings (article 51a CCP).

The claim may comprise material and immaterial damages. The heirs of a victim who died as a result of the criminal offence may join the proceedings as well. There is no statutory maximum amount that can be claimed when joining the proceedings, but the claim must be clear and not too complex to be dealt with by the criminal court.

The joiner as a rule is effected by a form in the pre-trial phase to be handed to the public prosecutor and, in the trial phase, to be handed to the court containing personal data of the injured party and information on the grounds for the claim and the content of the claim. For the proper preparation of the claim, the injured party has access to the police files of the case. In claiming compensation from the offender, the victim is not assisted by the State, but may be assisted by counsel or by a proxy.

The State does not assist the injured party in the effective recovery of his claim. To avoid the situation that recovery of the claim is impossible due to the unwillingness of the offender, the court can either impose a partly suspended sentence under the condition that the offender pays compensation (article 14c CC), or can impose a compensation order (article 36f CC). Compensation orders are enforced by the State.

7   The system of sanctions

7.1   Sentencing

The Dutch judiciary is vested with the widest discretionary power when sentencing.

The very few statutory rules that guide the court in this process are general and do not limit the court in choices of type and severity of the sanctions in individual cases.

The statutory framework of sanctions is set very broadly. The statutory minimum term of imprisonment is one day and is the same for all crimes, regardless of the generic seriousness of the offence.

Maximum terms of imprisonment are specified and reflect the gravity of the worst possible case. Few crimes are subject to life-imprisonment, but instead of life-imprisonment a fixed-term prison sentence of up to twenty years or a fine can be imposed.

7.2   Classification of penalties

The current Dutch sanctions system for adults distinguishes between penalties and measures. Penalties are aimed at punishment and general prevention. Punishment means that the offender, through the penalty, is made to suffer in reaction to the harm caused by his offence to others. In the penalty, revenge plays a role. Due to this element of revenge, the length of imprisonment must be proportionate to the level of blameworthiness.

Measures, on the other hand, are aimed at the promotion of the security and safety of persons or property, or at restoring a state of affairs. A measure differs from a penalty in that it can also be imposed when there is no question of criminal responsibility, in the sense that the person cannot be blamed for having committed a crime (e.g. in cases of insanity).

The Criminal Code furthermore distinguishes between principal penalties and accessory penalties, which originally only could be imposed in conjunction with a principal penalty. Since 1984, accessory penalties may be imposed as principal sentences as well.

For all offences, the maximum of the statutory penalty is specified by the Act which defines the particular offence. This maximum penalty reflects the gravity of the worst possible case and is thus high for the most serious offences, e.g. twelve years for rape, six years for domestic burglary, nine years for extortion and four years for simple theft.

Capital punishment for ordinary crimes was abolished in 1870. For military crimes and war crimes, capital punishment was abolished in 1983 (article 114 Dutch Constitution), but in practice had not been used since 1950. The Netherlands ratified Protocol no. 6 to the European Convention on Human Rights on the abolition of the death penalty.

7.3 Principal penalties

1. Imprisonment

The most severe penalty in the Dutch penal system is imprisonment, which can only be imposed for crimes. The most severe form is life imprisonment, which is relatively rarely imposed. Around twenty crimes carry life imprisonment as a statutory penalty, but the Criminal Code does not prescribe compulsory life imprisonment in any circumstances. Crimes, such as murder or manslaughter under aggravating circumstances, carrying life imprisonment, also carry a fixed-term prison sentence of up to twenty years. Furthermore, since 1983 a fine may be imposed as the sanction for any crime, even those which carry life imprisonment as statutory sanction.

A life sentence is deprivation of liberty for an indeterminate period. Parole or release arrangements are not applicable in the case of a life sentence. Life sentences, however, may be converted by way of pardon into a fixed-term prison sentence, for example for twenty years. After such conversion, the offender may be considered for early release. As a rule, a life sentence means about fifteen years of effective imprisonment.

The fixed-term prison sentence is the most frequently applied form of imprisonment. The statutory minimum is one day and the statutory maximum is fifteen years. In certain circumstances, the maximum may be twenty years. Unlike the situation in other countries, none of the offences carry a special statutory minimum term of imprisonment. Thus, for example for murder, a minimum prison sentence of one day is theoretically possible.

When an offender is sentenced to imprisonment for several offences committed concurrently or consecutively, the court may impose a prison sentence which may exceed by one third the maximum statutory prison sentence for the severest offence.

2. *Detention*

Detention is the custodial sentence for infractions. The minimum duration of detention is one day and the maximum duration is one year. In special cases, e.g. in cases of recidivism, the maximum can be increased to sixteen months. Originally intended as a *custodia honesta*, detention is deemed a lighter sentence on the sentencing scale than imprisonment, although the two hardly differ in the manner of their implementation.

3. *Task penalty*

The task penalty is one type of the community sentences increasingly used to reduce the incidence of custodial sentences. Additional forms of community sentences such as electronic monitoring and penitentiary programs are alternative forms for the implementation of deprivation of liberty *(executiemodaliteiten)*. The development of community sentences started in the 1970s with the establishment in 1974 of the Committee on alternative penal sanctions. This Committee was set up to advise the government on new sentencing options in order to reduce the number of short-term prison sentences.

In 2001, the provisions on the community service order (CSO) have been considerably reformed. The CSO has been replaced by the task penalty *(taakstraf)* which is no longer a substitute for a short-term prison sentence but a distinct sanction option considered to be a restriction of a person's liberty that is less severe than the custodial sentence and more severe than a fine. A task penalty may consist of a work order, a training order or a combination of both orders.

A task penalty may not exceed a total of 480 hours of which the work order is 240 hours maximum. The task penalty must be completed within twelve months. Extension of the completion term is possible. When imposing a task penalty, the court has to state the term of default detention in case the task penalty is not complied with. The default detention is at least one day and the maximum is eight months. Every two hours of task penalty count for one day default detention. When part of the task penalty is complied with, the length of the default detention is reduced proportionally.

The prosecution service is responsible for overseeing compliance with the task penalty and information may be requested from individuals and organizations involved in probation work for this purpose. In appropriate cases, the prosecution service may change the nature of the work to be carried out, or the kind of education to follow. When the prosecution service is satisfied that the task penalty has been carried out properly, it must notify the person convicted as soon as possible.

If the person convicted has not carried out the task penalty properly, the prosecution service may order implementation of the default detention mentioned in the sentence, taking into account the number of hours of the task penalty that has been carried out properly. The person convicted can file an appeal against the order to implement the default detention. The appeal is dealt with by the court which imposed the task penalty. The order to implement the default detention must be given within three months of the end of the completion period.

The probation service is responsible for administering task penalties and coordinators have been appointed in each of the nineteen jurisdictions who canvass for workplaces where the work order can be carried out. The work order must benefit the community. It can be with public bodies like the municipality or private organizations involved in health care, the environment and the protection of nature, and social and cultural work.

4. *Fine*

The fine is the least severe of the principal penalties. Originally, the fine was exclusively intended for infractions and minor crimes.

Since the 1983 Financial Penalties Act, all offences, including those subject to life imprisonment, may be sentenced with a fine.

The 1983 Act furthermore expresses the principle that the fine should be preferred over the prison sentence. Article 359 CCP requires the court to give special reasons whenever a custodial sentence is ordered instead of a fine.

The minimum fine for all offences is € 2. The maximum fine depends on the fine category into which a crime or infraction is placed. The 1983 Act created six categories with maxima of € 225, € 2,250, € 4,500, € 11,250, € 45,000 and € 450,000 (article 23 CC). Infractions come under the first three categories and crimes under categories II through V. Category VI fines can only be imposed on corporate bodies and on individuals under a few special criminal laws, such as the Economic Offences Act and the Opium Act.[8]

The Act urges the courts to take into account the financial position of the offender when imposing a fine sentence in as far as this is necessary to arrive at an appropriate sentence without the offender being disproportionately affected in his income and capital (article 24 CC). There must be a two-pronged proportionality test, between the crime and the fine and between the fine and the ability to pay.

7.4 Accessory penalties

The accessory penalties are:
- deprivation of rights and disqualification from practicing professions;
- forfeiture; and
- publication of the judgement.

---

8. *Wet op de economische delicten*, and *Opiumwet*, respectively.

The deprivation of rights concerns: the right to hold a public office, the right to serve in the army, the right to vote and to be elected, the right to serve as an official administrator and the right to practice specific professions (article 28 CC).

Forfeiture consists of deprivation of objects or money (article 33 CC). Objects that may be forfeited are those obtained by means of the criminal offence, or in relation to which the offence was committed or which are manufactured or intended for committing the crime.

7.5 Measures

Measures can be imposed on offenders, regardless whether they can be held criminally responsible for having committed an offence, since measures are not aimed at punishment but at the promotion of safety and security of persons or property or at restoring a state of affairs.

Among the measures laid down in the Criminal Codes are the following:

1. *Withdrawal from circulation (article 36b CC)*
   During a police investigation objects may be seized. Certain objects which are dangerous or whose possession is undesirable may be confiscated.

2. *Confiscation of illegally obtained profits (article 36e CC)*
   Since the 1993 Criminal Code law reform (the so-called Strip-them Act), the court may impose an obligation to pay to the State Treasury an amount that equals the financial gain obtained by committing criminal offences.

3. *Obligation to pay compensation (article 36f CC)*
   The 1996 Compensation Order Act introduced the possibility for the court to impose an obligation upon a person who is convicted of a criminal offence to pay the State Treasury a sum of money for the benefit of the victim of the crime.

4. *Psychiatric hospital order (article 37 CC)*
   If a defendant cannot be held responsible for the crime because of a mental defect or mental illness, the court may not impose a penalty, but the court may order that the defendant be committed to a psychiatric hospital for up to one year, provided that the person is a danger to himself, to others, to the general public or to property in general. The court shall only issue the order after submission of a reasoned, dated and signed opinion of at least two behavioural experts – one being a psychiatrist – who have examined the defendant.

5. *Entrustment order (article 37a CC)*
   If the court considers that a defendant, despite his mental defect or mental illness, can be deemed responsible, the court may impose a penalty in combination with this measure. An entrustment order may be imposed for crimes carrying a maximum statutory penalty of at least four years of imprisonment and provided

that hospital care is necessary in order to protect the safety of other people, the general public or property. The hospital care is carried out in a special private or state institution where the person is treated, the so-called *terbeschikkingstelling* (TBS). The order lasts for two years, but may be extended by one or two years. For certain violent offences, a further extension is possible as long as the safety of others requires so. Regular reviews of the entrustment order have to take place.

7.6 The suspended sentence

A suspended sentence means the non-implementation of (a part of) an imposed sentence.[9] Since its introduction in 1915, the rules for the suspended sentence have been radically revised a number of times. The last major reform took place in 1986, when the scope of application of the suspended sentence was substantially expanded.

The reform was inspired by a 1983 report of the Committee on Alternative Penal Sanctions and was strongly influenced by the need to reduce pressures on prison capacity. The reform simultaneously responded to a need, which had long been recognized in practice, to make a partial revocation of a suspended sentence possible.

Since the 1987 law reform, a suspended sentence is possible for all principal sentences, with the exception of the task penalty. A prison sentence of up to one year, detention and fines may all be suspended totally or in part. A prison sentence between one year and three years may be suspended only for one-third of the sentence. A prison sentence of over three years may not be suspended.

The suspended sentence can be applied to all offences and to all sentences to detention, fines and sentences of imprisonment for up to three years. Accessory penalties may be suspended as well.

---

9. Articles 14a-14k CC deal with the suspended sentence.

7 Drug Policy in the Netherlands

Maarten van Dijck

1 Dutch policy debated

1.1 Criticism and applause

The Netherlands are only a small country, on the geographical as well as on the political map. Yet, it has a reputation for its policies on issues like drugs and euthanasia, policies that are controversial and continuously topics of debate within the Netherlands and abroad. With regard to the issue of drug control the Dutch system and situation are frequently referred to, both by advocates and critics of the Dutch pragmatic approach. With regard to many controversial issues, such as drug policy and euthanasia, the Dutch favour a pragmatist approach which focuses less on the underlying principles and is more directed towards a practical solution that takes into account the limitations of a government to influence social practice. One might argue that such an approach is an unprincipled one and therefore cannot result in anything good. However, many of the advocates of a pragmatic approach refer to the actual success of this approach in daily practice, often claiming that such an approach, contrary to other policies, enables at least a minimum form of control and regulation. As a result of this argument, the focus in the discussion on the benefits of the pragmatist approach shifts almost inevitably to the field of empiricism. While advocates claim the success of the approach, often presenting the data that must justify this view, critics contest the success of the approach, often presenting opposite conclusions from different or even the same sources of empirical data. The debates on euthanasia and drugs – both issues in which the Dutch government has adopted a pragmatic approach that many deem highly controversial – are dominated by a 'battle of facts and figures'.

The efforts of the Dutch to control drug abuse simultaneously arouse applause and irritation, both from Dutch and foreign experts and politicians. International criticism has been strong ever since 1976 when the current pragmatic policy was adopted. However, the last decade shows a steady growth in the number of countries that have adopted similar policies and undertake similar experiments as the Dutch in combating drug abuse and addiction. Several countries, among which Denmark, Germany and Belgium have decriminalized cannabis use and the possession of small amounts; most European countries by now have adopted needle exchange programs to stop spreading the HIV virus and have made efforts to lower the threshold of addiction treatment. From an international perspective, the latest novelty is heroin prescription to addicts, which is already practiced in Switzerland and the Netherlands and is under discussion in the UK, Germany, France and several other countries. As the critique on the American 'war on drugs' model increases, the Dutch pragmatic approach becomes more and more popular and less criticized.

Though many of the Dutch think of the Netherlands as a guiding country and believe that the Dutch pragmatic approach reflects a balanced equilibrium between morality and rationality, the policy on drugs has increasingly provoked domestic criticism. Some of the Dutch experts openly raise doubts about the benefits of the system. The critique is threefold. First, according to some critics, the current drug policy is based on an archaic view on drug consumption and trade, stemming from the early 1970s. This old-fashioned view is unable to deal with the vast problems involved in large-scale organized drug criminality. Second, the inner incoherence of the soft drug policy has aroused some irritation, especially with the law enforcement authorities and municipality boards. Decriminalization and overt toleration of soft drug retail vending contradicts the criminalization and less overt condoning of soft drug supply. At the 'front door' of the coffeeshops, the 'customer' can freely obtain small amounts of soft drugs. At the 'back door', the shop owner is forced to become a partner in crime, for the supply of soft drugs is still illegal and, in contradiction to the retail of small amounts, not *officially* condoned by the local authorities. Although the supply is *actually* condoned by the legal authorities, there is no legal basis that backs the position of the shopkeeper or his suppliers. The shopkeeper therefore is forced to remain in limbo between respectable entrepreneurship and criminality. Some municipalities proposed to legalize a controlled chain of production and supply of cannabis, which would end the back-door-front-door inconsistency and enable the local authorities to gain control over the entire chain of production and trade. But the petition in which the municipalities expressed their concerns and requested for permission to set up a system of controlled supply, was turned down by the State Secretary of Justice.[1] The third major point of critique transcends the particularity of the drug policy. During the last decade, an increasing appeal has been made on strict law enforcement. As the Dutch policy on cannabis is based on a more 'loosened' approach of law enforcement, this policy is also put under pressure by the legalist movement that advocates repressive law enforcement and zero tolerance policy.

1.2 Prohibitionism versus anti-prohibitionism

The drug policy debate is dominated by the controversy between the prohibitionist and the anti-prohibitionist viewpoint.[2] In its pure form, prohibitionism and anti-prohibitionism are the two extremes of an imaginative scale. Standpoints with regard to the question which policy would serve best in combating drug abuse can be analyzed in prohibitionist and anti-prohibitionist components.

---

1. *Drugbeleid: Notitie Het pad naar de achterdeur*, Den Haag, Tweede Kamer der Staten Generaal, 2000, p. 1-18.
2. See also D.J. Korf, *Dutch Treat* (diss.), Amsterdam: Thesis Publishers 1995, p. 9.

Prohibitionism in its pure form favours a repressive criminal control of drug use and trade. Prohibitionists focus on the intrinsic negative consequences of drug use and stress people's incapability to consume drugs in a limited and controlled way (which is called the abstinence paradigm). According to the prohibitionists, drug consumption creates problems for the consumer in particular and for society as a whole. Criminal prohibition and repression of illicit drug use and trade diminish drug consumption and abuse rates and eventually society might be able to entirely root out drug abuse. If in practice the effects of such a repressive approach are disappointing, success must be expected from an even more repressive approach. Paradigmatic for the prohibitionist viewpoint is a zero tolerance policy as reflected in the 'war on drugs' as advocated by the United States drug enforcement agencies.

Anti-prohibitionism, in its pure form, does not deny the intrinsic risks of drug consumption and abuse, but neither does it expect any substantial benefits from criminal prohibition and severe repression. From the anti-prohibitionist viewpoint, it is stressed that a repressive policy is counterproductive to the goals of drug control. Criminalizing drugs has caused, and will cause, an increase rather than a decline in drug abuse. Moreover, it contributes to unwanted side effects that have become worse than the actual problems. The level of criminality has increased to enormous proportions as a result of the illegality of drug consumption and trade. Statistics point out that at least 16.5% of the prison population is sentenced for a drug related crime.[3] High risks (resulting from actual criminalization) involve high profits, which will attract criminal rather than respectable entrepreneurs. In order to hide drug trafficking and trade from the eye of the legal authorities, drug offences are embedded in non-specifically drug related criminality. The lucrative character of the drug market makes the drug scene a crowded one, which in turn results in an increasing number of violent clashes between different players in the field. Criminalization of drug consumption and trade have pushed retail prices to a maximum, which in turn provoked an increase of so-called acquisition criminality. As a result, more and more drug addicts have become involved in criminality and are registered in police records. Anti-prohibitionists stress that to a large extent drug related criminality would not exist if drugs were legalized and criminal repression of drug related activities would come to an end. In addition, the anti-prohibitionist view claims that legalizing narcotics to the extent that these narcotics are freely available, will not result in a significant increase in drug consumption and abuse rate.

1.3   Decriminalization and legalization

As it is the prohibitionist versus anti-prohibitionist controversy that dominates the debate on drug policy, it seems wise to specify the relation between three of the key expressions in the debate: 'criminalization', 'decriminalization' and 'legalization'.[4]

---

3.   See note 9.
4.   See also D.J. Korf (1995, p. 8, see note 2).

When it comes to the notion of social change and the provocation of this change, it is not uncommon in sociology to differentiate between formal and informal control. In contrast to informal control that originates from within society itself, formal control is generated by authorities that represent the state. Criminalization, decriminalization and legalization all represent various kinds of formal control or the refraining thereof. Criminalization is the act or process in which deviant behaviour becomes liable to public prosecution and criminal punishment. One can distinguish between statutory criminalization and actual criminalization. Statutory criminalization is the result of a statutory change that encompass a raise in the degree in which certain behaviour is liable to criminal prosecution. Actual criminalization occurs when the actual enforcement of an existing law is intensified.

The arrow of decriminalization points in the opposite direction: former deviant behaviour is seen as less deviant or at least less liable to criminal punishment. Statutory decriminalization is the result of a change in legislation or statutory interpretation. Actual decriminalization is the actual decrease of the level in which deviant behavior is prosecuted and sanctioned, without regard to the question of what has caused this change. If an Act of law prohibits certain activities, but on the level of law enforcement low priority is given to the actual investigation and prosecution, then the result is the actual decriminalization of these activities, for the prohibiting law is left untouched.

Legalization goes one step further as it is the positive expression and acknowledgement of the non-deviant character of the behaviour by legislative change. This change by definition would be the entire or partial abolition of the prohibition of a certain type of behaviour.

1.4 Evaluation criteria

Evaluation of any drug policy requires a clear set of criteria. In the light of the international diversity of drug policies and the prohibitionist controversy, one would not expect to find a universal criterion to measure the success of the various policies. Yet there is. First, both prohibitionists and anti-prohibitionists presuppose a causal relation between anti-drug legislation and the level of drug consumption and trade. The prohibitionist view is based on the belief that (actual) criminalization of drug offences will result in a decline in drug consumption. The anti-prohibitionist view stresses the opposite: criminalization will increase drug consumption and cause additional negative side effects. Second, both prohibitionism and anti-prohibitionism agree on the intrinsic negative consequences of drug consumption and abuse. Drug consumption causes problems for the individual consumer as well as for society in general and these intrinsic problems occur regardless of the criminalization of drug offences. As a result, each policy can be evaluated by the rate it contributes to the prevention or suppression of the wrongs intrinsic to drugs and by the rate it contributes to the prevention or repression of the non-intrinsic wrongs of drugs.

Pointing out the negative consequences of drug use is a more difficult task than it may seem in first instance. Several problems of a methodological and conceptual nature jeopardize the objective determination of the problems. As will be discussed in detail in the next paragraph, illicit drugs are associated with three problem types. The first problem type concerns the harm that drug consumers inflict on themselves by using psychoactive substances. These problems range from all kinds of physical trauma to social deterioration. The second type of problems concerns the harm that is inflicted by drug users on others, i.e. anti-social behaviour, public nuisance, vandalism and acquisition criminality. The third type of problems concerns the large-scale production and trafficking of illicit psychotropic substances. Under current international law, these activities are by definition of a criminal nature and entrepreneurs involved in drug criminality often make use of 'regular' illegal means to run their illegal business.

2   Drug related problems in Dutch society

2.1   Health risks

One of the main international treaties dealing with drug use and trafficking is the United Nations Single Convention on Narcotic Drugs, which in 1961 replaced a multitude of international conventions and agreements by one multilateral treaty. The Single Convention begins with a statement about the benefits of narcotic drugs:

> 'The Parties, concerned with the health and welfare of mankind, recognizing that the medical use of narcotic drugs continues to be indispensable for the relief of pain and suffering and that adequate provision must be made to ensure the availability of narcotic drugs for such purposes.'

Many of the qualities that make a drug useful for medical use, make the very same substance a dangerous narcotic that can have a devastating effect on the health and the well-being of the frequent consumer. The current lists of illicit psychoactive substances contain many different types of drugs all having their specific range of physical and mental effects. One can distinguish between direct and indirect effects. The former are a direct somatic or psychosomatic result of the effective substances in the drug, such as concentration problems, dehydration, dizziness, hallucinations, lung cancer, brain damage and death due to overdose. Indirect effects are long-term effects that correlate to the increasing level in which the drug user or addict has become dependent on the drug. Common indirect effects are emotional problems, relational deficiency, social disintegration, isolation and unemployment. A distinct category of indirect effects is formed by HIV infection due to shared use of infected needles. Although HIV infection is not caused by the drug itself, the increase in HIV infection among heroin addicts has become a real concern and in many countries has led to the acceptance of needle exchange programs.

The drugs that are the most addictive are deemed to be the most dangerous, though evidently the addictive quality of a drug loses significance if the drug inflicts little or no harm on the consumer's health. The core characteristic of an addiction is the growing dependence on the addictive substance: at a certain point, the addict will lack the capacity to quit the habit on his own accord. Drugs that are physically addictive alter the chemistry of the body, which slowly becomes accustomed to the psychoactive effects of the drug. Abstinence from drugs in case of a physical addiction is related to withdrawal symptoms: physical inconveniences like headache and shivers that can make the process of detoxication very painful and hard to endure. In case of a mental addiction, the dependence on the substance is not essentially of a physical nature. The drug addict has become accustomed to the mental state of mind caused by the drug. Drugs like LSD and heroin are known as 'pleasure drugs' and 'escape drugs' because they, much like alcohol, are often consumed to take refuge from reality.

As mentioned in the former paragraph, the Dutch policy on drugs is based on the assumption that not all drugs are equally dangerous. In 1972, the Baan Committee on request of the Dutch government issued a report in which it advised on drug control policy.[5] The most important recommendation in the report concerned a policy differentiation on the basis of the differences in risks that evolve from consumption of different types of drugs. Since 1976, the year in which the Opium Act was revised to the model of the Baan recommendations, Dutch drug policy distinguishes soft drugs (cannabis products like marihuana and hashish) from hard drugs (such as cocaine, heroin, LSD, speed, XTC and amphetamines). While the latter involve an 'unacceptable risk' to society in general and to the consumer in particular, the former do not.

Though the findings of the Baan Committee were based on empirical investigation, the differentiation thesis is not at all unquestioned. The medical debate on drug effects is dominated by a lack of consensus on the actual health risks of the different types of drugs. Disagreement between experts exists on the level of hard drugs as well as on the level of soft drugs. As it is mainly the Dutch policy on *soft* drugs that is subject to criticism, I will focus on the problems regarding the health risks of this class. While some claim that cannabis products are quite harmless and not at all addictive, others claim the direct opposite. Two issues will be highlighted in the following section: the controversy on the 'quality' of soft drugs products and methodological problems in investigation drug effects.

The psychosomatic effects of cannabis products correlate to the level of THC that determines the 'quality' of the product. Many believe that the THC level has increased during the last two decades as a result of improved cultivating techniques and know-how. Cannabis products would in general have become stronger, more unhealthy and more addictive. In addition, recent investigations get rid of the myth that the average 'joint' causes less lung cancer than a regular cigarette, claiming that it even contributes more than its non-psychotropic equivalent. Advocates of legalization of soft drugs contradict the increase of the level of THC in cannabis products, and claim that there are no reliable data of recent date that support the opposite assumption.[6]

5. P.A.H. Baan, *Achtergronden en risico's van druggebruik: rapport van de Werkgroep Verdovende Middelen*, Den Haag: Staatsuitgeverij 1972.
6. British Lung Foundation, *A smoking gun, The impact of cannabis smoking on respiratory health*, British Lung Foundation, 2002, p. 1-15.

Investigation into the consequences of drug use is confronted with methodological problems inherent in socio-demographic and medical research. One of the main difficulties concerns the scientific proof of a causal link between a certain drug and the effect it is assumed to cause. Consumption of psychoactive substances normally occurs under a complex of interrelated social, emotional and physical circumstances and isolation of the 'drug factor' from other plausible causes is barred by practical limitations. The fact that frequent drug consumers often experiment with two or more different drug types at the same time (including alcohol and tobacco) makes it even harder to correlate registered effects to a specific drug. Experiments with rats have more or less compensated for the impossibility to experiment with human being in an isolated lab setting. But the scientific profit from animal experiments is relative, because of the differences between animal and human anatomy.

However, even the unlimited possibility to measure effects of drug use cannot provide all the answers. Health problems and especially mental health problems by definition have a subjective component. Drug effect investigation shows some divergence between the perceptions of respectively medical science and social care. In general medical science tend to focus on aspects of physical addiction while social care workers are primarily preoccupied with the mental and social aspects of drug addiction. Opposite claims about the addictive (and therefore dangerous) nature of soft drugs contradict each other, regardless of the possibility that both claims are based on substantive empirical research. According to sociological research regular users of cannabis consider themselves more frequently the victim of an addiction than is supported by claims about the addictive nature of cannabis from medical science.

As a consequence of the disagreement between experts with regard to the issue of soft drug health hazards, any drug control policy implies some kind of political commitment. The strong belief of the Dutch government and legislator in the validity of the findings of the Baan Committee and in the correctness of the differentiation thesis, cannot disguise the politically contingent nature of the policy. However, any other policy suffers from the same contingency and may therefore be considered politically biased as well.

2.2 Public nuisance and drug related criminality

The second category of drug related problems concerns the wrongs that are inflicted by drug consumers on others. This category consists of two subcategories: disturbance of the public order and petty offences. Drug vending and consumption cause public nuisance in several ways. Typical of the Dutch policy is the condoning of coffeeshops: legal selling points of soft drugs. Coffeeshops function like ordinary pubs, but instead of alcohol they serve and sell small packages of soft drugs, which is legal as long as the shopkeeper limits the amount to a maximum of five gram per instance. Some buyers leave the establishment after purchase and consume the substance in private accommodations, others stay in the shop or in the near surroundings and consume right on the spot. Coffeeshops are as much a cause of public nuisance as any regular pub, except for two slight differences. First, pubs are open and visited mostly in the evening and at night; coffeeshops are open during the day. Second, regular pubs lack the penetrating cannabis odor one can often smell in the near surroundings of the coffeeshop. In the centres of the larger cities, coffeeshops are as ordinary as regular pubs and part of street life. In the smaller towns and villages, this is not the case; some villages do have one or a small number of coffeeshops, other have none. As a result, the emotional and sometimes actual resistance against coffeeshops is stronger in the province than in the urban regions. Especially in municipalities that have little or no coffeeshops, the establishment of one can easily arouse feelings of distress among the neighbourhood. The alleged 'Dutch tolerance' is contrasted by the NIMBY principle: 'not in my back yard!'.

Far more serious is the public nuisance caused in places that are regularly visited by hard drug addicts, the so-called heroin squares. Some of these places have gained a notorious reputation and are avoided by people who have no specific business in that particular area of the city. It can be easily imagined how these places attract more drug users as well as street dealers; the former may find a secure spot to 'trip' in the company of his or her companions, the latter may be attracted by the amount of potential customers. It is not uncommon for heroin addicts to be homeless and the heroine squares form a significant part of their residential space. Now and then, the local authorities organize raids to sweep the place clean, most often with little effect: the drug addicts will find a new place to settle down, be it spread out through the whole city centre or again concentrated in one particular spot. Though in recent decades heroin was considered one of the most problematic drugs for the devastating effect it has on the heroin addict's life and for the increasing popularity of the drug, lately the emphasis has shifted from heroin towards more modern types of drug and drug use, such as XTC and other 'party drugs'. Heroin addiction has become less of a problem: new generations of youngsters generally reject heroin as a 'loser' drug.

Drug tourism is another phenomenon that causes public nuisance and feelings of distress. Because the Dutch authorities – in contradiction to the international standard – tolerate the controlled vending of soft drugs, customers and dealers from abroad are attracted to the Netherlands. Major Dutch cities like Amsterdam and Rotterdam and border municipalities like Arnhem, Heerlen and Venlo are popular destinations for users and vendors from abroad. Legal purchase of cannabis often goes hand in hand with illegal activity such as large quantity purchase, street dealing and hard drug trade and trafficking. The Dutch liberal policy on soft drugs has aroused the irritation of several European countries close to the Netherlands. The diplomatic relations between France and the Netherlands have suffered to some extent from the French critique of the Dutch system and its alleged influence on the French juvenile consumers. The French critique ceased only when it became clear to the French that high consumption and addiction rates in France had less to do with Dutch coffeeshops and more with French domestic soft drug policy.[7] As more and more countries alleviate the repression of cannabis offences, international critique of the Dutch policy decreases; nevertheless, the free availability of cannabis in the Netherlands is still a matter of controversy.

---

7. See also T.B. van Solinge, 'Dutch drug policy in a European context', *Journal of Drug Issues* 1999, vol. 29 (3), p. 511-528.

The critique is not only restricted to foreign origin. Some Dutch municipalities close to the German border suffer to a great extent from drug tourism. Cities like Arnhem, Heerlen and Venlo are frequently visited by foreign drug buyers, dealers and prostitutes. The inhabitants of Heerlen, a relatively small town near to the border with Germany, have witnessed the deterioration of the city. Expensive foreign cars with blinded windows drive in and out of the city area, creating an unpleasant atmosphere of criminality. Prostitutes and addicts gather at public meeting points and needles used by heroin addicts and possibly infected with HIV linger in the open, sometimes in or near children's playgrounds. All these things have affected the city negatively and caused feelings of distress to the local population. In Arnhem, the situation escalated when citizens blocked the streets of their neighbourhood to foreign 'tourists' and removed of their own accord drug addicts from the area.

On the boundary of public nuisance and plain criminality is the category of 'acquisition criminality'. In 1985 the Dutch Department of Justice issued a report under the name of Society and Criminality *(Samenleving en Criminaliteit)*. In this report, the Commission Roethof expressed its concerns about the increase of petty crimes, which according to the commission caused a lot of distress and feelings of insecurity among the Dutch people. The relation between petty crime and drug use and abuse had been repeatedly under investigation in the period before and after the report. One can distinguish between two types of drug related criminality. The first type involves criminality that is perpetrated under the influence of a psychoactive substance. These offences are more a matter of public nuisance than a matter of mere criminality. Driving under influence and causing accidents as a result may be seen as a distinct category of offences and do not qualify as 'plain' criminality in a more traditional sense. The second type involves what is called acquisition criminality. The general assumption is that many drug consumers and especially addicts get involved in criminality in order to finance the expensive habit or addiction. The addictive nature of many illicit drugs makes many addicts prefer a criminal career above limiting or quitting drug use. Although it is a fact that many drug consumers are in some way or other involved in criminal activity, there is no conclusive proof for the claim that drug use contributes to criminality. The reverse claim, that many criminals are frequent users of drugs and that criminality or a criminal environment stimulates drug use, seems equally valid. Yet, it can be assumed that the marginalization of drug use and the criminalization of drug offences result in the increase of acquisition criminality. The marginalization of consumption makes it easier for the buyer to cross the thin line that separates legal from illegal purchase and other activity. The criminalization of drugs pushes the retail prices to excessive heights and some of the more expensive drug addictions like cocaine and heroine simply require extra financial backing to maintain regular use. Social research has pointed out that most of the hard drug addicts are not in such a position that they can finance their consumption by legal means.[8]

---

8. K. Swierstra, *Drugscarrieres. Van crimineel tot conventioneel* (diss.), Groningen: Onderzoekscentrum voor Criminologie en Jeugdcriminologie, RUG 1990.

2.3   Organized crime

Drug manufacturing and trafficking has become an enormous transboundary market both from an economic perspective and from the perspective of law enforcement. Between 1994 and 2001, approximately 16.5% of all prisoners was convicted for a breach of the Opium Act.[9] Research and law enforcement statistics point out that the Netherlands are no less involved in organized drug criminality than other European countries. Many believe that a significant part of international drug criminality and trafficking involves activity on Dutch territory. As mentioned above, some believe that the pragmatic and tolerant approach to soft drugs has contributed to the increase of illicit hard drug activities on Dutch soil. On the basis of the available research data, it is difficult to estimate the exact proportions of the hard drug market and even more difficult to compare countries on this issue. Conclusions with regard to the extent soft drug policy has contributed to a flourishing hard drug market are void for the same reason. The extensive survey, carried out by the Fijnaut Committee in 1996[10] has shed some light on drugs criminality in the Netherlands. Three components of the Dutch involvement in international drug criminality can be highlighted: transportation, manufacturing and social infrastructure.

Rotterdam harbour is known as one of the largest gateways to Europe and the Netherlands is famous for its many transport firms that travel and deliver throughout the entire European mainland. It is not difficult to imagine how the Dutch transportation network is liable to abuse by criminal organizations. The same factors that make the Netherlands a transport nation of name make it possible for criminal entrepreneurs to run a successful smuggling business, using the same infra- and organizational structure as serves the legitimate distribution of legal goods. The assumption that Dutch infrastructure and the prominent Dutch market position in the international transportation branch have contributed to drug criminality is as problematic as the assumption that the liberal soft drug policy has stimulated hard drug related criminality. The liberal Dutch policy has facilitated the growth of an extensive semi-legal coffeeshop network. Some believe that this coffeeshop network has contributed to a parallel infrastructure used by criminal organizations to distribute hard drugs alongside the tolerated soft drugs. It must be acknowledged that the tolerant soft drug policy, issued in the 1970s by the Dutch legislator and carried out by the Department of Public Health and Justice, was based on a miscalculation of the future development of the soft drug market. The initial liberal soft drug policy focused on small-scale house dealers and autonomous coffeeshops and did not anticipate the commercialization and scaling-up of the soft drug market. The possibility of a commercial 'take-over' of the soft drug market and vending points by criminal organizations was not adequately taken into account.[11] Still, there

---

9.   Source: CBS Statweb, http://www.cbs.nl, 2 June 2003.
10. M. van Traa, *Inzake Opsporing* (Enquêtecommissie Opsporingsmethoden), Den Haag: Sdu Uitgevers 1996.
11. T. Blom, *Drugs in het recht, recht onder druk* (diss.). Deventer: Gouda Quint 1998.

is no convincing proof of any large-scale entwinement between the soft drug network and hard drug criminality. But, as there is neither ground for the opposite claim, rumours about a hard and soft drug market connection will not cease to exist and may proof justified in the future.

Other factors than the existence of a tolerated soft drug market can explain the existence of relatively well organized structures of criminal cooperation. It is assumed that the main large ethnic minorities, especially those who have been part of Dutch society for several decades or longer, have contributed to the rise of several criminal drug networks. Four groups can be distinguished in particular: the Turks, the Moroccans, the Chinese and former inhabitants of the Dutch Antilles and Suriname. All of these groups are organized in ethnic subcultures in which bloodlines constitute a natural hierarchy and sometimes even provide for a more or less natural 'chain of command'. The family structure – open to the inside, closed to the outside – provides for a relatively stable and durable organizational structure that suits the demands of an underground drug network. Complex labour division goes alongside the (natural) family order. Contacts with next of kin in countries of origin provide a direct and reliable relation with the manufactures or suppliers abroad. Morocco and Turkey are famous for their production and export of respectively marihuana, hashish and heroin. The Caribbean is famous for its coca production and the Chinese have a long tradition in opium cultivation, distribution and consumption.[12]

Beside these ethnic minorities that are part of Dutch society, other ethnically identifiable groups like the cocaine trading Colombians have chosen the Netherlands as one of their bridgeheads to the European market.[13] But it is not only groups of foreign origin that are involved in illicit substance trade and trafficking. In the 1990s, drug enforcement authorities were relative successful in dismantling criminal organizations that occupied themselves with international drug trade. Though these organizations often consist in cooperation of individuals of diverse origin, it is not uncommon for Dutch criminals to dwell in the highest ranks of the organizational hierarchy. A number of trials have received wide media attention and made several of the Dutch drug bosses, or at least their names, quite famous.

In addition to its role as a bridgehead and gateway, the Netherlands also play a part as a producer of illegal substances. In the last decades, there has been an increase in the manufacturing of two different types of drugs: cannabis ('Nederwiet') and synthetic drugs (XTC tablets). *Nederwiet* has become famous for its high THC level, which makes the drug popular for Dutch and foreign users. The weed plants are illegally cultivated in hidden and improvised localities. In 2002, local police authorities discovered the entire basement of an apartment building being used to grow weed, without the building inhabitants suspecting anything. Recent investigations estimate the number of private 'in-house' cultivation at several ten thousands.[14] Media reports frequently report the rounding up of smaller or larger

---

12. Van Traa (1996, see note 10).
13. Van Traa (1996, see note 10).
14. *Kamerstukken II*, vergaderjaar 1994-1995, 24 077, nrs. 2-3,
    http://www.drugtext.org/library/reports/wvc.

groups involved in XTC manufacturing and the dismantlement of the clandestine laboratories used by these groups.

3   Key characteristics of the Dutch policy

The primary objective of any drug policy is the diminishing of drug related problems as stipulated by the authorities. From the former paragraph can be concluded that the stipulation of the drug related problems – which presupposes these problems as directly or indirectly *caused by* drugs – is not as easy as it may have seemed beforehand. Such a stipulation necessarily involves decisions of a political nature which only to a limited extent can be backed by empirical data. In order to evaluate a policy on drug issues it is necessary to understand the key presuppositions that underlie that policy.

The analysis of the presuppositions that underlie the Dutch policy on drugs seems to validate the claim that a drug policy is partly based on political motives and partly on empirical data provided by scientific research. Some of the presuppositions on which the Dutch policy is based are subjective (but more or less shared) views on the moral aspects of drug use and abuse and on the role the State has to play in regulating society. Other presuppositions are in fact empirical claims that can be verified or falsified by empirical research. Over the last decades, a lot of empirical research has been done in the field of drug use and criminality. The limited scope of this chapter leaves only little room to elaborate on the results of these investigations.

3.1   The principle of autonomy

The first and perhaps most fundamental presupposition underlying the Dutch drug policy is related to the liberal notion of individuality and the individual's responsibility for the self. People are regarded as autonomous, meaning that they are allowed to do what they want as long as they do not cause harm to others. People are therefore free to consume any substance they like, regardless of whether this substance is considered to be healthy or unhealthy to the person's body or mind. Interference in these personal choices would result in paternalism, which liberalism generally rejects as a legitimate cause for the restriction of the freedom of the individual. If the State wants to diminish drug use by its citizens, it may use other forms of formal control than the legal prohibition of drug consumption. As far as drug consumption is concerned, government interference is restricted to education and social and medical aid. Drug addicts cannot be forced to participate in detoxication programs. Criminal legislation focuses on the supply side: manufacturing, trafficking and possession of illicit drugs are liable to criminal punishment.

3.2   Normalization

The second presupposition follows from the first. No moral judgement on drug use is expressed in anti-drug legislation. As stigmatization of drug users only increases the drug problem and subverts actual drug control, the Dutch policy is aimed at the de-stigmatization of (soft) drug use. Instead of counteracting drug use as deviant criminal behaviour from which society must be cleared, efforts are made to diminish the stigmatization of drug use and to lower the thresholds for social and medical care. Soft drugs may even be considered recreational drugs, much like alcoholic drinks and are in general associated with a predominantly juvenile subculture. This de-stigmatization and normalization paradigm does not imply the approval of drug use, as that would be a moral judgement the other way around.

Many Dutch people see little harm in the recreational use of drugs, although there is a general awareness of the risks that are involved. Though some of the Dutch do have moral objections against drug use, it is a more or less accepted as part of a (mostly juvenile) subculture. As is often the case, there is a striking difference between the enlightened views on the issue in the abstract and the actual restrictions that many of the parents subject their own children to. Parental control is a form of informal control and is not inconsistent with the thesis that the State has no business in condemning drug consumption. In most of the larger cities, smoking a joint is almost as normal as smoking regular cigarettes, but this does not imply that the former is equally tolerated. While most restaurants and schools do have smoking areas for regular tobacco products, no such thing exists for cannabis products and in-school smokers of marihuana are regularly expelled from school. Though there is in general an increase in smoking restrictions in public and private areas, joint smoking is even more restricted.

3.3   Market separation

The third presupposition deals with the separation of markets that distinguishes between two classes of psychotropic substances: soft drugs (marihuana, hashish and other cannabis products) and hard drugs (e.g. heroin, cocaine, LSD, amphetamines). As mentioned earlier, the Baan Committee in 1972 issued a report in which the differentiation between soft and hard drugs was defended on basis of the health risks of drug use. Since that report, hard drugs are considered to cause 'unacceptable risk' to society while soft drugs are not. Since 1976, the Dutch legislator and government have built a two-track system in accordance to the recommendations in the report.

The Dutch policy aims at separating the soft drugs market from its hard drug equivalent. Production and trafficking of hard drugs are heavily penalized and much effort is invested in prosecuting these offences. Production and trafficking of soft drugs is only moderately subject to criminal repression and in particular cases even overtly tolerated. Possession and vending of illicit drugs is formally liable to criminal punishment, but under the flag of priority reasons, little effort is made to prosecute possession and trade of small amounts for personal use. This is openly done in the case of soft drugs, less openly in the case of hard drugs. The Dutch policing and prosecution policy is concentrated on the key players that dominate the market from the supply side. Relative low imprisonment rates are compensated for by frequent high quantity seizures of narcotic substances and by frequent success in rounding up entire networks and organizations.[15]

Inherent to the separation thesis is the denial of the stepping stone thesis that is often invoked by opponents of the decriminalization of soft drugs. All stepping stone thesis varieties share the presupposition that unlimited availability of soft drugs will lead to an increase in hard drug use and addiction rates. Because hard drugs involve 'unacceptable risks' to society, the availability of soft drugs must be diminished to the utmost. A more extreme version of the stepping stone thesis adds one more level of decline: drug addicts often end up in a criminal subculture in which drug abuse and drug related criminality go hand in hand. The unlimited availability of soft drugs therefore indirectly contributes to an increase in (drug related) criminality and to the number of juveniles involved in criminality.

The separation thesis underlying the Dutch differentiated policy presupposes a different causal connection between soft and hard drugs. According to advocates of the separation thesis, hard drug addiction and the involvement in drug criminality is not caused by mere soft drug *consumption*[16] but correlates with the level of entwinement of soft drugs and hard drug scenes or *markets*. Market separation leaves room for a differentiated approach in which the soft drug scene is dealt with separately and in which soft drug users are not pushed into the hard drug scene and subsequently into criminality. A pragmatic and mild approach creates a more open and overt soft drug scene which leaves room for monitoring and control optimal social and medical care.

The policy of market separation presupposes the possibility of a separation of the hard drug from the soft drug scene. A main point of critique concerns the alleged link between the liberal Dutch policy on soft drugs and the leading position of the Netherlands as one of the centres of international drug trade and transportation. It has been assumed that the network of coffeeshops (that operate on the edge of legality) has provided a network which has not only served the controlled distribution of soft drug market, but also has been gratefully adopted by criminal organizations to distribute hard drugs alongside the soft drugs. The network of tolerated soft drug selling points may have contributed to an illegitimate hard drug equivalent. However, no proof exists of such a connection between the hard and soft drug markets. In fact, some surveys point out the opposite: coffeeshop owners have an economic interest in avoiding any connection with the hard drug scene and in general do not secretly deal in hard drug substances. However, it remains questionable whether the upper segment of the supply side shows a similar separation of actors and organizations.

---

15. See also Van Solinge (1999, see note 7).
16. See also J.C. van Ours, 'Is cannabis a stepping-stone for cocaine?', *Center Discussion Papers* 2001 (98), p. 1-29.

3.4   Harm reduction

As can be extracted from the former section, the Dutch policy is based on harm reduction, which implies the view that drug abusers are not regarded as delinquents but as citizens in need of medical care or social support. When drug abuse leads to criminal behaviour like petty theft, demolition of property or public nuisance, then of course on that ground drug users are liable to criminal prosecution and punishment. The criminal liability of the offenders of drug-related crime, however, results from the breaking of the law and not from the consumption of drugs. Criminal legislation is only one form of formal control by which means governments can influence society. Other forms of formal control consist in the creation of social and medical care facilities, financing campaigns to educate people, drug monitor projects, needle exchange projects, methadone issuance et cetera. Drug policy is primarily regarded as a matter of public health and it is the Department of Health that is primarily responsible for the execution of the Drug policy, leaving the Department of Justice only a supporting (but no less important) role. This is consistent with the Dutch view that criminal law is an *ultimum remedium*, the last resort to back social and legal policy. Formal control involves five organizations or organization clusters. Medical treatment facilities and other socio-medical care projects are governed by a program set out by the Department of Health and carried out by both governmental and private organizations. Criminal policy originates from the Department of Justice and the Public Prosecution Service, which is also responsible for the actual realization of the policy. The municipalities cooperate with the local branch of the Public Prosecution Service and the local police department responsible for law enforcement, which among other things means that the municipality councils must provide for a local soft drug policy. From the harm reduction perspective all departments deal with different kinds of harm. The Department of Public Health and the medical and social care organizations deal primarily with the harm that drug consumers inflict on themselves, the Department of Justice and the Prosecution Service deal with the criminal aspects and the local municipalities together with the local police mostly deal with matters of public nuisance.

The notion of harm reduction serves as a fundamental principle, not only as a motive to establish drug control policy, but also as the justification of such a policy as legitimate. The principle of autonomy outbalances the principle of harm reduction in case of collision between both principles. The drug policy does not interfere with the harm that is inflicted by the drug consumer on him or herself, unless he or she calls for help or at least is assumed to do or have done so. State interference is restricted to cases in which the subject agrees with the interference or in case harm is done to others. Drug offences are so-called victimless offences which is one of the reasons why prohibitionists argue against criminalization.

4   Three levels of regulation

Drug policy is related to three levels of regulation and legislation. The first layer consists of the international treaties that are more or less binding on the Netherlands as a member state of the United Nations and the European Union. The second layer consists of national legislation, particularly the Opium Act in which drug transport and trade are prohibited. The third layer consists in national guidelines for the prosecution in which some aspects of anti-drug law enforcement is dealt with in detail.

4.1   International treaties

The Netherlands is party to several international treaties that concern anti-drug legislation. The United Nations Single Convention on Narcotic Drugs of 1961 replaced a total number of nine international treaties that dealt with the matter before 1961. The Single Convention aims to protect the legitimate use of narcotic substances for medical purposes and aims at the repression of illegitimate drug production and trafficking. The treaty obliges Member States to 'give effect and carry out the provisions of the Convention within their own territories' and to 'co-operate with other States in the execution'. The convention distinguished four categories of illicit drugs, cumulating to no less than 24 different standards for the repression of drugs. Those substances that are on lists I and IV such as cannabis are subject to the most severe regime, but the Convention is not very specific about the consequences and obligations for the member states.

The increasing popularity of a new branch of psychoactive drugs such as LSD and amphetamines resulted in the United Nations Convention on Psychotropic Substances of 1971. The treaty does not criminalize specific forms of action, but the member state 'shall limit the use of substances in Schedule I' and 'limit by such as it considers appropriate the manufacture, export, import, distribution and stocks of, trade in, and use and possession of, substances in Schedule III and IV to medical and scientific purposes'.

The United Nations Convention against Illicit Traffic in Narcotic Drugs and Psychotropic Substances of 1988 deals with the drug related organized and transboundary crime, such as import and export, trafficking, and laundering of illegal profits. The purpose of the 1988 Convention is 'to promote co-operation among the Parties so that they may address more effectively the various aspects of illicit traffic in narcotic drugs and psychotropic substances having an international dimension'. This convention does not compel Member States to adopt measures that conflict with domestic legal provisions, as it explicitly expresses the sovereignty of the party states.

The Schengen Treaty of 1985 (implemented in 1993) is a pact between several European states to abolish border control and make free border crossing of persons and goods possible. The treaty has a separate section which includes agreements on international cooperation in fighting drug criminality and harmonization of anti-drug legislation.

4.2   Dutch legislation

Trade and possession of psychoactive substances are without exception liable to criminal punishment on the basis of the Opium Act. The substances are specified in two lists. The maximum punishments for offences concerning the substances on list II (soft drugs) are less high than for offences concerning substances on list I (hard drugs). List II mainly consists of cannabis products, such as marihuana and hashish. The highest maximum punishment applies to the deliberate import or export of list I substances in amounts that are too large to be considered as 'small amount for personal use'. The maximum punishment for this offence is twelve years imprisonment or a fine of the fifth category (€ 45,000). The mildest maximum punishment is one month of imprisonment or a fine of the second category (€ 2,250). This maximum punishment applies to all offences, including possession, regarding substances of list II of small amounts for personal use. The part of the Opium Act in which criminal behaviour is codified shows a complex matrix that combines the two enumerations of psychotropic substances with a multitude of offences with these substances. Despite this complexity, there can be no doubt about the criminal character of transboundary transportation, manufacturing, producing, enhancing and trafficking of soft drugs as well as hard drugs. The same goes for possession. How can coffeeshops exist under such anti-drug legislation? The answer is simple. The Dutch liberal policy on soft drugs is not solely based on the Opium Act, but also on national directives of the Department of Public Prosecution regarding the policy of enforcement of the Opium Act.

4.3 Prosecution directives

Dutch soft drug policy was reshaped by the Guidelines for Investigation and Prosecution with respect to cannabis, which have been in effect since 1976. The guidelines play a key function in Dutch law enforcement. The directives in the guidelines that are issued by the Board of Attorneys General are internally as well as externally binding to the public prosecutors. Internally binding means that the prosecutors are compelled to adjust their prosecution policy to the directives as a consequence of the organizational hierarchy of the Prosecution Service. Externally binding means that, once the guidelines have become known publicly, citizens can appeal to the guidelines in order to avoid prosecution of offence categories that in the directives are exempt from prosecution.[17] The guidelines that complement the Opium Act contain a number of directives that result in the actual decriminalization of cannabis possession, vending and the growing of hemp plants.

The legal basis for the guidelines is article 167 of the Dutch Code of Criminal Procedure. This article contains the expediency principle, which dominates criminal law enforcement from the phase of criminal investigation to the eventual decision on prosecution. Article 167 says: 'Criminal prosecution can be refrained from for reasons of public interest.' The expediency principle is the legal opposite of the principle of legality. The latter principle compels the prosecutor to prosecute if the law provides a legal basis to do so and if his case is strong enough to be taken to court. In a system based on the expediency principle, the prosecution service can

---

17. See also the Ruling of the Dutch Supreme Court on 19 June 1990, *NJ* 1991, 119.

refrain from criminal prosecution, even if a crime or infraction has been committed and no obstacles hinder a successful prosecution. It is up to the prosecutor to decide whether or not the prosecution of a specific case is in the interest of society and whether or not prosecution is opportune.

In the first half of the 20th century, legal doctrine gradually acknowledged the primacy of the expediency principle over the principle of legality. In the second half of that century, the interpretation of the expediency principle has made a turn from a so-called negative to a positive conception. At first, the expediency principle only functioned as a legal basis for exceptional non-prosecution in cases in which prosecution was evidently not the right answer. The principle functioned as a corrective in order to avoid evident iniquities. In the turbulent 1960s and 1970s the expediency principle became the legal basis of a wider and more structural policy of non-enforcement. Together with the rise of alternative means to sanction breaches of the law, such as the possibility of conditional non-prosecution and the financial transaction, the public prosecution increasingly refrained from prosecution of petty offence categories. In the 1980s this refraining from prosecution developed into a full-grown policy in which the prosecution service, due to several causes increasingly confronted with a lack of capacity, harmonized priority criteria on a national level. Offence categories were ranked by seriousness and by the level of public interest that demands action. Under the negative interpretation of the expediency principle prosecution was the rule and non-prosecution the exception that required explanation. Under the positive interpretation, it is the other way around: prosecution must be explicitly motivated as serving the public interest.

Under the principle of legality, the Prosecution Service is literally in the service of the criminal legislature. In a system based on the positive conception of the expediency principle, the Prosecution Service itself becomes a policy making power that can create criminal policy by means of internal directives. The expediency principle has thus contributed to the rise of a Public Prosecution Service that exercises its political power, albeit a power that is firmly embedded in the conception of the public prosecutor as part of the judicial branch. According to this conception, which is dominant in Dutch criminal law theory, the public prosecutor is as much a magistrate, concerned with the legitimate application of the law and the achievement of justice, as he is a crime-fighter, concerned with the effective handling of criminality in society.[18]

Parallel to this development, criminal policy became politically significant due to the 'reinvention' of criminal policy and criminal law as means to achieve political goals that extend beyond the traditional field of crime suppression. Criminal legislation gained importance as the cornerstone of all kinds of legislation, ranging from environmental law to economic and alien law. This development led to a significant increase of the tasks attributed to the law enforcement agencies and their workload. To cope with the increased workload in the perspective of a continuous lack of capacity, the law enforcement agencies are compelled to selective prosecution

---

18. A.C. 't Hart, *Openbaar Ministerie en rechtshandhaving*, Arnhem: Gouda Quint 1994.

and investigation policy. Notwithstanding the formal criminalization of cannabis offences, prosecution of these offences is given low priority. Dutch case law determined that the publication of directives in which the low priority is expressed changes the nature of the policy. On the basis of the guidelines, defendants can appeal against prosecution that contradicts the directives in the guidelines. Prosecution of certain categories of cannabis offences is no longer subject to the discretion of the public prosecutor, but a right that can be invoked by citizens. However, the 'right' to sell cannabis is not as unrestricted as it may seem, for the vending of soft drugs in coffeeshops requires a license of the municipality, a prerogative that can be denied without any substantial motivation.[19]

5 Towards legalization?

As mentioned before, the survey of the several negative consequences of drugs in society must differentiate between negative effects caused by the drug itself and those effects that result from the marginalization and criminalization of drug offences, drug consumption included. The first group of effects consists of two subcategories: the actual physical and mental harms that are the result of abundant drug consumption and the offences perpetrated under influence of a psychoactive substance. The rate of cumulated harm directly or indirectly caused by drugs is related to the level of drug consumption. This is what may be called the intrinsic wrongs of drugs.

For the second group of drug related harms, it is less clear whether these are intrinsic or non-intrinsic wrongs. At first glance, it is obvious that these harms result from the stigmatization and criminalization of drug consumption and trade. For example petty theft is a common crime among heroin addicts, not because the heroin makes thieves out of ordinary persons, but because the high retail prices of heroin force the heroin addict into the only alternative option of economic gain that is left open to him: theft. Drug manufacturing and trafficking are criminal activities *because of* the stipulation of these activities *as* criminal behaviour by way of legislation. In itself, there is no harm in cultivating and trading products that are to some extent dangerous to the unwise consumers' health, as there is no moral harm at all in consuming less healthy substances. It is the criminal prohibition that makes these activities legally wrong and harmful.

Furthermore, these activities are conceived as wrong and harmful partly because they are associated with other criminal behaviour, such as the use of excessive violence, liquidation, theft, fraud, tax evasion and money laundering. The only intrinsic wrong in drug trading is perhaps in the harm that is done by persuading youngsters to buy and use addictive and potentially dangerous drugs. Liberalism, which in general rejects paternalism, to some extent accepts paternalism as a ground for government action when the interests of non-adults are involved. Though the

---

19. See e.g. Dutch Supreme Court 7 November 2000, *NJ* 2000, 738 and Court of Appeal Leeuwarden 23 July 2002, *NJ* 2002, 451.

abuse of drugs among people of minor age is a vast part of the problem, it is wrong to evaluate drug policy in general on the basis of the paradigm of the asymmetrical interaction between adults (dealers and traders) and non-adults (consumers and potential fellow dealers). The possibility of an age-based restriction to the availability of drugs may tackle this specific problem and it is neither necessary nor very attractive to build a drug policy on this paradigm. On the other hand, if the potential harm done to juvenile drug users is one of the main arguments against the legalization of drugs – which is a very legitimate argument – then advocating legalization should focus on the question of to what degree actual restriction of availability for the under-aged can be expected.

The non-intrinsic wrongs of illicit substance manufacturing and trade form the basis of a widespread plea for legalization. However, it would be somewhat naive to believe that the legalization of drugs would put an end to these wrongs. A system in which drugs are obtainable legally would render much of the same problems. Such a system must necessarily put restrictions to the availability of narcotic substances, much as is currently the case with alcohol and tobacco. Any effort to limit the availability of drugs implies that the potential consumer must be stimulated *not* to buy and consume drugs, either by discouragement or otherwise. Incentives to refrain from drugs must be quite strong, for it may considered a fact that drugs have quite a strong appeal, especially, as experience shows, for adolescents. The options of the government to discourage drug abuse and to assure the recreational (i.e. non harmful) nature of drug consumption are quite limited, especially when criminalization is not to be taken into account. The raising of taxes, such as in most Western countries with regard to alcohol in combination with some kind of education and propaganda program, would be the most likely course to be followed. The artificially raised prices will leave room for criminal entrepreneurs to set up a black market of untaxed and therefore much cheaper alternatives to the drugs that are legitimately obtainable. More or less the same argument is applicable to controlled availability, such as the requisite of a doctor's prescription. Any legalized drug market must somehow limit availability in order to avoid too abundant a consumption rate and an increase in the number of drug addictions and other abuse. Any formally limited market will create its black or gray equivalent, attracting less bona fide entrepreneurs that aim at making profit from the price gap and availability gap between legally and illegally obtainable drugs.

However, any theorizing on actually legalizing the (soft) drug market is at this moment purely academic, for it is generally acknowledged that there is no international political basis for any such experiment. It is evident that the legalization of (soft) drugs must be a transboundary operation that involves at least all countries of the European Union. Free availability of drugs in but a few countries would increase the problems instead of diminish them, cumulating the problems of a system of criminalization of drugs with the problems of a legalized market.

As long as actual legalization is a political impossibility, the Dutch pragmatic approach might be a good alternative to those countries that have lost their belief in the war on drugs and seek for better and more practical solutions to the drug problems they are facing. Such a pragmatic approach may seem incoherent and lacking in principles, its success in harm reduction outweighs any of these contra-arguments, which are essentially about esthetics. The relative success of the Dutch approach, if one is willing to acknowledge it, must however not be the only reason to adopt a similar system. Here, the relativism of Montesquieu seems applicable: what are good laws for a country depends on the specific features of the country and of the situation and conditions specific to that country in that era. What may work for the Dutch may not yet or not at all become a success in the United States, France or Sweden. If not on a global scale, then at least on a transatlantic or European scale, are we compelled to a common approach to the drug problem. The discussion about what approach should be adopted has not yet come to a close.

Part IV

Private Law

8 The Outlines of Dutch Private Law[*]

1 Introduction

Citizens who need the law to manage their affairs must first of all turn to private law: the part of law that governs the relationships between private persons. Dutch private law applies to all dealings between persons, companies, associations, et cetera, except relations with the State's institutions in an official capacity. In this chapter, one of the main parts of Dutch private law is discussed: patrimonial law, i.e. the law concerned with rights and obligations that are valuable in money.[1] Apart from the importance of patrimonial law for social and economic issues, there are specific Dutch and European reasons for extensive discussion, because this part of private law has undergone important developments recently. The main event for Dutch law in the last twenty years has been the recodification of the patrimonial part of the Civil Code *(Burgerlijk Wetboek)*, books 3, 5 and 6. In this recodification, many of the developments in case law of the 20th century were laid down in statutory rules.

In this chapter, the most extensively discussed area of Dutch patrimonial law is the law of obligations. One of the reasons to focus on this area is its international relevance. The main parts of the law of obligations, tort law and contract law, often have aspects that transcend the national level, which makes it interesting for foreigners to know the Dutch law on these subjects.

The international context most relevant to Dutch law is the European dimension. Because of the European Union and the intense economic relations between the countries that are part of it, private law is not merely national private law. Recognition of this development has led legal scholars all over Europe, including Dutch scholars, to study the possibilities of moving towards a European private law. This has led to comparative studies, but also to proposals for new rules. Sometimes with reference to the *ius commune* of the Middle Ages, efforts are made to unify parts of private law, most successfully in contract law. In 2000, the so-called Lando principles, principles of European contract law, were published, by which the makers mean to express the common core of the contract law of European countries. A more ambitious project has been started at the initiative of the European Parliament, exploring the possibilities of a European Civil Code. Of course, directives of the European Union already influence the national systems profoundly and a European Civil Code could in part be based on existing directives. There are, however, many

---

[*] Many thanks to Geertje van Schaaijk for her comments.
1. The next chapter discusses another important area of private law: family law.

legal scholars who are sceptical about the need for a European code or the possibilities of achieving a common law of Europe.[2]

Although this chapter mainly explains important institutions and features of the law of obligations, as they can be found in legislation and case law, I want to indicate a few considerations about the context and values that surround the positive law. Some years ago, the legal scholar and philosopher, Langemeijer, devoted a small book to the idea of justice in Dutch private law.[3] He analysed the developments of private law in terms of justice, which he understood as the fair recognition of relevant interests. From this perspective, he saw three developments as particularly significant: recognition of the need to protect the weaker party, the growing importance of good faith, or reasonableness and fairness, and the growing attention to allocation of risks. These are general considerations playing a role in the continuing efforts to make private law a just and workable system, which form the background to the more specific explanations that follow.

The remainder of this chapter is structured as follows. Section 2 is a sketch of the outline of the Civil Code and the main distinction between the law of property and the law of obligations. In section 3, tort law is discussed. Section 4, the longest, is a description of the main features of contract law. Section 5 has a more theoretical character and contains a discussion of the principle of reasonableness and equity as a key to the open system of Dutch private law.

2   The Dutch Civil Code

In January 2003, Book 4 of the Dutch Civil Code, on the law of succession, was replaced: one of the last big instalments of the revision of the Civil Code. For almost a century and a half, the Netherlands used a civil code from 1838, a slightly altered translation of the French *Code Civil*. Halfway into the 20th century, pleas began to be heard for a new codification: a revision of the code to bring it more up to date, especially to incorporate insights from case law which had been steadily interpreting the statutory law more freely. In 1947, the Dutch government appointed E.M. Meijers, law professor at Leiden University, to design a new civil code. The first half of his draft was published in 1954. Because Meijers died suddenly in the same year, the drafts were finished by a number of other jurists. In 1958, the draft of the first book was passed by Parliament; it came into force in 1970. The largest operation was the joint introduction of Books 3, 5, and 6 in 1992.[4]

The system of the code bears the clear mark of Meijers' views. He paid much attention to the systematic structure of the code. The old distinction between private

---

2. E.g. M.J. Bonell, 'The need and possibilities of a codified European contract law', *European Review of Private Law* 1997, p. 505-518.
3. G.E. Langemeijer, *De gerechtigheid in ons burgerlijk vermogensrecht*, (6th edition revised by E.J.H. Schrage) Zwolle: Tjeenk Willink 1994.
4. About the background of the new code, see E.H. Hondius, 'Recodification of the Law in the Netherlands: the New Civil Code Experience', *Netherlands International Law Review* 1982, p. 249-366.

law, governing the relations between citizens in general, and commercial law, governing commercial relations, is abolished in the Code. The first two books cover the law of persons: the law of natural persons and family law in Book 1, the law of legal persons, such as unlimited and limited companies, the foundation and the association, in Book 2. Books 3 to 8 cover patrimonial law, ranging from general provisions to more and more detailed rules. Book 3 contains general definitions and rules relevant to all property: e.g. how to acquire, transfer, or lose it; how to establish rights to property such as pledge and mortgage *(hypotheek)*. Book 4 contains the law of succession: how to make a will, who inherits when no will is made. Book 5 is the book on real rights: ownership and other rights concerning things, both moveable objects and immovable property such as land. Book 6 is about the general part of the law of obligations and includes general rules on tort and contract. Specific contracts are dealt with in Book 7, such as the contract of sale, of employment, et cetera. Book 7 is not complete yet: there are still some contracts such as the lease that are covered by old law, which are now gathered together in Book 7A. Book 8 contains the law on transport: shipping, transport of goods.

2.1 Property and real rights

One of the distinctive features of the Dutch Civil Code is the strict division between the law on property and the law on obligations. It follows the old Roman distinction between rights *in rem* and rights *in personam*: rights to an object versus rights to a performance by another person. The rights *in rem* consist of two categories: rights to tangible objects (ownership and limited rights derived from ownership) and rights to intangibles, such as copyright. The rights, directly concerning tangible objects, also referred to as real rights,[5] are the subject of Book 5 of the Civil Code. Of these rights, ownership is the most important category: it is defined as the most comprehensive right which a person can have in a thing. This implies the freedom to use it as one likes — within the limits of the law, of course — and it includes ownership of anything generated by the thing one owns, e.g. the fruit born by the tree in one's orchard. Apart from this comprehensive ownership, a thing can also be burdened with limited rights. For instance, the owner of the orchard can give the owner of the neighbouring property the right to use a path through the orchard: a servitude, or the owner can grant another person the right to the fruits of the orchard, to eat or sell them: usufruct.[6]

---

5. Please note that this distinction is different from the one between real and personal property, as made in the common law: real property refers the ownership of immovables such as land or houses, and personal property to movables such as furniture and cars. All of these can be the subject of real rights under Dutch law.
6. Strictly speaking, usufruct is not necessarily a real right (directly pertaining to a thing): it is also possible to establish usufruct regarding a non-real item, e.g. to give someone the right to the interest on a loan. The same double character is found in the rights of mortage and pledge. Because they are not necessarily related to tangible things, all these rights are treated in Book 3. There are some limited rights, such as servitude, which are by necessity real rights: they can only be related to real things.

Real rights have a special characteristic: they are absolute, meaning that they remain in existence even if the property changes hands. If the owner of the orchard sells it, the duty to respect the servitude to use the path now rests on the new owner. Because of their absolute nature, the system of real rights is a so-called closed system: the only rights that can be established are the ones explicitly created in the Civil Code. If someone wants to establish a different kind of right, it can only be a personal right, only binding the person establishing it.

In order to transfer property from one owner to another, the owner must be qualified to dispose of the property, there must be a valid title, and delivery of the property. A title can be defined as a legal relationship that justifies transfer. The most common title for transfer is the contract of sale: it is a set of obligations which obliges the seller to deliver the sold item and the buyer to deliver money in return. Once the seller has delivered, the buyer becomes the owner: there was a valid title and delivery. In case of movable property, delivery is achieved simply by giving the future owner (physical) possession of the thing. If I buy a book, the seller has to give it to me. In the case of immovable property, such as land or a house, delivery is more complicated: a notary has to make a deed of transfer, which has to be registered in the public registry. This is additional to the contract of sale: if someone wants to sell his house, he has to make a contract of sale with a buyer and together they have to go to a notary for the deed of transfer. The system of registration for immovable property is meant to make it easy for third parties, who are not involved in the transfer themselves, to gain knowledge of property rights: they can simply check the public register and regard as owner the person named in the register. The same holds for limited rights regarding immovable property: these must also be registered. If they are not, they cannot be invoked against third parties. For example, the new owner of a piece of land does not need to honour an unregistered servitude. Technically, this does not even exist as a servitude because it was not delivered as it should have been; it is then only a contract creating obligations between the two contracting parties.

2.2 The law of obligations

Whereas the law of property, Book 5 of the Code, is restricted to rights regarding things, the law of obligations has a much broader scope. It concerns all obligations a person can have, whether they follow from a contract, are based on a moral duty, or are connected by law to certain actions or events. In order for an obligation to be a legal obligation, the general kind it belongs to has to be recognized by law (article 6:1 *Burgerlijk Wetboek*).[7] This means that the obligation has to fit one of the categories created by the system of the Code. The courts do not interpret this rule very strictly, though: if an obligation is not specifically mentioned in a statutory provision but accords with the system as a whole it will be recognized.[8]

---

7. Further references to the *Burgerlijk Wetboek* (Civil Code) are abbreviated as 'BW'.
8. In a landmark decision of 30 January 1959 *(Quint v. Te Poel, NJ* 1959, 548) the Supreme Court recognized that obligations need not necessarily follow from statutory law or contract.

However, unlike the system of property rights, the law of obligations is an open system: because of the freedom of contract, people can determine the content of their own obligations, provided they do not act contrary to general legal and moral duties. Obvious examples of illegitimate obligations are selling yourself in slavery, or promising to break a provision of criminal law.

The main distinction made in the system of obligations is that between obligations created intentionally, by a juridical act, and obligations following directly from the law regardless of the intent of the person under obligation. Contract is the most important source of the first category of obligations and tort of the second. Other sources of obligations of the second kind, such as undue payment or unjustified enrichment, will not be discussed here.

Juridical acts can be unilateral or multilateral: in the first case, only one person's intention is involved; in the second case, at least two people are involved, i.e. a contractual relationship. An example of a unilateral act is the making of a last will and testament. Multilateral acts or contracts can place an obligation on only one person, e.g. the contract of gift, or be reciprocal with obligations on each side, e.g. the contract of sale. Later, when discussing contracts, I will also point out which aspects are shared by all juridical acts.

3   The broad scope of tort law

One of the most dynamic parts of Dutch private law has been tort law. It is the part of law dealing with damage resulting from unlawful acts. If a person commits an unlawful act, which can be imputed to him or her, causing damage to another, he or she is obliged to repair the damage (article 6:162 BW). An act can be imputed to a person if the act is his fault, or if he is answerable for it according to law or common opinion. Dutch law recognizes two basic types of tort liability: liability based on fault and liability based on risk. I will return to that issue later. For a standard tort case based on fault, four things have to be determined: whether there is damage, whether there has been unlawful conduct, whether this conduct is a person's fault, and whether there is a causal connection between the unlawful conduct and the damage.[9]

3.1   Damage

The first question to be answered is what counts as damage in Dutch law. Reparation of damage is covered in general by articles 6:95-110 BW. A general definition of damage is not given but two categories are mentioned. The main one is patrimonial, or material, damage, that is, all kinds of loss with a monetary value: economic losses, deprivation of income or profit, hospital costs, et cetera. Other, non-material damage, such as pain or emotional damage, also qualifies for reparation in certain

---

9. A fifth condition is that of relativity (comparable to the German *Schutznorm*): the violated norm must have as its purpose the protection from damage such as that suffered by the victim (article 6:163 BW).

cases. Material damage must in principle be repaired fully; immaterial damage is subject to a test of fairness by the judge. In practice, the court has to estimate the damages they award in every case and will do so with reference to amounts awarded in similar cases. Dutch courts have awarded fairly modest amounts in cases of emotional damage, rarely more than € 50,000.

3.2 Unlawful conduct

The second question is: when is conduct unlawful? Traditionally, Dutch law recognized two reasons why conduct can be unlawful: because it infringes a person's right or because it violates a statutory duty. If you accidentally break the window of your neighbour's house, you infringe his right to undisturbed enjoyment of his property which follows from his ownership. If a company dumps its waste in a river without a government permit, it violates the duty it has according to environmental statutes. The limited system of unlawfulness became disputed early on in the 20th century. There was the case of the lady from Zutphen in 1910, where a broken water pipe started to cause damage to leather goods in a warehouse.[10] To stop the damage from increasing, the main water tap needed to be closed. The tap was located in the dwelling of the lady living above the warehouse, who refused to cooperate by closing the tap or letting someone into her house to do it. The Supreme Court ruled that her conduct was not unlawful because she had no statutory duty to cooperate nor did she infringe anyone's right. The ruling was generally regarded as very unfair. The breakthrough came with another case before the Supreme Court in 1919: *Lindenbaum-Cohen*.[11] This was the case of two entrepeneurs engaged in fierce competition, which led one, Cohen, to bribe the employee of the other, Lindenbaum, to give him information about the offers Lindenbaum had made to his clients, which allowed Cohen to make a better offer. Although there was no explicit statutory rule forbidding this, the Court nevertheless ruled that Cohen's conduct was unlawful, because he had 'violated a rule of unwritten law pertaining to proper social conduct', to cite the words in which the decision was eventually codified in article 6:162 BW. Thus, taking due care with respect to the interests of others, as a generally accepted maxim of social morality and unwritten law, has now become a recognized criterion of unlawful conduct.

The *Lindenbaum-Cohen* decision expanded the scope of tort law significantly:[12] the third criterion of unlawfulness, not taking the care required by unwritten law, has since been used most often in court decisions. The range of cases in which this criterion has been used is broad. These are some of the types of cases covered by the due care criterion: creating dangerous situations – for instance by leaving open a

---

10. HR 10 June 1910, *W* 9038.
11. HR 31 January 1919, *NJ* 1919, p. 161.
12. The expansion of Dutch tort law parallels the development in other countries, see: T. Koopmans, 'Modern Trends in Tort Law: A Summary', in: E. Hondius (ed.), *Modern Tort Law: Dutch and Japanese Law Compared*, The Hague: Kluwer Law International 1999, p. 261-268.

trapdoor in the floor of a bar;[13] creating a nuisance for neighbouring property – for instance by dumping waste which attracts birds that also eat the fruit of the neighbouring farmer;[14] damaging a person's reputation or invading privacy.

3.3 Causality

The third issue to be determined is the causal relationship between the unlawful act and the damage. Usually, this is not a problem in cases where one person suffers the damage due to the conduct of one other. Problems arise when there are more causes of more than one party acting unlawfully. In the Dutch system, each party that contributes to the damage is liable for the whole. For instance, if there is a traffic accident between three cars where two drivers have made mistakes that caused damage to the third car, the driver of the third car can sue each of the two for the whole damage. It is essential, however, that they are each liable for the same damage: if a clear distinction can be made between the parts that each has caused, they are only liable for that part of the damage.

One of the most difficult situations regarding causality is when it is uncertain who precisely caused the damage: cases of alternative causality. The Supreme Court had to decide this issue in the case of the DES daughters.[15] These were women whose mothers had taken the medicine DES during their pregnancies to prevent a miscarriage. The medicine later turned out to cause cancer to the daughters. The causal connection between DES and cancer was clear, but DES had been produced by a number of pharmaceutical companies and it could no longer be determined which company had supplied it to which of the mothers. The daughters took ten companies to court: the Supreme Court ruled on the basis of article 6:99 BW that each producer of DES was liable for the whole damage, and it was their own responsibility to claim compensation from the other producers. The decision met with serious criticism, because it made one company liable for the faults of a whole producing market, which seems unfair. However, with the decision, the Supreme Court chose to protect the victims of DES by placing the risk and costs of further procedures on the producers among themselves.[16]

3.4 Fault and risk

The fourth question is whether the unlawful act can be imputed to the person, either because of fault or otherwise. This involves the distinction between fault liability and strict, risk-based, liability. The basic idea of tort law follows the moral intuition that every person should be accountable for the consequences of his own actions. Fault

---

13. HR 5 November 1965, *NJ* 1966, 136.
14. HR 10 March 1972, *NJ* 1972, 278 *(Vermeulen v. Lekkerkerker)*.
15. HR 9 October 1992, *NJ* 1994, 535.
16. Compare J. Spier et al., *Verbintenissen uit de wet en schadevergoeding,* Deventer: Kluwer 2000, section 239.

liability can be related to this intuition of outcome responsibility: if someone makes a stupid mistake or takes unnecessary risks, he should pay for the consequences.[17] It is the flip-side of profiting from the gain of one's own actions: by working you earn the right to be paid, by investing your savings the right to the profit of your shares. A person should bear the risks, both positive and negative, of his actions.

Although fault liability is plausible for standard cases, there are many situations in which it seems unfair, or it may be impossible, to hold a person accountable for his own deeds. Sometimes, it may even be the case that the tort is not the fault of a person at all. Exceptions to fault liability are often based on the idea of risk: if someone stands to gain from a risky situation, that person should also bear the losses. This is a basis for strict liability, regardless of fault, for damage caused by things and animals and also for the liability of an employer for the actions of his employees. If the roof of your house collapses and hurts someone, you are liable for the medical costs because the house you own is your responsibility. Similarly, if a raging bull damages a neighbour's fence, the farmer who owns the bull must pay.

Objects and animals make a simple category for strict liability, because they cannot be at fault themselves. Liability for the actions of other people is more complicated: here fault is at issue. With regard to the liability of an employer for torts committed by his employee, the fault of the employee plays an important role: the employee must have committed an unlawful act, imputable to him, in order to make the employer liable. Additionally, the employer must have the authority to give instructions about the actions concerned. It is not essential that instructions were in fact given, merely that a relationship of authority exists. If the plumber I hire to fix the shower in my house sends an employee who makes a mistake causing a leak in the drain, I can claim damages from the plumber I hired, regardless of the instructions given to the employee.

Parents are liable for the unlawful acts of their children. This is because the idea of fault is problematic in such cases: small children cannot foresee the consequences of their dangerous actions, so they cannot be said to be at fault. Since parents are in general responsible for the care and upbringing of their children, it is not so strange that they are liable for their unlawful behaviour as well. The way Dutch law determines when such liability arises is by applying a hypothetical test to children under 14: would a normal adult performing the same action have been liable in the situation? If the answer is affirmative, the parent or guardian of the child is liable. Children of 14 and 15 are held responsible for their own actions, but their parents are also liable, if they were capable of preventing the act. For instance, if a fourteen-year-old damages furniture at school, it was impossible for the parents to do something about it: then the child itself is the only one liable.[18]

---

17. See T. Honoré, *Responsibility and Fault*, Oxford: Hart 1999, p. 14 ff, about the idea of outcome responsibility.
18. Although this might seem to lay a heavy burden on teenagers, in practice most people have insurance against liability that covers the whole family.

3.5   Traffic accidents

A large number of tort cases arise because of traffic accidents. When an accident concerns two cars (or other motorized vehicles such as motor cycles or camper vans) it is covered by the general rules of tort liability, based on article 6:162 BW. This means that the person who causes the accident, for instance by not giving way to a car coming from the right, will be liable for the damage. If both drivers contribute to the accident, liability will be shared to the extent to which each contributed.

A very different set of rules applies when there is an accident between a motorized vehicle and a person who is not driving (or riding in) such a vehicle, e.g. an accident between a car and a pedestrian. In that case, the special rule of the *Wegenverkeerswet* (Road Traffic Act) says that the driver of the motorized vehicle is liable for damage suffered by the other person (pedestrian), with the exception of *force majeure* i.e. when there are circumstances beyond the control of the driver. This is not as straightforward as it looks, because, first, a defence based on *force majeure* is not often conceded, and, secondly, the own fault of the person suffering damage plays a different role than usual.

The interpretation given to *force majeure* by the Supreme Court in traffic liability is special, because it restricts the idea to situations when legally there is no culpability at all on the part of the driver. Circumstances excluded by the Court include defects of the vehicle and physical problems of the driver: these are not reason enough to conclude that there were circumstances beyond his control. It comes down to a distribution which places the burden on the driver, unless there is clear culpability on the part of the pedestrian. So when a pedestrian ignores a red traffic light on a busy crossing and is hit by a car, the driver of which maintains reasonable speed, this pedestrian will probably be liable. On the other hand, circumstances which are neither the fault of the driver nor that of the pedestrian will be borne by the driver.

So one can observe that *force majeure* and the own fault of the pedestrian have become linked. There is, however, another peculiarity concerning the own fault of pedestrians or cyclists, also engendered by the case law of the Supreme Court. This is the so-called 50% rule. Even when a pedestrian very clearly commits a traffic offence, and is therefore at fault, he will never be liable for more than 50% of the damage. When a young child is concerned, the own fault of the child does not come into play at all: the driver is liable for the full 100%. So here, the hypothetical test comparing the behaviour of the child to that of an adult in the same situation, which is used in standard tort cases, is not applied.

Not everyone regards the system as fair: traffic rules are not obeyed very consistently by pedestrians, and especially cyclists, in the Netherlands, which has been reason to argue that the 50% system creates a questionable licence to disobey the rules which moreover should not be at the expense of careful drivers. On the other hand, it has been argued that it is a good system because car owners are obliged to be insured against liability, so effectively it will be the insurance company that pays.

4   Contract law

In all modern legal systems, contract is the most important form to realize one's objectives through private law. In Dutch law, freedom of contract is recognized as the (unwritten) basic principle of the law of contract: a person is free to make contracts when, with whom and with the content he or she chooses. Of course, the rules of contract law impose limitations on this freedom, but there are also many rules which are better understood as ways to guarantee that contractual freedom has real meaning.

As was explained in section 2, in the system of the Dutch civil code, a contract is a subcategory of the juridical act, namely a multilateral juridical act. The rules regarding juridical acts in general are therefore also relevant to contracts. Because a juridical act is defined as an act *intended* to create legal consequences, I will in particular pay attention to the issue of intention. Discussion of contract law can easily follow the different phases of the 'life' of a contract: first, how it comes into being, secondly, what are the consequences when it exists and what rules govern its content, and, third, how it ends.

4.1   Intention and declaration

The subject of intention is most relevant for the first phase, the making of contracts: what do the parties who make a contract want and how do we know their will? Because all manner of legal consequences are attached to juridical acts, including contracts, it is important to know what a person intends when he or she performs a legal act. Because it is impossible to look inside someone's head at the time of making a contract, this raises the problem of how to determine what a person's intention is. Dutch law says that a juridical act can only be performed when the relevant will or intention is also made public by a declaration (article 3:33 BW). In principle, both the intention and its declaration are necessary, but it will at times occur that the declaration is not the same as the intention or that it is understood differently than intended by the other party. What prevails in such cases: the real intention or the declaration? In such a situation, the rule of article 3:33 BW clashes with another rule (article 3:35 BW) which allows the other party to rely on the declaration; the protection of the person who declared something perhaps mistakenly is at odds with the protection of others who need to be able to trust what was made manifest.

This conflict arose in the case of *Eelman v. Hin,* which concerns a person, Eelman, who was mentally disturbed and made his declaration under the influence of this disturbance. Eelman was the owner of a farm. He thought that there were ghosts haunting the farm and sold it to Hin in order to be rid of these ghosts. At the time, the price of farmland was determined by a public board, so a reasonable price was established. After the contract of sale but before the land actually changed hands, Eelman was officially declared mentally ill and put under legal restraint. His curator (who manages his affairs) tried to get out of the contract of sale. The argument was that Eelman did not really intend to sell his farm, but only did so under the mental delusion that there were ghosts. Was Hin allowed to rely on the declaration or should the real intention of Eelman have been honoured? Or, practically, can the contract of sale be considered final because of the declaration, or should it be annulled because of the lack of the real intention to sell? Dutch law chooses to honour the declaration, the outward appearance of the intention, and not the true intention. The justification for this is the importance it has for the smooth running of legal and socio-economic relations: without the certainty of taking a declaration at face value it would be difficult to conduct business. Under specific circumstances, the other party may be required to inquire what the real intention is, namely when the situation is so unusual that the other party should be suspicious. In the case of the haunted farm, it was relevant that Eelman received a good price for his farm. If, for instance, he had agreed to sell for a very small amount of money, then the other party should have understood that something might be wrong and have inquired what the real intention was. As it was, Hin could rely on the appearance of the intention in the form of the declaration.

Although this is a special case, in which the will was defective because of a mental delusion,[19] the principle of relying on appearances applies to all situations in which intention and declaration do not correspond: if the other party cannot reasonably suspect that the intention was defective, he is allowed to rely on the declaration. The general rules about the creation of juridical acts underlie more specific rules about the making of contracts.

4.2   Making a contract

Because contracts are made by two or more persons, the will of only one is insufficient: there has to be agreement between all the parties about the terms of the contract.[20] In Dutch law, the agreement between the parties is all that is necessary to create a contract: no formal requirements or procedures need to be observed.[21] This is also known as the principle of consensualism, because only a consensus between parties is needed. In case of a two-party contract, one party will start negotiations with an offer; when the other party accepts the offer, an agreement is reached and the contract concluded (article 6:217 BW). Offer and acceptance are needed, but what counts as an offer? If a bakery has loaves of bread on a shelf with the prices displayed alongside, that counts as an offer. But what about an advertisement in the paper in which a house is put up for sale?

Such an issue was at stake in the case of *Hofland v. Hennis*:[22] there was an advertisement in a magazine for a house at a certain price. The buyer Hennis wanted to buy the house at the price mentioned in the advertisement and argued in court

---

19. Article 3:34 BW governs the special case of mental disorder and gives the person who is suffering from a mental disturbance the right to annul a legal act if the declaration was made under influence of the disturbance.
20. The Dutch term for agreement: *overeenkomst* is used as the equivalent for the word *contract*. In the Civil Code, it is even the preferred term.
21. E.g. an oral agreement, without anything in writing is also a valid contract.
22. HR 10 April 1981, *NJ* 1981, 532.

that the advertisement was an offer, which he could simply accept to conclude the sale. He claimed before the court that the seller, Hofland was obliged to cooperate with the delivery of the house to him. The Supreme Court ruled that such an advertisement in the paper was no more than an invitation to start negotiations in which not only the price and conditions of the sale but also the person who buys are important factors.

The question whether an announcement counts as an offer is so important, because Dutch law in principle rules that, once an offer is accepted by the other party, it cannot be retracted. It is only different when a party explicitly says it is an offer free of obligations; in that case, it can be retracted if this is done immediately after acceptance. If an offer is made with a time limit, it is not retractable: for instance, if I offer to sell someone my piano for € 3,000 provided he accepts within two weeks, then I cannot retract the offer before the two weeks are over.

4.3   Negotiations

For important contracts, it is customary to have a substantial period of negotiating to reach an agreement. In business relations, this will often include the investment of time and money in preparing the contract and adjusting future business plans. That parties often go back and forth with different offers makes it hard to determine when exactly a contract is concluded. Simply applying the rule of offer and acceptance does not help here: often, there is agreement about some aspects of the deal and not about others, so it is unclear what has been accepted and what not. Dutch case law recognizes a basic contract *(rompovereenkomst)* when there is agreement about the essential parts of the contract. When one of the parties says that, or behaves as if, a certain part of the contract is so important to him that he wants to make it subject of further negotiations, there can be no basic contract.

But what happens when negotiations are broken off at an advanced stage and the contract is not concluded? In some cases, it may seem unreasonable to let one of the parties bear all the costs of investment. In Dutch law, the relation between negotiating parties is governed by the general principle of reasonableness and equity *(redelijkheid en billijkheid)*.[23]

In the case of *Plas v. Valburg*, the Supreme Court addressed the question as to when breaking off negotiations without compensation is unreasonable.[24] The city council of the town of Valburg had decided to build a swimming pool. Four interested building companies made plans and two of these companies, one of which was Plas, invested in specialized advice and redesigned on the basis of the list of demands prepared by the city council. The plans and offer of Plas were the cheapest of the four and were approved by the city officials, but in the final meeting for the decision of the city council, a fifth company (which had not competed before) was presented with plans that were slightly cheaper still. The town contracted the fifth

---

23. Since the judgement in *Baris v. Riezenkamp*, HR 15 November 1957, *NJ* 1958, 67. For discussion of this principle, see section 5.
24. HR 18 June 1982, *NJ* 1983, 723.

company and Plas went to court to complain. The Supreme Court ruled that the negotiations had advanced so far that breaking off the negotiations was itself contrary to the principle of reasonableness and equity: both parties had reason to expect that a contract of some kind would follow. In such a situation, there is room for awarding considerable damages: Plas could also claim some of the profit it failed to gain. In general, the Court distinguished three phases in negotiations: in the first phase, the risk of investment remains with each of the parties themselves and they are free to step out when they want; in the second phase, there is no duty to contract but breaking off negotiations can imply paying some of the costs the other party made in preparation. The situation in *Plas v. Valburg* was in the third phase: breaking off negotiations is no longer allowed and extensive damages can be awarded.

4.4   Failure: nullity and annulment

For lawyers, the interesting cases are the ones in which something goes wrong. With contracts and juridical acts, the most fundamental kind of failure concerns the lack of the real will to make the contract. The case of *Eelman v. Hin,* which I discussed in the context of intention and declaration, already addressed the issue: sometimes, there may be reason to doubt that someone really wants to perform a juridical act, for instance if that person is mentally ill.

In Dutch law, two categories of persons are protected against their own imprudent actions because they are considered incapable of performing juridical acts: children and persons with mental problems who have been placed under legal restraint. Legal restraint is achieved by court procedure and involves appointing a curator who manages the affairs of the incapable person. The incapability has to be registered and can thereafter be invoked against anyone who claims to have contracted with the incapable person.

A juridical act by an incapable person is either null in itself or can be annulled. It is automatically null when it is a juridical act which is not addressed to another person: for instance, the making of a last will and testament. An act can be annulled when it is two-sided (such as a contract) or, when one-sided, when it is addressed to a specific other party (e.g. termination of a rental contract). Because annulment is no more than the active invoking of nullity by a person, the result of an annulment is nullity: meaning that the act does not have the intended legal consequences and, if there have already been consequences, these need to be undone; the situation must be brought back to the way it was before the juridical act was done. In case of an incapable person, the curator has to invoke the annulment. The main exception regarding their incapacity is that incapable persons can act if they have the permission of their representative.

The incapability of a person is not the only reason why a juridical act can be subject to nullity or annulment: it is a consequence in general of defects concerning the formation of juridical acts. Many such defects concern a faulty determination of one's will, for instance, because it was formed on the basis of the wrong information or under the pressure of difficult circumstances. Dutch law recognizes four kinds of these so-called 'defects of the will': error, fraud, threat, and abuse of circumstances.

4.5   Error and fraud

Error is the defect of will following from a misunderstanding, or lack of relevant information; as a result, the contract will not correspond to the wills of both parties and is subject to annulment by the party who is in error (article 6:228 BW). Of course, the system of contract law would be terribly inefficient if every slight misunderstanding were reason enough to annul a contract; therefore, a set of criteria is applied to decide whether the claim based on error should be granted. The first important criterion concerns how important the aspect of the contract is about which there is a misunderstanding: is the error about an *essential* part of the contract? For instance, consider a person buying a second-hand car and the buyer forgetting to mention that the brakes do not work. Being able to stop the car is such an essential part of driving that defective brakes could be reason enough to annul the contract.

However, it is also a requirement that the other person involved knows, or should know, that the part of the contract is essential to the person in error. There are many aspects of contracts of which it is obvious that they are essential, but this is not always the case. If a person has very specific wishes but does not mention these to the contracting party, the claim of error can be unjustified. Imagine a couple who order pink flowers for the church in which their wedding is held and who notice on the day itself that the shade of pink is much darker than that of the sample flowers they saw weeks earlier. For the bride, this is a disaster because the darker shade does not match her pink wedding dress. They had, however, failed to mention to the florist that they wanted this particular pink because it matched the dress, so he did not know it was essential to them. In such a case, the error claim may be unjustified.

In cases of error, either of the contracting parties may be at fault for not doing enough to prevent the error: the party in error because he failed to make his wishes known or to inquire whether the contract answered his wishes, the other party because he failed to provide all relevant information. There is a tension between the *duty to investigate* of the first party and the *duty to inform* of the second. Precisely this issue was at stake in the case of *Booy v. Wisman.*[25]

Wisman needed a crane to move goods from a ship to the quays. He tells Booy, who runs a company that sells such cranes, that he needs to transport the crane over the road from one harbour to the other, so it is important the crane is able to move and that he gets a licence to transport it over the road. Booy tells him that he has sold similar cranes which all got licences without a problem. After the sale, Wisman applies for a licence for the crane, which is refused because the crane is slightly too heavy and too wide to take onto the road. Was Wisman allowed to rely on the information given by Booy about licences, or should he have investigated himself? The Supreme Court ruled that parties have a duty to prevent their own error by investigating, but this is combined with a right to rely on the information given by the other party, especially if the other party has expert knowledge. In this case, the

---

25. HR 21 January 1966, *NJ* 1966, 183.

salesperson Booy had expert knowledge about cranes, and Wisman was allowed to rely on his information. Wisman was justified in annulling the contract.

In some cases, the character of the contract can be such that an error claim is excluded by the contract itself: for instance, the buyer of an antique object often accepts the risk that it turns out to be a fake antique. Because that is a kind of situation in which the buyer calculates the risk of his purchase being worth much more or much less than the price he paid, the error is also at his risk. In Dutch law, the rejection of annulment based on error for these cases is justified with reference to common opinion: people in general believe that the risk has to rest with the party in error.[26]

Closely related to error is the defect of will called fraud: this could be described as a special case of error, namely error based on the intentional deception of the other party. Fraud can consist in intentionally giving the wrong information, in intentionally suppressing information, or another trick by which someone is induced to perform a juridical act (article 3:44 BW). The legal difficulty of using fraud as a basis for an annulment is how to prove that someone was *intentionally* misleading: when fraud cannot be proven, a claim based on error can be successful because that also covers unintentional misleading.

4.6 Threat and abuse of circumstances

Article 3:44 BW gives two other defects of will: threat and abuse of circumstances. Like fraud and error, threat and abuse of circumstances are related. Threat occurs when someone is induced to perform a juridical act by being illegally threatened with harm. A well-known example is the way the mafia forces shop owners to buy 'protection' from them, namely by threatening to damage the shop if they do not pay the protection money. In such a case, the threat is clearly against the law because the threat is a criminal activity. But what if a person feels threatened by someone using perfectly legal means? This happened in the case of *Van Meurs v. Ciba-Geigy*, concerning the end of an employment contract.[27] In this case, the former employer threatened to retract the promise to provide a policy for the pension savings of the former employee Van Meurs if he did not agree to their final reckoning of all obligations deriving from the employment contract. The pension policy was extremely important to Van Meurs because his own savings were insufficient. The Supreme Court ruled that it is not necessary to threaten someone with violence: circumstances such as these can also count as threat, because a normal person would feel the pressure and be influenced in his behaviour.

---

26. In the case of the so-called Kantharos, someone sold a silver cup for a small price, about which the buyer made inquiries and discovered that it was a very valuable old Roman cup. The Supreme Court rejected the claim based on error, because according to common opinion such a seller has given up the chance that it was valuable by selling it, and it was the effort of the buyer that made its value apparent (HR 19 June 1959, *NJ* 1960, 59).
27. HR 27 March 1992, *NJ* 1992, 377.

As can be seen in this case, threat can come very close to abuse of circumstances (also called: undue influence): this fourth defect of the will gives the possibility of annulment to someone who performed a juridical act because of special circumstances of which another party takes advantage. This includes taking advantage of someone's inexperience, dependence, psychological weakness, et cetera. The decisive factor here is whether another party uses the circumstance to achieve an unfair result. For example, an insurance adviser convinces a woman with psychological problems and financial need to give him, in exchange for a loan, an option to buy her house for a set low price. The court ruled that he had taken advantage of her difficult circumstances.[28] The key difference between threat and abuse of circumstances is the following: for the first category, the condition is that the other party takes the initiative to persuade the threatened party; for the second, the other party makes use of already existing circumstances.

As mentioned before, all of these defects of the will can be cause for annulment of a contract. Annulment works retroactively: the contract does not have the intended legal consequences any more, or if obligations have already been fulfilled, the consequences need to be undone. If this is impossible, the court can award damages.

4.7   The content of contracts

Because the basis of Dutch contract law is the freedom of parties to determine their own joint will, the most important part of the contract consists of the explicit agreement between parties as it has been laid down in the clauses of the contract. Problems arise when parties later find out that they only thought there was agreement when the contract was concluded, while later circumstances or events give cause for disagreement. In what way should the explicit clauses of a contract be explained in such cases? The most simple solution would seem to be to rely on a grammatical interpretation: the meaning the clauses have in normal speech. This solution has the drawback of possibly creating unfair solutions, especially if both parties understand a term in a non-grammatical, e.g. in a technical sense. The Dutch Supreme Court has therefore opted for a different solution: even if the wording of a contractual clause is clear grammatically, the central question is what meaning the parties could reasonably give to the clause in the specific circumstances and what they could reasonably expect of each other in this respect. Factors that influence the answer to this question are the part of society the parties belong to and the legal knowledge they have.[29] This means, for instance, that the technical language used in a business contract in a specific branch of industry will be interpreted differently than the everyday language used in a contract between two private persons.

Apart from the explicit clauses of the contract, there are other sources of obligations between parties. First of all, statutory law is such a source. There is a

---

28. Van *Elmbt v. Feierabend*, HR 29 May 1964, *NJ* 1965, 104.
29. This solution was first given in the *Haviltex* case (HR 13 March 1981, *NJ* 1981, 635).

difference between two kinds of statutory rules: rules that are obligatory, meaning that parties must follow them (on penalty of nullity if they do not) and rules that are permissive, meaning that parties can arrange things differently if they want. The second category only plays a role when parties do not make their own arrangements: for instance, if the place of the delivery of goods is not determined in a contract of sale, article 6:41 BW determines where the goods have to be delivered.

A second source of obligations is customary law: the unwritten rules that are accepted by the group in society in which there are frequent contractual relations. There are areas of commerce in which custom still plays a role, e.g. a sale at an auction is still concluded by raising one's hand at a given price. The courts will honour these rules, unless it is clear that the parties to a contract wanted to depart from the custom.

A third, steadily more important, source is the principle of reasonableness and equity *(redelijkheid en billijkheid)*. We already encountered the principle when discussing negotiations about contracts; it is relevant to all aspects of the law of obligations. It is explicitly connected to the content of contracts in article 6:248 BW: reasonableness and equity can supplement what parties have agreed to and it can set aside contractual clauses. Because of the special and pervasive role of this principle, I will come back to its meaning in section 5.

A special situation in which it is difficult to know what the obligations under a contract are, is a situation in which something happens which was not foreseen by either party. Is it fair to completely uphold the contract when there are such unforeseen circumstances? On the one hand, one might say that contracts are made with the implicit understanding that they will only be valid if there are no radically different circumstances (in the old European law, this was called the *clausula rebus sic stantibus*). On the other hand, one might say that contracts are made to ensure that all parties can depend on the contract to know what the other's obligations are, which is also, maybe even more, necessary in unforeseen circumstances. Dutch law takes the position that a judge should be able to (partly) set aside a contract, if there are unforeseen circumstances of such a nature that the other party could not reasonably or equitably expect the contract to be upheld (article 6:258 BW). This means that there must be a serious change in circumstances in which it is clear to both parties that performance of the contract would be unreasonable. As is apparent from the terminology ('reasonably and equitably'), this article of the Code is a special elaboration of the principle of reasonableness and equity, i.e. a *lex specialis*.

Until now, I have only spoken of the rights and obligations of the parties to a contract, but sometimes, a contract will also have consequences for others who are not involved in its making, for third parties. Dutch law accepts that a third party can derive a right or obligation from a special clause in a contract, if the contractual clause about this right or obligation has been accepted by the third party. For a situation that is the other way around, i.e. in which a party to a contract invokes a contractual term *against* a third party, acceptance is not an issue: then, it is a matter of what the third party should reasonably be bound to. One case in which the court judged that a third party was bound, concerned the storage of onions. The company who was storing the onions in its warehouse, noticed the onions were affected by insects and, with the permission of the owner of the onions, ordered the Roteb, the city's insect control service, to gas them with a kind of pesticide. Unfortunately, this also spoiled the onions, making them inedible. Roteb had excluded its liability only in the contract with the warehouse owner, but the court ruled that Roteb could also invoke this clause against the owner of the onions because he had given permission to take measures against the insects.[30] In short, there have to be substantial extra reasons to bind a third party to a contract between others.

4.8 Standard terms and consumer protection

A special kind of contractual terms are the so-called standard terms or general conditions: a standard set of rules made by one of the parties, which uses them in all its contracts of the same kind. General conditions have to be distinguished from the core clauses of a contract which define the core performance. Especially in consumer contracts, general conditions are an important and large part of the contract. If you buy a train ticket or open a bank account, the railway company or the bank will have a book full of general conditions that apply to your contractual relationship. Such standard terms are very useful for making commerce more efficient: it is not necessary to think about standard issues with every new transaction. There are, however, some drawbacks: because one of the parties did not have any influence on the making of the general conditions, there is the risk that the conditions will only be to the advantage of the party who makes them. The risk of unfair advantage is made even greater by the circumstance that general conditions are usually accepted without being read by the other party.

Because of the asymmetry in such contracts, there is detailed regulation of general conditions in Dutch law. General conditions may be used if they have been accepted by the other party, even if that party clearly did not know the content of the terms. However, a clause is subject to annulment, either if it is unreasonably onerous for the other party, or the user of the clause did not give the other party the opportunity to read the general conditions (article 6:233 BW). The most important ground for annulment is the first: an *unreasonably onerous* clause. This means that the clause is, in the circumstances of the particular contract, to the disadvantage of the other party, placing an unreasonably heavy burden on that party. Again, there is a link to the principle of reasonableness and equity: the rules about general conditions are seen as an elaboration, a *lex specialis*, of the principle for this particular kind of contract.

What kind of terms is seen as unreasonably onerous? On this point, a distinction must be made between consumer contracts and business contracts. For consumers, the legislator has drawn up two lists of terms of what is considered unreasonably onerous. The idea of making such lists was taken from German law which also uses this system. The so-called black list contains clauses which are forbidden because they are clearly unreasonable (article 6:236 BW). On this list are clauses like the

---

30. HR 7 March 1969, *NJ* 1969, 249.

following: clauses that exclude the right of the other party to set aside the contract, or that give the user the right to decide whether he has failed to perform. The second list, the grey list, contains clauses that are presumed to be unreasonable (article 6:237 BW). It includes clauses that give the user an extremely long period in which to perform, or that exclude the legal right to damages. The important difference between the two lists becomes apparent in court; a judge will always set aside a clause that is on the black list, while the user of a grey-listed clause has the opportunity to prove that it is not unreasonable in the circumstances. The burden of proof is on the user, but a grey-listed clause may be accepted if the judge finds the proof convincing.

The two lists are only applicable to consumer contracts, meaning a contract between a private person and a company. General clauses in business-to-business contracts can also be declared unreasonably onerous, on the basis of the general rule of article 6:233 BW, if the clauses are used by a large company in contracts with a small company (with less than fifty employees).

A special feature of the regulation of general clauses is the extra opportunity to complain that was created for consumer or branch organizations. They can ask the court of appeal in The Hague to declare a clause unreasonably onerous without a specific contractual relationship, i.e. to test the clause in the abstract. This opportunity has been used by the Dutch consumers association *(Consumentenbond)* against an electricity company which used the clause that it was not liable for damage resulting from a temporary power failure. The Supreme Court ruled that this was unacceptable.[31] The possibility of such complaints by representative organizations gives consumers extra protection; by creating such a right, the Dutch legislator underscores the importance they attach to protecting weaker parties in contract law.

4.9   The end of a contract

Contracts do not exist forever and many end as soon as they are made. The natural end for a contract is by performance: each party fulfils its obligation by performing what he promised to do. If I buy a bread at the bakery, the making of the contract coincides with its end: I promise to pay € 1 and the baker promises to deliver a loaf of bread, while simultaneously I hand him the money and he gives me the loaf. Of course, for us jurists, such contracts are fairly uninteresting: we like to consider the way things can go wrong. What happens when performance does not take place?[32]

In case of non-performance, the important issue is whether the non-performing party can be blamed for not fulfilling his obligation. If an artist has made a contract of sale concerning a particular painting and fails to deliver it at the agreed time, it makes a difference whether his failure or non-performance is due to the fact that he has already sold and delivered it to someone else or to the fact that lightning struck and destroyed the painting. In the first case, it is clear that the non-performance of his obligation can be attributed to the artist; in the second case, there is an outside

---

31. HR 16 May 1997, *NJ* 2000, 1 *(Consumentenbond v. EnergieNed and Vewin)*.
32. See C.J.H. Brunner & G.T. de Jong, *Verbintenissenrecht algemeen*, Deventer: Kluwer 1999, p. 98 ff.

cause for non-performance for which the artist is not to blame. The difference is important for the possible legal actions of the other party.

Another important question is whether performance is permanently impossible or just temporarily. In the example of the painting, both situations involved permanent impossibility: the painting already belonged to someone else in the first case, and it no longer existed in the second. Often, however, performance is only impossible for the time being, for instance, because a shipment of goods did not arrive in the harbour on time. The question is important because a creditor is obliged to notify the debtor that he is in default when there is temporary non-performance, while this is not required when non-performance is permanent. Notification of default is also necessary when impossibility is not an issue at all, i.e. if the debtor does not perform without a good reason.

A creditor has a number of rights he can exercise in case of non-performance (depending on the kind of non-performance), of which the following four are the most important. First, in case of temporary non-performance, he can demand specific performance, asking the debtor to do exactly what he is obliged to do. Secondly, the creditor can postpone his own performance: if the goods are not delivered on time, he can postpone paying for them. For the right to postponement, it is necessary that the two obligations are closely connected: if a creditor still needs to pay money for an earlier shipment of goods, he cannot postpone that payment on the basis of non-delivery of the later shipment.

Thirdly, the creditor can set aside the contract. This means that the obligations undertaken in the contract by both parties are ended. Setting aside the contract can be done whenever the performance by the debtor is lacking, regardless of the cause for non-performance. Setting aside the contract needs to be distinguished from the annulment of a contract discussed above. Annulment has retroactive force, because the contract should never have come into being due to some defect. Setting aside the contract merely ends the obligations. If one of the parties has already performed, there is a duty to repay when the contract is set aside. The difference between setting aside and annulment is relevant when a party goes bankrupt. If a painting is sold and the buyer goes bankrupt, the seller can get it back in case of annulment: it is as if the contract never existed and he was always the owner. In case of setting the contract aside, the seller merely has a claim on the buyer to return the painting as one of many creditors.

For the fourth right of a creditor, the right to claim damages, the cause is important: if the non-performance is not attributable to the debtor, the creditor does not have the right to damages. Damages can be claimed as a substitute for the performance and also for losses resulting from a delay or from attributable non-performance. Attributable non-performance is comparable to attribution of a tort in the sense that there is a similar distinction between fault and risk (article 6:75 BW). If a debtor is at fault, meaning that he clearly did not take the care he should have, non-performance is attributable. It is also attributable if the cause is at the debtor's risk, for instance, if a sub-contractor fails to perform or some equipment fails. To determine for what the debtor is responsible, Dutch law refers to the general opinion in society. For example, if an inexperienced carpenter builds a shed, his inexperience is no excuse for not building it right: we generally think that he should not have made the contract if he could not do the job properly.

5 The open system of Dutch private law

In the discussion of the law of obligations, a number of important legal rules have been discussed that can be characterized as open norms, i.e. as vague rules that are filled in flexibly when they are applied. Examples are the rule on tort (article 6:162 BW), or the rule on unreasonably onerous general clauses (article 6:233 BW): what counts as unlawful conduct, including violation of rules of proper social conduct, is an open category which is constantly being filled in specific cases; similarly, what is unreasonable to demand in a contractual general clause is also dependent on assessments of particular contractual relationships.

Because of the flexible character of open norms, they are regarded as a mechanism to achieve individual justice in law. Legal rules are abstract and general rules, which have to be applied equally to similar cases. An important disadvantage of general rules is that they do not fit the particulars of a case completely. Sometimes, this means that important details have to be neglected because they do not fit the description made by the rule and application of the rule does not do justice to the case. An open norm makes room for a correction of such unfair results.

In this respect, the most important open norm of Dutch law is the principle of *redelijkheid en billijkheid* or reasonableness and equity, which is invoked in many provisions throughout the Civil Code. Many other legal systems include a similar open norm functioning as a mitigating influence. As is to be expected in the case of an open norm, the Code does not give a definition of reasonableness and equity, although it does contain a number of things to take into account when one is trying to determine what is reasonable and equitable: general principles of Dutch law, current Dutch views about law and the societal and personal interests involved (article 3:12 BW). The broad scope of these considerations shows how 'open' the norm really is: it makes room for application of all legal principles and for the weighing of interests. The principle has a more prominent place in the current Dutch Civil Code than it had before, and since this part of the Code came into force, more reference is made to it in case law than before.[33]

The principle developed out of the Dutch notion of 'goede trouw', which is literally good faith, or *bona fides*. The Dutch concept of good faith has since long been divided into two components: subjective good faith and objective good faith. Subjective good faith refers to the state of mind of individual persons; for instance, a person buying a stolen bicycle without knowing that it was stolen buys in good faith. Objective good faith refers to a norm of conduct to which a person should conform: conduct contrary to good faith is conduct that goes against the norm that one should behave reasonably and equitably towards others. The principle of reasonableness and

---

33. Whether the rise of open norms is good or bad, is a matter of debate among Dutch jurists. I will discuss the debate later on in this section.

equity is based only on the second component, on objective good faith.[34] In the current Civil Code, only subjective good faith is called 'goede trouw', objective good faith is always referred to as 'redelijkheid en billijkheid'. Such a distinction in terminology for the subjective and objective component, is also made in German: *guter Glauben* and *Treu und Glauben* respectively. Other legal systems do not make the distinction in precisely the same way, although many continental European systems contain the idea of good faith either in general or more specifically as subjective good faith.[35]

5.1   The two functions of reasonableness and equity in contracts

A distinction has been made, first in case law and now in the Code, between two functions of reasonableness and equity: it can supplement or derogate from, or correct, (contractual) obligations (article 6:248 BW). With regard to the first function, the principle can supplement a contract whenever a problem arises for which there is no specific provision in the contract; then, a judge can use reasonableness and equity as a source for the obligations between parties and thus fill the gap in the contract. An example of this function is the case of a French wine seller who had a distribution contract with a Dutch import company and who wanted to end the contract. The relationship had existed over a hundred years and there were no explicit contractual conditions about ending it. The Supreme Court ruled that, on the basis of reasonableness and equity, the contract could only be ended if the wine seller had a good reason, which he did not.

The supplementary function has since long been accepted in Dutch law, but this is not the case with the second function of reasonableness and equity: the derogating or corrective function. This is because this second function means that reasonableness and equity is used against the explicit clauses of the contract: a clause can be set aside if its application is clearly against what is reasonable and equitable. It was first explicitly recognized by the Supreme Court in the case of *Saladin v. HBU*.[36] Saladin was a client at the HBU bank and often asked their advice on buying shares in the stock market. On one occasion, they advised him, without a request, to buy certain shares, saying that this was a 100% safe investment. The shares lost their value in the market and Saladin suffered a serious loss. The bank, however, had excluded liability explicitly. Although the Supreme Court ruled that HBU could invoke the exclusion of liability in this case, it also acknowledged the possibility that, under certain circumstances, reasonableness and equity can require that a party cannot invoke such a term in a contract even if it is an explicit part of the contract. Relevant circumstances are, among others: the seriousness of the blame of the party in the bank's position, the kind of contract that the term is part of, the degree to

---

34. See M. Hesselink, *De redelijkheid en billijkheid in het Europees privaatrecht* (summary in English), Deventer: Kluwer 1999, p. 27 ff.
35. See R. Zimmermann & S. Whittaker, *Good Faith in European Contract Law*, Cambridge: Cambridge University Press 2000.
36. HR 19 May 1967, *NJ* 1967, 261.

which the party in Saladin's position understood the meaning of the term. The corrective function of reasonableness and equity, as used in this case, has been codified, as mentioned, in article 6:248 BW. The catalogue of relevant circumstances that the Supreme Court gave in *Saladin v. HBU* is the beginning of a series of court cases in which different circumstances were recognized that can determine when the terms of a contract should be set aside on the basis of reasonableness and equity.

Although these two functions constitute the general role of reasonableness and equity in contract law, the principle has a broader scope, both within contract law and beyond. As I have indicated in the section on contract law, there are many specific provisions that have developed out of application of reasonableness and equity into a more specific rule of what is reasonable in a certain context. Examples of such contexts we already encountered are: precontractual negotiations, unforeseen circumstances and general conditions. Outside of contract law, the principle is also applicable; article 6:2 BW is the foundation for its application to the whole of the law of obligations, while article 6:216 BW stipulates that the rules on contract, including article 6:248 BW, are also applicable to multilateral juridical acts other than contracts. This means that reasonableness and equity is also relevant to company law, establishing limited or unlimited companies or partnerships and to parts of family law, such as the patrimonial aspects of marriage.

5.2   A debate on open norms

The central role of reasonableness and equity and the growing importance of open norms in general has given rise to a debate among legal scholars about the desirability of this development. The general discussion centres on the question whether open norms are good means of achieving development in law. The claim of proponents of open norms is that they enhance the flexibility of the law and therefore make it easier to accommodate change and achieve individual justice. Opponents of open norms claim that such norms obscure legal reasoning and thereby impede development and threaten legal certainty: reference to an open norm as a basis for a judicial decision does not really show the specific reasons for that decision and makes it difficult to use the decision for guidance about the way to behave in future. It also makes it difficult to criticize the decision. If a judge formulates a detailed rule in his decision, it is much easier to say precisely what is wrong with it, or so the opponents claim.[37]

Recently, the debate took a new direction with a specific focus on reasonableness and equity. A critic of open norms, Hesselink, argued that the special norm of reasonableness and equity is so open that it fails to give direction and is no more than a cover for the tasks of a judge. According to Hesselink, supplementing, correcting and interpreting contracts are simply things a judge has to do in cases about contracts; moreover, the open norm of reasonableness and equity does not tell him how to do it. The problem with this open norm is that it is too vague to give

---

37. J.M. Barendrecht, *Recht als model van rechtvaardigheid* (summary in English), Deventer: Kluwer 1992.

guidance to a judge. The only function the principle has, is to provide a cover for the creative activities of judges: they can say that what they decide is required by reasonableness and equity, while they are really only doing what they think best.[38]

This view has not gone unchallenged: especially the claim that reasonableness and equity is too vague to give any guidance has been disputed. Although it is recognized that the principle of reasonableness and equity alone is never sufficient to justify a legal decision, such authors say that a combination of the principle with a reference to the circumstances that make reasonableness and equity relevant can suffice. They also advance the argument that reasonableness and equity is not really such a vague norm, because it is embedded in the system of private law as a whole.[39]

Although opinion continues to differ about the exact nature of reasonableness and equity and its merit, it is clear that the principle is an important aspect of present Dutch private law. To grasp the system of this part of Dutch law, it is essential to understand the role of this principle.

5.3 Characteristics of Dutch private law

To conclude, I will return to the developments mentioned in the introduction to this chapter. One of these, the importance of reasonableness and equity, has just been explicitly addressed and is generally recognized as a distinguishing feature of Dutch private law at present. The other two, the protection of weaker parties and the allocation of risks, have remained more in the background.

Risk allocation is an idea that is most prominent in tort law: we saw that risk-based liability has a prominent place in the Dutch law of torts. The decision who has to pay for damages has become more related to the question in whose sphere of responsibility the consequences of the act should be placed than to the question whose fault the action is. However, the notion of risk is not limited to tort cases; it also plays a role in contract law. An important function of legal rules is to create certainty in legal relationships, so that people know what to expect and can rely on the rules to plan future activities. This also influences the allocation of risks; for instance, the regulation of error reflects the idea that someone who takes a gamble and does not investigate carefully has to bear the consequences himself. Contracts are also a means to spread risks: a smart person tries to minimize his own risk and liability and transfer it to the other party. One of the aims of the legal rules is to make sure that this does not unfairly burden the other party, as we saw in the discussion of the corrective function of reasonableness and equity.

The possibility of an uneven balance between parties brings us to the other trend of private law: protection of weaker parties. In contract law, there are many mechanisms that strengthen the position of persons who start off with a disadvantage. This is done at the level of groups who are vulnerable, such as consumers or

---

38. Hesselink, ibid (note 34), p. 443-448.
39. P. van Schilfgaarde, 'System, good faith and equity in the New Dutch Civil Code', *European Review of Private Law* 1997, p. 1-10.

employees, or at the level of the individual in a contractual relationship, such as a person who is in error. The principle of reasonableness and fairness may also be invoked in the interest of a vulnerable party. In tort law, the protection of weaker parties is clearly a leading principle in the regulation of traffic accidents.

A common characteristic of these developments, and one already recognized by Langemeijer, is the openness of private law to which they draw attention. Not only the existence of open norms, but also the reasoning in terms of interests makes room for moral and economic considerations which are not strictly part of law. Jurists in the Netherlands are becoming more aware of the importance of such fields, both practically and academically.

9 General Trends in Dutch Family Law

The Continuing Influence of Human Rights Conventions upon Dutch Family Law

Paul Vlaardingerbroek

1   Introduction

Before giving an impression of Dutch family law and the possible equalities and inequalities, it is good to note, that the Netherlands is just a very small (and flat) country (41,548 km²), but it is one of the most densely populated countries in the world. More than 16,2 million people live on these 42,000 square kilometres (thus more than 385 people per square kilometre). In 2002, we had 82,298 marriages and 33,643 divorces that were inscribed at the registrar's office. To give some more figures: in 2002, 203,194 children were born alive; 58,764 were born outside marriage (this is almost 29%; in 1994, almost 15% from all children were born outside marriage). The total number of couples living together outside marriage was 695,680; while 197,606 couples were living in a living arrangement with one or more children. In 2002, we had a total number of 410,553 single parent households with one or more children. The number of singles is also growing (in 2002: 2,354,302 persons).

Although we live in a small country, we form a mixture of tolerance and conservatism. Very conservative (for instance orthodox religious groups) and very modern groups can be found in our country, usually living next to each other peacefully. As a result of this large mix of cultures and beliefs, many different political and broadcasting unities exist in the Netherlands. The Netherlands have always been a multicultural society. From the religious viewpoint, Protestants were the majority in the North, whereas in the South the Catholics were the majority. Now, most of the Dutch do not go to church. Diversity also typifies professional activities. The Netherlands are not a homogeneous cultural whole. Diversity in terms of religious values and professional activity is its outstanding characteristic. This diversity can also be found in the broadcasting corporations and political groups. Even the last decade, the Netherlands can be seen as a country where the Islamic belief has rapidly grown among our inhabitants, thanks to the great number of inhabitants coming originally from Marocco, Turkey, China, Irak, Iran, Somalia, Vietnam, et cetera.

Thus, it is interesting to see how, in such a diverse country, family law has been codified and whether our family law (still) lays the foundations for this inequality between sexes, races and origins. Before we go to the general theme of this chapter, general trends in family law in the Netherlands, we have to be aware of the fact that in many other countries, family law is in motion too. At a supra-national level, the activities of the Council of Europe and the United Nations are important for us, especially because Dutch law can be superceded by international law. The impact and influence of the international conventions upon our Dutch law has been and still is very great. I will give examples of this later on.

The Council of Europe has many activities concerning the family, usually because the Committee of Ministers or the conferences of specialised ministers ask for action. Usually, the purpose of the Resolutions agreed by the Committee of Ministers, is to find general solutions to general family problems in the different Member States and to seek unity where possible.

For example, the purpose of Resolution (78)37 on the equality of spouses in civil law, is not to impose a particular system but to encourage each State to select, where appropriate, from among the solutions proposed, all of them non-discriminatory, the one closest to national customs associated with historical, social, economic and religious factors. When we look at the proposals, we can see the following:

– civil law should contain no provisions whereby one spouse is put in a more advantageous position than the other spouse by being designated to act as the head of the family or by being given the sole right either to take decisions concerning the other spouse or to represent this spouse;
– both spouses should have equal rights as regards freedom of movement, choice of occupation and choice of the common residence;
– equality in the choice of a family name;
– the removal of discrimination between spouses as regards marriage contracts and dotal property;
– equality of the spouses as regards contribution to household expenses;
– equality of rights and obligations as regards maintenance;
– equal responsibilities for their children, particularly in regard to their children's property, the choice of their surname and their legal representation.

With regard to most of these recommendations, there are interesting developments in Dutch family law.

In the Netherlands, there is not a specific Family Code, although a part of the Civil Code is reserved to family matters (Book 1 of the Civil Code). Besides this part of the Civil Code, family law (including child law) can be found in a lot of other codes and regulations.

In the following, I will give an overview of the most important issues in Dutch family law, such as the law on affiliation, marriage law and the law on divorce and the law with regard to parental authority. Besides, I will also deal with the impact of the human rights conventions on Dutch Family Law. Because it is impossible to describe the case law for every subject, I will limit myself to the most important trends and subjects. Before dealing with the legal aspects of family life, I will first spend a few words on family life in the Netherlands.

2   Family life in the Netherlands

In the Netherlands, 'family' and 'family life' are not limited to traditional concepts of the family. Apart from the traditional family of a man and a woman who are married and have children, the notion of a 'family' is – in the words of one of the former ministers – also used to describe *other primary living units in which the care and upbringing of children takes place*. As examples can be mentioned: single parent families, mostly a mother with her children, or persons living together, married or unmarried, of two opposite sexes or of the same sex. Regardless of the composition of the people living together, as soon as there are children to be raised, they are called 'a family' in the Netherlands.

The number of singles is growing, which can have several causes, such as the choice of people who live as a single, a growing number of divorced persons, widows and widowers, et cetera. As said before, in the Netherlands, there are already more than 1 million single parent families and there is a widespread tolerance in our society for unmarried couples. As for people of the same sex who prefer to live together, more than 30,000 homosexual and lesbian couples are living together – unmarried, married or as registered partners – on a durable basis, also caring for children.

In the opinion of the Dutch government, family life is considered to be an *absolutely private affair*. It is not considered to be the job of the government to interfere with the way in which people shape their life or their family life, *unless there is a very good reason like the interest of the children*. Recently, the government has made violence in the family (usually against women and children) into a new target of interference. Usually, interference in family life to protect these children is allowed in case parents or other educators maltreat or abuse their child(ren).

With regard to basic cultural values and beliefs, there is general acceptance in the Netherlands of the freedom of choice for the form of relationship. Cohabitators are generally seen and treated as equivalent to married couples. The Dutch Supreme Court decided on 19 October 1990[1] that there had been unjustified discrimination against homosexual couples, compared to heterosexual couples, in the right to marry, but the Supreme Court did not think it was the task of the judiciary to change this situation. The legislator then took the initiative to make new regulations for homosexual couples. At first, legislation made it possible for couples to register as partners at the registrar's office. This registration of partnership was allowed for homosexuals who could not marry and heterosexuals who did not want to marry. The registration of partnership did not have any effect for children who would be born in such a registered partnership.

However, notwithstanding these trends, the vast majority of people prefer for themselves the so-called 'traditional' arrangements. Interestingly, the family ethos is extremely strong concerning two core values: monogamy and (the intention of) staying together for a lifetime. In brief: the general adherence to family values is seen as a personal choice and therefore, in general, such a choice is tolerated.

---

1. *NJ* 1991, 129.

The consequence of structural changes in family life is that the sequences of a given standardized family cycle (marriage – children – empty nest – death of one spouse – living alone) are not followed in this order in a number of families. The number of families that transit through other life forms has increased. Hence the number of new kinds of households and other primary-life forms, wherein the child is no longer the main concern, has increased.

Nuclear families represented only 35% of all household forms at the beginning of the 1980s. In the near future, one third of all households will be of the nuclear family type, one third will be of the one-person variant and the remaining third will be made up by other household forms. If social policy remains unchanged, it is expected that, at the beginning of the 21st century, half of all households in the Netherlands will be of the one-person type. These changes and forecasts are not different from those found in other Western European countries.

3   Family life and the law

The rules on family law can be found in Book 1 of our Civil Code (BW). This code was enacted in 1838 and is based on a mixture of Roman, French and old national Dutch law. This Civil Code was modernized several times, but since we have had a growing influence of human rights on the Dutch legal system in the last few decades, the legislator is confronted with great problems to adjust our code to the case law, especially in the field of family law. Although Dutch law is based on statute, it is interesting to note that judge-made law is becoming ever more important. The influence of human rights on Dutch law has been enormous, but especially article 8 of the European Convention on Human Rights and Fundamental Freedoms (ECHR) has had a great influence on Dutch family law.[2] The impact of the International Convention on the Rights of the Child is growing.

In the last 25 years, the Supreme Court in the Netherlands *(Hoge Raad)* has given extensive interpretations to some rather rigid laws by applying especially the ECHR and the International Covenant on Civil and Political Rights (ICCPR). The scope of the human rights conventions that have been ratified by the Netherlands, has been and continues to be widened in such a way that the sky seems to be the limit. Important issues that have been dealt with by the Supreme Court are: equality between men and women, the legal status of children born within and outside marriage, the legal position of the biological father, access rights of family members to children, the consequences of child protection measures, the legal consequences of divorce, the rights of the mentally disabled, et cetera. In this chapter, the examples of these trends in case law, usually followed by legislation, are taken from the fields of affiliation, surname, custody, access and marriage.

The ECHR is frequently invoked in the Netherlands, as it is a directly applicable law by virtue of the Constitution, and therefore takes precedence over national

---

2. Articles 12 and 14 ECHR and article 26 of the International Covenant for Civil and Political Rights (ICCPR) play an important role too.

legislation. Hence the Convention is often used to challenge the validity of legislation. This is also necessary because the Convention must be invoked before the domestic courts to preserve the option of a subsequent appeal to the European Court of Human Rights.

The Convention is designed to secure the 'collective enforcement' of human rights and fundamental freedoms. 'Respect for family and private life' within the meaning of article 8 ECHR means primarily that public authorities must refrain from arbitrary interference in the lives of individuals and families. This negative obligation on public authorities is set out in article 8(2) ECHR. But 'respect' for family life may also include a *positive obligation* on the part of public authorities. In *Marckx* (at paragraph 31 of the judgement), the European Court decided that in so far as a positive obligation exists, it constitutes an incentive for the (Belgian) government to bring its legislative system in line with the Convention. This opinion has been repeated in many other decisions.

The problem with this approach is that the whole Dutch code has to be changed to achieve conformity with the case law of our Supreme Court and of the Court of Human Rights in the field of family law, as article 8 itself seems to contain a whole code of family law. In many cases, the Dutch judges must make their own decisions, because statute does not provide answers to new problems such as surrogate motherhood, access rights of persons other than the divorced parent of the child and parental rights for unmarried parents, or because the legislation has become obsolete. In *Marckx*, the UK judge of the Court of Human Rights, Sir Gerald Fitzmaurice, dissented from the view that article 8 is not intended to settle the legal position of infants. He spoke of 'a misguided endeavour to read – or rather introduce – a whole code of family law into article 8 of the convention'.

Without doubt, article 8 ECHR, often read in conjunction with article 14 ECHR, has been the most important factor in the Netherlands, generating changes in the field of case law and leading to efforts to modernize legislation in the field of family and child law. However, articles 5, 6, 12 and 13 ECHR have also been important. The same can be said of article 26 of the International Covenant on Civil and Political Rights (ICCPR) and several articles in the UN Convention on the Rights of the Child (UNCRC).

Article 8 ECHR is a rather vaguely formulated right. Its contours are unclear, but that also makes it possible to develop its interpretation. Article 8 ECHR says:

'a. Everyone has the right to respect for his private and family life (...).
b. There shall be no interference by a public authority with the exercise of this right except such as is in accordance with the law and is necessary in a democratic society (...) for the protection of health or morals, or for the protection of the rights and freedoms of others.'

Although the (former) European Commission and the European Court of Human Rights have both interpreted the concepts of 'family life' and 'private life' quite strictly, the Dutch courts, led by the Supreme Court, have broadened the scope of article 8. A key requirement is a link which can be considered to establish family life.

This means that there must have been a close relationship, a kind of 'effective family life'. Or, in the words of the European Court in *Keegan vs Ireland* 26 May 1994, PubECHR A 290, NJ 1995, 247:

'44. The Court recalls that the notion of the "family" in this provision is not confined solely to marriage-based relationships and may encompass other de facto "family" ties where the parents are living together outside of marriage (see, inter alia, the Johnston and Others v. Ireland judgment of 18 December 1986, Series A no. 112, p. 25, § 55). A child born out of such a relationship is ipso jure part of that "family" unit from the moment of his birth and by the very fact of it. There thus exists between the child and his parents a bond amounting to family life even if at the time of his or her birth the parents are no longer co-habiting or if their relationship has then ended (see, mutatis mutandis, the Berrehab v. the Netherlands judgment of 31 June 1988, Series A no. 138, p. 14, § 21).
45. In the present case, the relationship between the applicant and the child's mother lasted for two years during one of which they co-habited. Moreover, the conception of their child was the result of a deliberate decision and they had also planned to get married (...). Their relationship at this time had thus the hallmark of family life for the purposes of Article 8. The fact that it subsequently broke down does not alter this conclusion any more than it would for a couple who were lawfully married and in a similar situation. It follows that from the moment of the child's birth there existed between the applicant and his daughter a bond amounting to family life.'

In *Kroon v. the Netherlands* (27 October 1994, PubECHR A 297-C) the European Court decided:

'30. A child born of such a relationschip is ipso jure part of that "family unit" from the moment of its birth and by the very fact of it (see the Keegan judgment, ibid.). There thus exists between Samir and Mr Zerrouk a bond amounting to family life, whatever the contribution of the latter to his son's care and upbringing.'

Other decisions of the European Court also recall that although the object of article 8 is essentially that of protecting the individual against arbitrary interference by the public authorities, it does not merely compel the State to abstain from such interference: in addition to this primarily negative undertaking, there may be positive obligations inherent in an effective respect for private life:

'These obligations may involve the adoption of measures designed to secure respect for private life even in the sphere of the relations of individuals between themselves (X and Y v. the Netherlands, 26 March 1985, Series A no. 91, p. 11, § 23). The boundaries between the State's positive and negative obligations under Article 8 do not lend themselves to precise definition. The applicable principles are nonetheless similar. In particular, in both instances regard must be had to the fair balance which has to be struck between the competing interests; and in both contexts the State enjoys a certain margin of appreciation (Mikulic cited above, § 58).'[3]

The consequence of such a relationship is that for example the non-custodial parent will have the right of access to his or her child. The mutual enjoyment by parent and child of each other's company constitutes a fundamental element of family life. Article 8 of the ECHR is now used in almost every case, where the claimant seeks the right to a remedy which is not currently available under national law. In the following sections, we shall see several examples of the importance of case law in this respect.

'Family life' in article 8 is an autonomous concept, which refers not only to family life *de jure*, but also to family life *de facto*. Family life comprises all kinds of close relationships, such as kinship and foster parenthood. The mutual enjoyment by parent and child of each other's company constitutes a fundamental element of family life. The notion that these legal ties (the family relationship) will not be terminated by reason of the fact that the child is educated elsewhere (e.g. because it is taken into public care or lives with foster parents), has generated *a whole code of judge-made law* in my opinion.

So, the importance of especially the European Convention has been and still is enormous. However, there are more treaties which may have a direct influence upon national laws. Other international family law standards are also applied in the European States, such as treaties or rules from the United Nations, like the Convention for the recovery of maintenance for children, the nationality of married women and the Convention on the Rights of the Child. Also the Hague Conventions of the Hague Conference on private international law are very important (like the conventions on intercountry adoption and international child abduction). These Hague conventions provide solutions to family law problems with a foreign element, in particular dealing with jurisdiction, recognition and enforcement and cooperation between the States. The work of the International Commission on Civil Status is promoting international cooperation in the field of civil status and assisting States to improve the functioning of their civil status services. Looking at the impact for national family law in the different states, the role of these international conventions must not be underestimated, although these conventions always form a compromise between more modern and more traditional opinions. Some countries in Europe tend to be of others ahead in the field of family law. Nevertheless, notwithstanding the different languages, different legal systems and different cultures between the States in Europe, a general trend is the growing cooperation in trying to find and develop Europan standards. This is done by assisting and encouraging the (nowadays 40) States of the European Council.[4] But, as said before, all Council of Europe States are bound to comply with certain minimum standards. So, different legal systems or traditions will not be sufficient reasons for non-compliance. The standards that are

---

3. See *Odièvre v. France*, 26 February 2003, Appl. No. 42326/98, in consideration nr. 40.
4. Margaret Killerby, Family Law in Europe, in: *Liber Amicorum Marie-Thérèse Meulders-Klein, Droit comparé des personnes et de la famille*, Bruxelles: Bruylant 1998, p. 353.

developed, must be applied in all countries, although at present in some countries, the national law may discord with these standards. It is the task of the European Commission and the European Court to protect the human rights of the individual citizens in these countries. If a State really infringes the rights set forth in the European Convention, the State will be condemned. In severe cases, the State will even have a problem with its participation in the Council if the State's policy is to violate the human rights (e.g. public discrimination of ethnic groups). In the field of family law, the European Social Charter is also important, where Part 1-16 provides: 'The family as a fundamental unit of society has the right to appropriate social, legal and economic protection to ensure its full development.'

4 Trends in the law on affiliation

In all western industrialized countries, the 1960s marked a turning-point, especially in matters of demography: a decline in the birth rate, fewer marriages and more cohabitation, a growing number of separations and divorces and consequently an increasing number of children born outside wedlock or living with only one parent or with a parent and a stepparent. At that time, it was a straightforward task to describe the rule of affiliation. The following is a brief summary of the legal issues.

Articles 7 and 8 of the UN Convention on the Rights of the Child indicate that children shall be registered immediately after birth and shall have the right to know their parents and the right to preserve their identity including family relations as recognized by law. In most European countries, it is a problem to find a good solution to improve the status of the child born out of wedlock, because it is difficult to make arrangements for the position of the father. The establishment and legal consequences of parentage are one of the main issues in European family law at the moment. Any discrimination between children born inside marriage and children born out of wedlock should be forbidden. Article 10 of the European Convention on the legal status of children born out of wedlock states: '(...) the marriage between the father and the mother of a child born out of wedlock shall confer on the child the legal status of a child born in wedlock.' Article 10, paragraph 1 of the European Convention on adoption states: 'Adoption confers on the adopted person in respect of the adopter the rights and obligations of every kind that a child born in lawful wedlock has in respect of his father and mother.' And more broadly, article 8 of the European Convention on Human Rights protects the rights of children born out of wedlock, especially the rights of inheritance. If the rights of inheritance of a child born out of wedlock are restricted, the European Court has held that this is a violation of the Convention.[5]

In all societies the status of the father in legislation has been under discussion. The starting point in this discussion has always been the same natural phenomenon,

---

5. In *Marckx v. Belgium* (1979), *Johnston and others v. Ireland* (1986), *Vermeire v. Belgium* (1991) and *Inze v. Austria* (1987).

namely procreation. The diversity of social, legal and cultural standards has lead to different solutions to the questions:
– Who decides on procreation?
– To whom is the child affiliated?
– Who exercises authority over the child?

In general, the mother plays a key role in these issues. The law relating to parentage and its effects is essential in all societies and in all ages, whether it is laid down in statutes, in case law or in unwritten law. The usual triad: father-mother-child has changed into a new triad: social parents-genetic/biological parents-child. Thanks to the case law of the European Court, the status of the social parents has improved. Where in the old days the biological/genetic parents had all the rights, now more attention is given to the rights of those who have 'family life' with a child. But we should also note that a difference must be made between the biological mother (the woman who gives birth to a child) and the genetic mother (the child was born from her egg). In the Netherlands, the legislation makes a difference between the biological father and the begetter. The begetter is always the biological father, but the biological father is not always the begetter. The Dutch legislator made this difference to allow a difference in legal consequences between semen donors and begetters. A begetter is (financially) responsible for his child, whereas a semen donor (who did not have sexual intercourse with the mother) cannot be sued for child support.

In theory, maternity is always known and in almost all European countries it results automatically from the fact of the birth, or of the registration of the name of the mother on the birth certificate,[6] the establishment of maternity by recognition or legal proceedings (Belgium, Italy, Luxemburg and Spain) or by the possession of facts in proof of civil status (the so-called 'possession d'état' in France and Luxemburg). In France, it is possible for a woman in need to have her child discreetly fostered or adopted. In that case, the name of the biological (and/or genetic) mother is unknown.[7] So in some countries, the child can be registered as a child 'born of an unknown mother' or 'under X', i.e. to keep the maternity secret on the birth certificate. However, this possibility enables the mother to deprive the child of his mother and also of his father. The child is therefore condemned to live its life without knowing its roots, as 'nobody's child'. The question arises, if this possibility is in accordance with the right of the child to know its identity, which to my opinion includes the right of the child to know its origin.

In general, it can be said that maternity can be established more easily than fatherhood. Establishing fatherhood raises far more complex problems and this is the case in all European countries. With regard to fatherhood, the law has to work with presumptions and with facts. The presumption of the paternity of the husband is laid

---

6. This is not the case in France and Italy, when the mother is unmarried.
7. The European Court of Human Rights has recently decided that this anonimity of the mother is not against article 8 ECHR. See ECHR in *Odièvre v. France,* 26 February 2003, Appl. No. 42326/98. I regret this decision because the child is an object of its mother's decision and can be seriously traumatized by not mentioning the name/identity of the biological parent(s).

down in most legislation. Paternity of the husband is established in case the mother is married at the time of her birth. The man to whom she is married becomes the legal father of the child. This is the case in all countries. However, in some countries, a more liberal approach to the establishment of true (i.e. biological) paternity can be seen. If the husband is not the biological father of the child, the question arises who is authorized to contest the legal paternity. Is it possible for the true father, the mother, the child or a third party to contest paternity?

In some countries, it is possible to abolish the presumption of paternity by way of a judgement or a petition in proceedings for divorce or legal separation. This is the case if the child has been born after this judgement (the Netherlands) or if the child is born more than 300 days after the spouses' judicial separation order and less than 180 days after the final rejection of the petition or the condonation (article 313 French Civil Code). In more general terms, the presumption does not apply when the spouses are living apart, legally separated or engaged in divorce or separation proceedings at the time of conception[8] or even, under certain conditions, if the child was conceived before marriage, as is the case in Denmark, Portugal and Spain.

In all cases where presumption of paternity of the husband does not apply, there is the possibility of substituting another paternity. This can be done voluntarily or legally.

In some countries, the presumption of paternity cannot only be contested by the presumed legal father, mother or child, but even by third parties. The true father may let his paternity be substituted for the husband's without first contesting it. The proof of non-paternity can be provided by all means, especially medical tests (blood test, DNA test). However, in some countries, it is impossible to sue to contest paternity when the husband has consented to artificial insemination (or any other act intended to result in procreation, or by giving his authorization to sexual intercourse from his wife with another man; approval of adultery). The time for the mother to contest the paternity of her husband is shorter than that allowed to the husband or to the child. The idea behind this discrimination is that the mother is always aware of the birth and the underlying facts (although it is possible that she does not know exactly who was the begetter of her child, e.g. when she had sexual intercourse with several men around the time of conception).

To conclude, in most countries, we can see a growing tendency to make use of two principles to establish paternity. The first consists of more openness to everyday reality in establishing paternity, i.e. ongoing interaction between the relevant persons is one of the founding principles of paternity. This in turn offers more possibilities to contest paternity for the persons involved: father, mother and child. The second principle might be called 'the biological way', which consists of a more liberal attitude to establish paternity.

Paternity in case of birth outside wedlock
As we have seen before, the European Convention on the Legal Status of Children

---

8. This is the case in Denmark, Ireland, the United Kingdom and Spain.

born out of Wedlock and the European Convention on Adoption require the laws of States to treat children born out of wedlock and adopted children as children born in wedlock, for most purposes. The same can be said of the UN Convention on the Rights of the Child and of the European Convention on Human Rights.

Of course, it is easier to establish parentage if the mother is married by presuming that her husband – at the time of birth of the child – will be the biological father of her child. It is still the case in every legal system that a father is automatically acquired by the fact of the mother's being married at the time of conception (or birth), whereas paternity outside marriage has to be established by an act or by judicial proceedings. Paternity outside marriage never having been presumed, the usual methods of establishing paternity have been voluntary recognition (acknowledgement) and legal decision.

New legislation now widely accepts suits to decide paternity and proof by all methods. If the mother so desires, the father can thus always be sued, at least for child support.

In Europe, three different models to establish paternity outside marriage can be distinguished, namely: free recognition, compulsory paternity, or recognition with consent of the father, the mother and the child.

In case of free recognition, the child can only be recognized if the father wishes to do so. This is only forbidden in the case of children born of adultery or incest. It is not needed that the mother (and/or the child) consents with the recognition. They do not have the right of veto (this is the case in French law).

In the Nordic countries, paternity can be established, even against the will of the mother and the child, e.g. by threatening her to diminish financial support by the local authorities. The idea behind this approach is to protect the mother and the child from the irresponsibility of the father. A second idea behind this may be the need of the State to diminish as much as possible the financial expenses of the State. Another reason can be found in German law: according to article 6.5 and 2.1 of the Basic law, children have a constitutional right to know their origin.

The third, and most widespread, approach to legal recognition is the right of the mother and the child (when the child has reached a certain age; in the Netherlands: 12 years) to consent or the right to veto the recognition. In the countries which know this system, the child will be represented by a special representative (legal guardian, guardian ad litem or special curator) and in some countries the consent of the mother and of the child can be replaced by a legal decision at the request of the man who wants to recognize. The basis of this system, although there can be many differences between the different countries, can be found in Belgium, Germany, Greece, Ireland, Luxemburg, the Netherlands and the United Kingdom.

In the Netherlands, until 1 April 1998, the mother had to give consent to a man to recognize her child (she had the right of absolute veto). However, with regard to the right of family life of the biological father in Dutch case law, a change has been introduced in the event of the mother refusing without a valid reason. In that case, the man has to state that there has been 'family life' between himself and the child (HR 8 April 1988, NJ 1988, 170; HR 18 May 1990, NJ 1991, 374 & 375). The so-called 'absolute veto' of the mother of the child had become a 'veto with a suspensory effect'.

At the request of the man who wants to recognize her child and who can prove that he has enjoyed 'family life' with the child, the judge may decide that the mother's consent may be overridden by a decision of the court. This case law has been laid down in the new law on affiliation which entered into force on 1 April 1998.

Articles 7 and 8 of the UN Convention on the Rights of the Child provide that every child shall have the right from birth to a name and the right to preserve his or her identity including the name. Most of the laws relating to family names differ considerably in Europe. Therefore, the question of the choice of family name has been dealt with by a number of Europan instruments. The general idea is now that both legal parents have equal rights as to the family name to be given to their children. Paragraph 17 of Resolution 37 on the equality of spouses in Civil Law recommends that the States

'be guided for instance by one of the following systems:

i. when the parents do not have a common family name:

a. to allow the child to take the family name of the parent whose name he was not granted by law;

b. to allow the family name of the children to be chosen by the common agreement of the parents;

ii. when the parents have, by the addition of their family names, a common family name: the choice of a common family name must be in agreement with the other spouse, in particular the family name which has been either chosen by them or by the operation of law, the omission of part of this family name should not lead to discrimination concerning the choice of the family name or names to be omitted'.

To conclude, in most countries, we can see a growing tendency to more truth in establishing paternity, with more possibilities to establish paternity and to make it possible that the biological father will be the legal father. Another trend is to give the parents more freedom in choosing the surname of the child. In the traditional law of most European countries, the name of the legal father was decisive for the child's surname. Only if the child did not have a legal father, would the child bear his mother's surname. Now, in a growing number of countries, the parents have an equal right to choose the child's surname, which is usually a choice between the name of the father and the name of the mother and not a free choice. The right of non-discrimination entails that the parents should be given discretion in choosing the child's family name. Discrimination between children born out of wedlock, adopted children and children born in wedlock has been diminished as much as possible. Children born out of wedlock, adopted children and children born in wedlock have, with some exceptions,[9] obtained the same rights as children born or conceived within marriage.[10]

---

9. These exceptions pertain to the access to inheritances and to the father's relation to the child. So, in some legal systems, parental authority is a prerogative of the unmarried mother, to be shared with the father only with her consent or in which the parental authority can only be transferred to him in exceptional circumstances.

10. Harry Willekens, Longterm developments in Family Law in Western Europe, in: John Eekelaar & Thandabantu Nhlapo (ed.), *The Changing Family. Family Forms & Family Law*, Oxford: Hart Publishing 1998, p. 54.

4.1 Paternity and affiliation in the Netherlands

Legal maternity and paternity
Since 1 April 1998, Dutch written law no longer distinguishes between legitimate and illegitimate children. However, the unjustified discrimination between them already disappeared after the so-called *Marckx* decision.[11] We now speak of children with legal ties to the mother and to the father or only to the mother and of course to their family members.

Mother is the woman who gives birth to a child or the woman who adopts a child (article 1:198 BW).

Father is the man:
– who is married to the woman who gave birth to the child at the time of its birth;
– who has died less than 306 days before the birth of the child (the presumed paternity of the husband of the child's mother);
– who has recognized a child;
– whose fatherhood has been determined in court;
– who has adopted the child (article 1:199 BW).

Contesting paternity
If the child is born within marriage or within 306 days after the death of the man with whom the mother of the child was married, the man automatically becomes the father of the child. However, if he is not the begetter of the child or did not give his wife permission to an act which led to the pregnancy and birth of the child, his paternity can be contested before the district court, provided that the father is not the biological father of the child. This contest can be done by the mother, the father or the child itself. Of course, if there is any doubt, the court can order a DNA test.

The mother can contest marital paternity within one year after her child's birth. The legal father can do the same within one year after the moment he became aware that he is possibly not the biological father of the child. The child can contest the marital paternity of his father within three years after becoming aware of the fact that his legal father is not his biological father; when the child is a minor and he finds out that his father is not his biological father, he can contest the paternity within three years after having become adult.

The court will reject the claim if the father has consented to donor insemination or to another deed that could have led to a child being conceived, or if the father knew about the pregnancy before he married the woman, unless she deceived him about the identity of the begetter (article 1:200 BW). If the claim is adjudicated, it means that the child loses its legal father.

The biological father himself cannot contest another man's (presumption of) legal paternity.

---

11. ECHR 20 June 1979, Series A.

In general, the filiation itself cannot be contested if the child has a *de facto* status of this parent or these parents (article 1:209-211 BW).

Recognition

Another possibility to establish fatherhood between the child and a man, who is not married to the child's mother at the time of its birth, is the recognition of the child. Recognition is a legal act aimed at establishing legal filiation links with a child, irrespective of its biological link with the child, or just an acknowledgement of an already existing link between them. However, if the man who recognized is not its biological father, his paternity can later be contested because he is not the biological father of the child. The law stipulates certain requirements, a violation of which renders the recognition void (article 1:204 BW).[12]

Recognition is only possible if the child does not have two legal parents. Any man older than 16 years and unmarried may recognize the child if the child does not have two parents.

Recognition is not valid if there is an absolute marriage impediment between the mother and the man, e.g. if they are brother and sister or father and daughter. The mother (until her child has reached the age of 16) and the child itself (if it is 12 years or older) must give written consent to the recognition. If each of them, or both, refuses to give consent, such consent can be substituted by the consent of the district court, provided that the man is the begetter of the child and the recognition would not disturb the relationship between the mother and her child and is not against the child's best interests. Another requirement for valid recognition is that a married man cannot recognize a child born outside his marriage, unless the court has established that this man has, or has had, a marriage-like relationship with the mother of the child, or that the man has a close bond, family life according to article 8 ECHR.

The man, who recognized the child, provided that he is not its biological father and the recognition was the result of duress, mistake, fraud or abuse, can reverse the recognition. The mother and the child almost have the same rights as the presumed father to deny the parenthood of the father, with retrospective effect till the date of birth or the date of the recognition.

Judicial establishment of paternity

Another way to create paternity between the child and his father is the judicial establishment of paternity.[13] Article 1:207 BW provides for the possibility of judicial establishment of paternity concerning the begetter or the partner of the mother who consented to a deed that could have led to a child being conceived (e.g. donor insemination). The court is empowered to order a DNA test if the man refuses to acknowledge that he is the biological father of her child. The mother can bring a

---

12. See further: Masha Antokolskaia, Recent Developments in Dutch Filiation, Adoption and Joint Custody Law, in: *Familia, Anno II*, fasc. 3-2002, p. 781-805.
13. Not to be mistaken with the possibility for the mother to sue the biological father for maintenance for her child, according to article 1:394 BW. The sole result of this procedure is the support of the child by its father.

paternity suit before the court within five years after her child's birth, or within five years after she found out the real identity or right address of the begetter. However, she can only sue him until her child has reached the age of 16. The child itself can commence proceedings without any time limits.

Judicial establishment of paternity is not possible if the mother of the child and the man are related within the prohibited degrees of consanguinity, or against a man who is under the age of 16.

The judicial establishment has a retroactive effect till the day of birth of the child.

Legal consequences of filiation
The law gives many legal consequences to legal parenthood, such as:
– the fact that both parents are invested with joint parental authority (article 1:246 BW) and that they can choose between both their surnames for their first child;
– the fact that parents and children are mutually obliged to pay for the costs of living, care and education (article 1:392 sect. 1 BW);
– the fact that parents and children are mutually and totally entitled to each other's inheritance according to testate succession rules (Book 4 of the Civil Code).

4.2 Adoption

General remarks
Originally, adoption was introduced in 1956 in Dutch law as a measure of child protection. Since then however, adoption has become more and more a special legal construction of filiations. An adoption can only be granted providing that it is in the child's best interests and it is clear that the child has nothing more to expect from its parents. The adoption is established by a decision of the district court and not by contract between the natural and the adopting parents (article 1:227 BW).

Conditions for adoption
On 1 April 1998, the (rather) old limitation of adoption by married couples only was set aside, and adoption is now equally available for cohabiting (married or not) couples and for singles. With the introduction of same-sex marriage, Dutch legislation on adoption has also changed since 1 April 2001. Two women or two men may adopt a child as of that date.[14] However, this applies only to children who are habitually residents in the Netherlands. Adoption of a child from another country will still only be possible for married couples of different sexes.

Social parents can adopt 'their' child. This possibility makes social parents into legal parents. In most cases of adoption by singles, the partner of the parent will adopt her/his child (so called partner-adoption and formerly called stepparent-

---

14. The government answered the question of whether this new Adoption Act is not rather a means for homosexual couples to create parenthood, by stating that the law of descent concerns relationships which are the result of a biological link between the parents and the child, while in the case of adoption, the relationship between the parent(s) and the child is based upon care, which relationship justifies legal recognition.

adoption), i.e. adoption by the partner or new partner of the child's mother or father. In case of partner-adoption, the new partner of one of the parents adopts the child. The family ties with this parent remain in existence. Only the family ties with the other parent (if that parent or that tie is present, e.g. in the case of a legal father) are broken. In practice, the partner was often already living as a family with the parent and one or more children. The duration of cohabitation and caring for the child are therefore the same for the partner (stepparent) as for adoption by two persons. The stepparent must have been living with the other parent for at least three years and must have cared for the child for at least one year. This last demand is not necessary if the child is born in a lesbian relationship and the female partner of the mother wants to adopt the child. A single must have taken care of a child for at least three years (article 1:228 sect. 1 sub f BW).

The interests of the child are paramount and come first. Another important condition is that the child has nothing more to expect from its birth parent or parents in their capacity as parent. A couple wanting to adopt must be able to prove that they have lived together for at least three years and have cared for the child for at least a year.
A child of 12 years or older has the right to veto adoption, while a younger child can be heard if the judge determines that it is aware of its interests. From the side of the parents, it is sufficient that they do not contest the adoption and that they do not have custody at the time of the adoption procedure. Under certain conditions, objections by the parents can be overruled (article 1:228 sect. 2 BW).

Adoption leads to cutting off the links between the child and its former parents to establish new legal links with the social parents. In case of adoption by the then partner of the parent, we call this partner-adoption. Thanks to adoption, new legal family ties come into being between the child and the adoptive parent(s). The family ties with the original parent(s) cease to exist. This makes adoption a drastic measure. The starting point in the legislation is that adoption must only be possible if the original family ties cannot be maintained. For this reason, adoption may only take place if a number of conditions are met. The request for an adoption must be submitted to the court. The help of a solicitor is necessary.

The conditions for the *adoptive child* are the following:
- The child must be a *minor*.[15]
- It must *not* be a legal *grandchild* of one of the adopting parents, i.e. in the Netherlands, a grandparent's adoption is not permitted.
- From the age of 12 onwards, the child has an absolute right to *veto* his/her own adoption.
- Children of 12 *years* and older have to be *heard* by the judge about the intended adoption. In this hearing, the judge tries to establish an opinion on whether the child has been adequately informed about his/her position as a foster child who

---

15. The Court of Appeal in Amsterdam however allowed an adoption of a girl, who was 20 years old at the time of the first demand for adoption (Hof Amsterdam 16 March 2000, *NJkort* 2000, 39).

probably will be adopted in the near future. The philosophy behind this kind of information gathering is that the child might be traumatized severely if an outsider were accidentally to tell him about his/her adoptive status. It is thought much better for adoptive children to be told by their adopting parents that they are in fact not their biological children. This *information duty* is not laid down in the statutes; it has been developed in legal practice.[16]

Consequences of adoption

With the adoption order, the child acquires the legal status of a child of the adoptive parent(s) (article 1:229 BW). The child loses all legal ties with his/her original biological parents and family. Revoking an adoption is possible. The only person who can revoke an adoption is the adopted child itself, two years but no longer than five years after he/she reaches majority. The revocation has to be in the best interest of the young adult (article 1:231 and 232 BW). Revocation hardly ever happens. Adoption of stepchildren of the other partner is possible (article 1:228 sect. 2 BW). Most Dutch adoptions nowadays concern foreign children, especially from China or from South American countries. Those adoptions are not so much a matter of private law regulations as of the policy in respect of aliens. The future adoptive parents have to deal with the ministerial circulars concerning aliens and the Act on the placement of foreign children for adoption (1988) operative from 15 July 1989. This law provides not only the conditions to adopt for the future adoptants but also rules pertaining to persons or agencies that mediate in cases like these. There is a licensing system in this respect.

5   Trends in custody/parental authority

In Paragraph 1 of Principle 1 of Recommendation No. R 4 on parental responsibilities (European Parliament), the parental responsibilities have been defined as 'a collection of duties and powers which aim at ensuring the moral and material welfare of the child, in particular by taking care of the person of the child, by maintaining personal relationships with him and by providing for his education, his maintenance, his legal representation and the administration of his property'. These responsibilities not only seek to ensure the welfare of the child but also to respect equality between parents. The Recommendation provides that parental responsibilities for a child of their marriage should automatically belong jointly to both parents. However, some of these principles do distinguish between married and unmarried couples. It is allowed that States make differences for children born out of wedlock, for instance by restricting an automatic attribution of parental responsibilities to the mother.

One of the most far-reaching trends is the question of joint parental authority after divorce. Here again, the UN Convention on the rights of the child is leading, where article 9 (I) provides: 'A child shall not be separated from his or her parents against their will, except when competent authorities subject to judicial review determine, in

---

16. See Masha Antokolskaya, ibid, p. 796-799.

accordance with applicable law and procedures, that such separation is necessary for the best interests of the child.' Usually, a child will reside with both parents. However, there may be certain exceptions such as when a child over a certain age (usually at the age of 16) has the right to determine his or her residence, when the parents of a child are separated or divorced or when the child is to live with others than the parents (i.e. with foster parents or in a children's home).

In 1984, the European Commission decided in the case of a complaint by two unmarried parents who could not receive joint custody (EC 9519/81, 15 March 1984, *X versus FRG,* not published), that: 'it is not discriminatory to pass special legislation concerning the care and custody of children born out of wedlock, such legislation is justified by the greater difficulties met by these children if the relationship of their unmarried parents ends' (ECRM 15 March 1984, No. 9639/82, D and R 36, p. 130; ECRM 15 March 1984, No. 9519/81).

Under the influence of article 8 ECHR, however, in many countries, judges granted joint custody to both parents or even imposed it on them if it was in the best interest of the child. They even extended this to the principle in law that, in case of legal separation or divorce, the judge had to award the exercise of parental authority to only one of the two parents, whereby the other parent only retained the right to supervision, the right to personal contact and/or the right to be informed or consulted by the other parent. So, judges opened up the possibility of maintaining the situation in which both parents have the parental authority also in situations where the marriage has ended in divorce.[17]

Parental authority in case of unmarried parents
Later, judges in some countries even gave a further interpretation of the concept of parental authority, determining that, even in cases of cohabitation, parents could obtain an order giving parental authority on condition that it is in the best interests of the child and there are family relations between both parents and the child.[18] The mother automatically has a legal connection with any child born to her; for the father, this arises when he recognizes the child. In this case, the Supreme Court in the Netherlands justified its decision by reference to the protected rights which result from the concept of 'family life'. The Supreme Court found that the Dutch

---

17. The Civil Court of Appeal in France 21 March 1983; in the Netherlands the Supreme Court 4 May 1984, *NJ* 1985, 510; in Germany the Federal Court 3 November 1982, *NJW* 1983, p. 101; In the United Kingdom: the introduction of the 1989 Children Act provided for the continuation of retaining full parental responsibility if the parents separate or divorce. They may exercise it as if they were still married.

18. In the Netherlands, this was decided by the Supreme Court 21 March 1986, *NJ* 1986, 585. The interest of the child was the most important criterion by which the joint request of the parents had to be reviewed. The requirement of a family relationship remained, as a result of the advice given by the Council of Europe concerning parental responsibility, issued by the Committee of Ministers on 28 February 1984, Recommendation No. R(84)4 concerning 'parental responsibility', Strasbourg, 1984.

legislation, which accepts parental authority only during marriage was out of line with prevailing views in society.

It is interesting to show by an example how judges dealt with this new principle of parental authority for social parents, which was not laid down in statute law and what they did with demands of other carers.

In spite of the extension of the national legislation mentioned above, the argument has been taken further, as the nature of the family relationship between parents and child became the focal point of discussion. In a number of judgements, the Supreme Court in the Netherlands has explicitly recognized a broad concept of family life. In the first case, the request came from two women who considered themselves to be social parents of the child, as it was they who were providing everyday care (HR 24 February 1989, NJ 1989, 741). One of the carers was the mother of the child. In their opinion, it was possible that, in spite of the absence of a family tie between the mother's partner and the child, there was in fact family life (as defined by article 8 ECHR) between the adult and the child. The Supreme Court was of the opinion that the requirement that there must be a (legal) family relationship between the adult and the child was not incompatible with article 8 and 14 ECHR.

Another case concerned a man who was in the position to recognize a child, but – as this would (under the old laws) have the consequence of the child's family name changing – he and the mother did not wish to do so, because they wanted the child to have the mother's family name (HR 24 February 1989, NJ 1989, 742). Again, the Supreme Court rejected this petition by using the same reasoning as in the first case, namely the lack of legal parenthood. Since 1 January 1998, the modernized Civil Code in the Netherlands offers fairer solutions to cases such as these. In the case of a heterosexual or homosexual partner of the parent, the carers have the possibility of shared parental responsibility, i.e. shared parental authority. This will lead to child support obligations for the partner of the parent of the child. So, this means that the social parent is entitled to joint authority. Although this does not give this parent exactly the same status as the legal parent, it certainly strengthens his or her legal position *vis-à-vis* the child. In the second case set out above, recognition no longer affects the name of the child: the parents now have discretion in choosing the child's family name.

To conclude, in western Europe, we are moving towards a more open legal system, in which the legislator (and society) is trying to find a new balance between the legal recognition of the child's genetic origin and the fact that those who act as parents for the child (the social parents or carers) are not always the child's biological parents and should be given a legal status adequate for the parental responsibilities they voluntarily assume.[19] In the old days, the general situation was that paternal authority was exercised almost exclusively by the father. This changed gradually and

---

19. Jaap E. Doek, The Nuclear family: Who are the parents?, in: John Eekelaar & Thandabantu Nhlapo, *The Changing Family. Family Forms & Family Law*, Oxford: Hart Publishing 1998, p. 552.

the general trend moved 'towards joint exercise of what has now become "parental" authority by the father and the mother, with the father's view carrying greater weight in the case of disagreement, and arrive, in the 1970s at joint or concurrent exercise of parental responsibility by the father and/or the mother, with possible recourse to the law by one or other in the event of disagreement in the interests of the child'.[20] So, in many European countries, we can see similar trends to reduce the legal priority of the father and to give mothers and fathers equal rights. In the Netherlands, we saw that since 1 January 1998, it is possible for a child's legal parent to share custody with another person who is not the child's parent and even for two non-biological parents to share the guardianship.

Looking at the Dutch law on parental authority and custodianship, the following must be mentioned:

6   Parental authority and custodianship in the Netherlands

While a minor child is always under someone's authority, this can be parental authority or custody. Three aspects have to be distinguished:
1. the person of the child;
2. the legal representation of the child; and
3. the child's property (article 1:245 BW).

Parents are obliged to look after and care for their minor children. They are responsible for their mental and physical well-being and the development of their personalities (article 1:247 BW). The same goes for the custodian and the foster parent (article 1:248 BW). The minor has to take into account the rights of the parents and the interests of the other family members (article 1:249 BW). The parents represent their child in legal cases. In the case of conflicting interests, the court can appoint a third person as a 'special guardian' (article 1:250 BW) to represent the minor and to look after his interests. If the two parents with joint parental authority do not agree on specific issues with regard to the education of their child(ren), they can ask the juvenile judge to mediate between them or to give a decision himself, e.g. in the choice of a school.

Parental authority during marriage or in a cohabitation without marriage and the authority after divorce
During marriage, the parents exercise parental authority jointly. After divorce, the parents will continue their joint parental authority, but each of them can request sole custody. If one or both parents did not request this, the court decides which of the parents will be entrusted with the authority (article 1:251 BW). Parents who are not married nor even have lived together, can jointly exercise parental authority if they

---

20. Marie-Thérèse Meulders-Klein, The Status of the father in European Legislation, *The American Journal of Comparative Law*, Vol. XLIV, 1996, no. 3, p. 507-508.

have registered their combined request in the custody register (article 1:244 and 252 BW).

The authority of the unmarried parent
The unmarried mother (of age) alone is entrusted with the authority over her child (article 1:253b BW), but the unmarried father can ask the court to change this situation, if he is convinced of the desirability of such a change (article 1:253c BW). The court can change these authority rules (e.g. after the death of the parent entrusted with the authority) because of new, altered circumstances (article 1:253h BW). If the parents place their child in a foster family, where it is looked after and cared for and if this situation has lasted one year or longer, the (biological) parents cannot change the residence of their child without the consent of the foster parents. This so-called blocking right is meant as a protection both of the foster family and the child. Only the substituted consent of the juvenile court can overrule the blocking (article 1:253s BW).

Joint responsibility
Since 1 January 1998, one of the parents may exercise responsibility for the child together with his or her partner (who is not the parent of the child). This may involve the mother and her male or female partner with whom she forms a family, or the father with his male or female partner with whom he forms a family. Joint responsibility gives the non-parent the same rights and duties of parental responsibility as it does the parent(s). He or she is then in all respects responsible for the care and upbringing of the child. To obtain joint responsibility, the parent and his or her partner must jointly submit a request to the court. The help of a lawyer is necessary.

Because children are only born into marriages and registered partnerships that include at least one woman, a male co-parent who wants to share the legal and financial responsibilities with the father of the child, will still need to go to court to ask for joint parental authority and maintenance duties.

A gay or lesbian co-parent who wants to have full parental *status* to complement these responsibilities, will have to go through the adoption procedure.

When marriage was opened up for same-sex couples on 1 April 2001, one important distinction remained between lesbian and heterosexual marriages. If a child is born in a heterosexual marriage, the child automatically has the husband of the mother as its legal father, and that father and mother both automatically share all legal and financial responsibilities over the child. Such joint parental authority plus joint parental maintenance duties do not arise automatically if a child is born in a lesbian marriage (nor where a child is born in a lesbian or heterosexual registered partnership). These responsibilities could only be obtained by petitioning the court. But this changed on 1 January 2002 when the law of 4 October 2001 (amending various articles of Book 1 of the Civil Code; which was published in *Staatsblad* 2001, nr. 468) entered into force. Any child born from that date into a lesbian marriage (or into a registered partnership of two women or of a man and a woman) will automatically, from the moment of birth, have two fully responsible adults: its mother and her spouse or registered partner. That spouse or partner will still not be deemed to be the 'father' (nor 'parent' or 'second mother') of the child, but will have an equal share in the *parental authority* over the child and in the *maintenance duties* towards the child.

Interference in family life

There are several situations in which state intervention in the family is necessary, because parental authority is not exercised according to principles of accepted morals and public order. For example, if a child grows up under circumstances which threaten it in its moral, mental or physical interests and other non-compulsory measures to change this situation have failed, the court can order a *family guardianship* (article 1:254 BW). This means that an organization for family guardianship is appointed which will advise the parents and the minor and help them with the educational problems for the time of one year (article 1:256 and 257 BW). This term can be extended. The family-guardianship society may give (written) instructions that have to be followed by the parents and the minor (article 1:258 BW). The court can suspend, abrogate or withdraw the instructions (article 1:259 and 260 BW). If necessary, the court may authorize the organization to place the child in residential care for the duration of one year at most, but an extension of one year is always possible (article 1:261, 262 and 263 BW). During the family guardianship, the appointed organization can take all kinds of measures concerning access to or contracts of the minor with third persons or concerning medical treatment (article 1:263a, 263b and 264 BW).

Dutch law knows *two ways of ending parental authority* (relief and dismissal). If a parent is unfit or unable to fulfil his/her parental duties, the court can order the parent to be *relieved* of his/her authority over the underage children. The parent has to sign a declaration of no-objection (article 1:266 and 268 sect. 1 BW). In a few cases, the court can order relief even if the parent(s) object(s), e.g. in the situation where the parent is mentally so disturbed that he/she is not be able to make up his/her mind or understand the meaning of the declaration of no-objection (article 1:268 sect. 2 sub c BW). A third party guardian, usually a *family-guardianship society*, will take care of the children in the period during which the parent(s) is (are) relieved or dismissed of their parental authority.

The second way to lose parental authority is by a *dismissal* ordered by the court. The grounds are:
- abuse of the authority or serious neglect of the care for one or more of the children;
- misconduct;
- a conviction for committing a crime with the minor, or for committing a crime against the minor.

The dismissal is meant to be an intervention by the court in the best interests of the child as is (compulsory) relief.

In principle, relief and dismissal continue until the child has reached majority or until the court is convinced that the child can be returned to his/her parent(s). In such a case, the court can pronounce a reinstatement of parental rights or a trial reinstatement of at most six months. Usually, this precedes definite reinstatement. During this period, the child lives again with its parent(s) (article 1:277 and 278 BW).

Third party custody
In his/her last will or by special notarial act, a parent can designate a third party (a person and not an institution) to exercise custody over his/her minor children after his/her death. If both parents have made such a provision and they both die without it being clear who died first, the local division of the district court *(Kantonrechter)* decides whose choice will be followed (article 1:292 BW). This last will custody has been criticized because quite a long time may have lapsed since the drafting of the last will before both parents die. The designated person may have vanished from the family circle and the best interests of the minors concerned can require for another guardian. The court cannot really put to a test the guardian chosen by the parents in their last will, but this person has to give his written agreement before the court. When parents are dismissed or released from their authority over the children, the district court has the competence to appoint a guardian. In cases like these, the court usually calls on guardianship societies or foundations. Those private organizations have the special task to care for and educate the children of released or dismissed parents. The guardianship societies have to be accepted as such by the Government. They receive subsidies from the local and provincial authorities but they mainly rely on private initiative (article 1:295 and 302, 306 BW).

7 Access rights

Although, especially after divorce, problems may arise between the parents concerning contact of the child with the parent with whom the child is not habitually resident, account must be taken of the great need for children to have contact with both parents and other family members, like siblings, grandparents, et cetera. Principle 8 of Recommendation No. R (1984) on parental responsibilities recommends the European States to give at least the possibility of maintaining personal relationships with the child to the parent with whom the child does not live, unless this relationship would be seriously harmful to the interests of the child. This idea has also been laid down in article 9 paragraph 3 of the UN Convention on the Rights of the Child which provides that States Parties 'shall respect the right of the child who is separated from one or both parents to maintain personal relations and direct contact with both parents on a regular basis, except if it is contrary to the child's best interests'.

In the old days, one parent had no legal right to maintain contact with the children who were in the custody of the other parent. In many countries, the initial statutory amendments gave the judges only a discretionary power to make arrangements between the child and the *divorced* parent, who did not have custody. The judge was free to determine the grounds on which a request was to be granted or denied. No grounds for legal review were enacted, nor was there a right for parents and children to have access. Furthermore, the act was only applicable in cases of divorce.

It is not surprising, therefore, that case law has led to a further interpretation and extension of the right to access. Back in 1957 and 1961, the European Commission had accepted that the parental right to access after divorce follows from the right to family life. Breaking off the relationship between the parents does not end the tie between the child and his or her parents (ECRM, Application No. 172/56, X v. Sweden, Yearbook I, p. 211; ECRM, Application No. 911/60, X v. Sweden, Yearbook IV, p. 198).

In 1980, the European Commission concluded (ECRM 13 March 1980, NJ 1981, 121) that 'according to its established case law, the right to family life also contains the right of a parent to have access to or contact with the child on the understanding that the State may not interfere with the exercise of that right otherwise than in accordance with the strict conditions set out in paragraph 2 of the article', that says 'protection of health and morals' and 'protection of the rights and freedoms of others'. In this respect, it is important that the Berrehab case (Berrehab v. the Netherlands), which was dealt with by the European Court, had a great impact on the rights of biological parents. In this case against the Netherlands, the issue concerned the father and daughter Berrehab, who could not have contact with each other, because the father had not received permission to remain in the Netherlands and had been deported. The farther and daughter enjoyed family life according to the European Court. The Court held:

> 'The Court likewise does not see cohabitation as a sine qua non of family life between parents and minor children. It has held that the relationship created between the spouses by a lawful and genuine marriage (...) has to be regarded as "family life". It follows from the concept of family life on which Article 8 is based that a child born of such union is ipso iure part of that relationship; hence, from the moment of the child's birth and by the very fact of it, there exists between him and his parents a bond amounting to "family life", even if the parents are not then living together. Subsequent events, of course, may break that tie (...).' (paragraph 21)

In Europe, parents and children are entitled to have contact with each other, unless such contact would be seriously harmful to the child's interests. The right of access is in some countries restricted to parents, brothers and sisters and/or grandparents. The question arises if the right of access should also be given to third parties who claim to have (had) 'family life' with the child, like former step parents, former foster parents, et cetera. The general interpretation in the case law is 'the necessary existence of a concrete family relation for a certain period, continued contact with the child after breaking off the relationship with the parent and a demonstrated interest in and care for the child' (HR 4 January 1991, NJ 1991, 253). According to the case law of the European Court of Human Rights, 'family life' must lead to access rights, even if the contact between the person involved (the appellant) and the child has been broken for quite a while. As a result of the wide interpretation of 'family life', the circle of people who are able to apply for a right of access has increased substantially.

The next question which must be answered concerns the justness of the arrangement of the parental access in the actual case. The rights and interests of other people, also involved in the relationship between the child and the parent who wishes to have visiting rights, will be balanced, because the right to access will also influence the child's other relationships. The judge will reject the request when, generally speaking, access would be against the child's best interest. For example, the contact with the parent who does not have custody over the child can cause serious damage to the development of the child. Another reason can be the unsuitability of the parent. Article 1:377f of the Dutch Civil Code gives this right to anyone who has a close personal relationship with the child and is a relative in the second degree or its biological parent. Also the so-called 'social parent' who has educated, raised and taken care of the child, treating him as belonging to his family for at least one year, can apply for access to the child. With the words 'close personal relation', the legislator is linking Dutch law to the case law of the European Commission and Court, which gives an interpretation of family life as 'a relationship (...) sufficiently close to constitute family life' (European Commission, 8823/78, 12 March 1980, unpublished). The grandparents or separated brothers and sisters are possible candidates for the right to have access and I believe that even a mother who cares for other people's children will be able, in certain circumstances, to appeal to her close personal relationship with the child in order to obtain certain access rights.

One further right has also been given a legal basis in some European countries. The parent who has custody can be obliged to give information to the other parent about important facts and circumstances concerning the child. The following information can be supplied: school reports, a photograph of the child(ren), details of illnesses, et cetera. In some jurisdictions, it is even possible to ask third parties (professionals, like the school, the doctor, etc.) for information about the child.

Fortunately, we can see a growing tendency to ask the child's opinion in cases where the child is involved in questions of religious education, school career, medical treatment, et cetera. Article 12 of the UN Convention on the Rights of the Child guarantees that States Parties shall assure to the child who is capable of forming his or her own views the right to express those views freely in all matters affecting the child, the views of the child being given due weight in accordance with the age and maturity of the child. Parents, legal guardians or other persons legally responsible for the child, must provide, in a manner consistent with the evolving capacities of the child, appropriate direction and guidance in the exercise by the child of his rights. And, in the case of (any) judicial and administrative proceedings affecting the child, the child shall in particular be provided with the opportunity to be heard, either directly, or through a representative or an appropriate body, in a manner consistent with the procedural rules of national law.

A remaining problem concerns the enforcement of the judgement. Because we are dealing with people and problems of access and information arising from the breakdown of a relationship or a marriage which is not harmonious, it is very difficult to devise legal provisions for these practical problems. Possible methods of enforcement of court orders are:

1. a financial penalty: however, in most cases the mother has to cooperate, but she is also financially the weakest party;
2. imprisonment: the consequence is that the child's educator will not be able to look after it;
3. setting aside of the obligation to pay maintenance: this is unlikely to lead to an alteration in the financial position of the mother if she obtains her money from social welfare;
4. placing the child under supervision: such a measure can be excessive in these circumstances.

Only very exceptionally will one of these decisions be taken. The main reason is that it will cause distress to the child. In almost 25% of marriages involving minor children which end in divorce, the dissolution of the marriage does not bring to an end the quarrel between the former spouses.[21] A solution might be contact houses, which already exist in Belgium, France and in the UK (and since 2000 in the Netherlands), in which parents and children can meet in a neutral place under the supervision of social workers. Of course, this supervised contact is not ideal, but in very difficult ex-partner relations, it can solve problems and it may lead to better contact between the parents (and former partners). It is not surprising that action groups (mostly of divorced fathers) claim more rights and try to fight for their rights in the media, et cetera. On the other hand, we must note the fact that the judge is entitled and obliged to give an order at the demand of one of the parents. However, I want to raise the question of whether it is a judge's task to intervene in these private matters if parents cannot solve their own problems and do not want to listen to each other nor to the judge.

8 Marriage law, registered partnership and homosexual marriage

Marriage is a legally durable community between a man and a woman. It is a legal institution and has certain legal consequences. Since the introduction of divorce legislation in the republic of Ireland in 1996, in all European countries, divorce has become a legal possibility to end an unhappy marriage.

Concubinage or analogous relationships outside marriage usually do not have the same consequences as marriage. Nowadays, however, it is generally assumed that the choice of a man and woman[22] not to marry should be respected and legal consequences should be attached to these types of relationships. The protection awarded by article 8 ECHR is not restricted to legal marriage. In some jurisdictions, *de facto marriage* (cohabitation) is made equivalent to marriage in certain cases. This is the case in the Scandinavian countries (registered partnership), the Netherlands

21. Judith S. Wallerstein & Joan B. Kelly, *Surviving the Breakup: How Children and Parents Cope with Divorce*, New York, 1980. Richard A. Gardner, *The Parental Alienation Syndrome*, Creskill, NJ, USA: Basic Books 1998.
22. Or in modern societies of two people of the same sex.

(registered partnership) and France (pacte civil de solidarité; PAC). However, (also in other countries) concubinage has become a part of social life. Social recognition of cohabitation often leads to recognition in administrative and civil law, by putting into the code a definition of this de facto situation and by attaching rights to concubinage, such as the duty of maintenance, pension provisions and the law regarding matrimonial property.

The fact that it is very difficult to reach an agreement on the various issues in question leads to problems. For instance, should cohabitation be settled in the same way as a marriage? And if so, are cohabitants willing to be responsible for each other's existence? Should the cohabitation be registered and if so, in what manner? And what sort of cohabitation can be regarded as equivalent to marriage?

With regard to homosexual marriage, for instance, various attempts have been made, using the Convention to convince the judges that homosexuals should also be entitled to contract a civil marriage with each other. It must be kept in mind that it may constitute an inadequate justification simply to link a specific legal consequence to marriage and not to two people of the same sex living together. Until now, judges in many countries have declined these applications, justifying these decisions on the grounds that the Convention is based on the traditional matrimony joining a man and a woman. The judges did not have any say in this matter and referred the applicants to the legislator. In the Netherlands, the Supreme Court decided that two women or two men cannot marry and that this Dutch rule was not against article 12 and 14 ECHR. In another decision the Supreme Court ordered that joint parenthood is only possible in the case of two unmarried people, who live together, who are of opposite sex and who are registered as the parents of the child, but the court said that this matter was a political issue and had to be ordered by the legislator.

On 8 July 1999, a legislative proposal was sent to Parliament which, after enactment, would make it possible for same sex couples to marry and to convert a registered partnership into marriage and vice versa. Parliament accepted this bill on 21 December 2000 and from 1 April 2001, it is possible for two homosexuals to marry;[23] nonetheless a number of provisions in the legislation on matrimony have been declared applicable to registered (homosexual) couples. In practically all respects, marriage for same sex couples will be the same as marriage for man and woman, but the marriage between a same sex couple will have no effects upon the legal relationship with children.

---

23. Until recently, it was generally assumed that article 12 and also article 23 ICCPR were intended to protect the traditional marriage between two people of opposite sexes. This was also the case in the Netherlands. 'One of the characteristics of a marriage is that the partners are physically capable of having sexual intercourse in such a way that it could bring about sexual reproduction.' In its conclusions, the Supreme Court pointed to the judgement of the European Court of Human Rights (17 October 1986, *NJ* 1987, 945) in which article 12 ECHR is cited as being concerned only with the traditional marriage of two people of different sexes.

8.1 Marriage and registration of partnership in the Netherlands

Dutch family law has originally (1838) been greatly influenced by the French Code Civil, so the separation of religion and State is one of the main principles. Only civil law marriages are valid (article 1:30 BW).

Since 1 April 2001, the Dutch legislation with regard to marriage has changed, so that since that date two *(heterosexual, lesbian or homosexual)* people can marry. In practically all respects, marriages for same sex couples are the same as the marriage of a man and a woman, but the marriage between a same sex couple will have no effects upon the consequences of affiliation if a child is born during the marriage of a lesbian couple. Another difference between heterosexual and homosexual marriages is that the international effects of the marriage between a same sex couple differ from the effects of a marriage between a man and a woman.

A man or woman can only be married to one other person at a time. The rules for marriage are also applicable to the rules with regard to registered partnership.

The age of consent as regards marriage is 18 for both men and women (article 1:31 sect. 1 BW). An exception is made for those who wish to marry and who have reached the age of 16 and:
– if the woman can show a medical statement of her pregnancy; or
– if she has already given birth to a child (article 1:31 sect. 2 BW).

Dispensation by the Minister of Justice is possible in all other circumstances (e.g. in the case of a younger person), though in practice it is seldom granted (article 1:31 sect. 3 BW).

No marriage is possible for a mentally disabled person who is incapable of determining his or her free will or of understanding the meaning of the statement (article 1:32 BW).

A minor (i.e. a person under the age of 18) cannot marry without his or her parents' consent (article 1:35 BW). But if the parents refuse consent, the minor can request the district court, local division (a special section of the district court) for substitute consent (article 1:36 BW).

A person under tutelage because of a mental handicap is only allowed to marry with the consent of the district court, local division (article 1:38 BW). If this person is put under tutelage for reasons of dissipation or alcoholism, he has to get the consent of his guardian in order to marry. If he refuses, the district court, local division may be requested to give substitute consent (article 1:37 BW).

Another impediment to marriage is the one that makes it impossible for people to marry if they are related to each other within the prohibited degrees of consanguinity in the ascending or descending line. The same absolute prohibition holds as well for brothers and sisters. Dispensation by the Minister of Justice can be granted for a brother and sister related to each other by adoption (article 1:41 sect. 1 and 2 BW).

One can never be forced to marry or to register as partners, even on the basis of a once given promise. After a simple breach of promise, one cannot sue either for the solemnization of the marriage or for damages. Only if the wedding has been announced formally, may the jilted party claim real costs and material damages, such as the costs of the photographer, the restaurant that had to be cancelled, et cetera. *Immaterial damage* (sorrow, the loss of a good party) is not compensated (article 1:49 BW).

Dutch people who want to celebrate their wedding in another country can do so and ask the registrar for an official qualification to marry abroad. Such a qualification is valid for a sixmonth period (article 1:49a BW).

8.2 Suspending a marriage

If the legal requirements between two people have not been met, some people have the right to prevent the actual wedding celebration by 'suspending the marriage'. They can do so by issuing a summons against the Registrar. This competence belongs to direct lineal members of the family, brothers, sisters, guardians, curators and trustees of each of the future spouses (article 1:51, 52 and 54 BW). The Public Prosecutor is obliged to suspend a planned marriage, if he knows of any legal impediment or if, in his opinion, the marriage is meant to be a bogus transaction. Such a sham marriage is only intended to obtain admission, for a party of foreign nationality or a refugee, to the Netherlands (article 1:50 and 53 BW).

The person who wants to go through with the wedding has to take legal action and address him- or herself to the district court. In the meantime, the planned marriage will remain suspended (article 1:55 and 56 BW).

The same rules are applicable in the case of a registration of partnership.

8.3 The solemnization of a marriage

Marriages are solemnized in public in the official municipal town hall in the presence of the Registrar and at least two or at most four adult witnesses (article 1:63 BW). If one of the parties cannot go to the town hall (e.g. because of illness or imprisonment) the marriage may be solemnized in a 'special building' (hospital or prison). In that case, *six* witnesses have to be present at the wedding. The Minister of Justice can give permission for a marriage by proxy under special circumstances (article 1:65 and 66 BW). This hardly ever happens anymore.

The same rules are applicable in the case of a registration of partnership.

Religious confirmations of marriages can only take place after the solemnization of the civil marriage in the town hall (article 1:68 BW).

8.4 Decrees of nullity

Though the Dutch Civil Code contains a provision on annulment of marriage, this provision is very rarely applied. The reason is that the registers are very accurately kept and mistakes are seldom made. However, the district court can pronounce a decree of nullity because of the absence of one of the requirements of marriage. Fewer people are competent to file a petition for annulment of a marriage than there are people able to suspend a planned marriage. Only ascendants of the spouses and the spouses themselves have the ability to file such a petition. Furthermore, third parties who have a direct legal interest in the annulment are competent to file such a petition *after* the dissolution of the marriage. The Public Prosecutor, however, is competent in this matter, as long as the marriage has *not yet* been dissolved. At the request of the Public Prosecutor, a marriage can be declared void, if it is proved that the marriage was entered into with no other intention than to acquire a right of residence in the Netherlands (a so-called sham marriage). This is possible even after the dissolution of that marriage (article 1:71a BW).

Each one of the spouses has the right to file for annulment on the basis of intimidation or a mistake as to the identity of the other party or a misunderstanding about the real meaning of the solemn vow to take the other party as his or her spouse (article 1:71 BW).

The rules for annulment are also applicable in case of registered partnerships.

8.5   Spousal rights and obligations

General provisions

Dutch law contains provisions concerning the more immaterial *personal relations* between spouses as well as the material *regime governing property*. The same counts for registered partners. The spouses owe each other fidelity, help and support. They are obliged to supply each other with the necessities of life (article 1:81 BW) and they have the duty to bring up, educate and support the (minor[24]) children of the family (article 1:82 BW). They are not obliged to live together.

There exists a mutual duty to bear the costs of the household and the liabilities evolving from this duty to third parties (article 1:84 and 85 BW). Both parties have the duty to provide the other with housekeeping money. In conflicting situations, an appeal to the court is possible.

Irrespective of the regime concerning the property between them, the spouses need each other's consent for some legal acts, e.g.:
– contracts to dispose of certain goods, to mortgage property or to give it in use; any action by either or both spouses, that tends to end the use of the house as living quarters, or any action that tends to end the use of the goods or the furniture that come with the house in question;
– for gifts and donations except the usual, modest ones;
– for contracts, made outside the exercise of his/her profession or employment for which one of the spouses has to give a collateral or provide a guarantee or any other form of security;
– for a contract for purchase in installment (article 1:88 BW).

The consenting party does not have to be present in person; a written authorization suffices.

---

24. If their children study or are in need, the parents have to support them until they are 21 years of age.

Legal community of goods and marriage settlements
As far as the relationship of two spouses or registered partners towards property is concerned, the Dutch legal system has a rather unique position among the other countries. If the spouses did not make any arrangements before the wedding, they are married in *community of goods*. This complete community comprises all present and future property and also all debts from the moment of the solemnization of the marriage (article 1:93-96 BW). There are only a few exceptions to this complete community of property: firstly, it does not include those objects for which the donor or testator decided that they should be excluded from the community. Secondly, it does not cover those goods and debts that are specially attached to one of the spouses (article 1:94 BW). Lastly, since the new law on the equalization of pension rights came into force in 1994, the pensions do not fall in the community of goods anymore (article 1:94 sect. 4 BW). The administration of a property is in the hands of the spouse who brought it to the community. Spouses are obliged to inform each other about the state of the goods and the debts of the community (article 1:97 and 98 BW).

The community of property is dissolved by:
1. the end of the marriage;
2. a legal separation;
3. a court decision dissolving the community;
4. a post-nuptial settlement to dissolve the community (article 1:99 BW).

This means that the community is divided into two equal parts, one half going to one spouse (or registered partner) or his/her heirs and one half going to the other spouse or his/her heirs. However, after the dissolution, each of the spouses remains liable for the total of the common debts for which he or she was liable previously and each spouse or registered partner is still liable for half of the other debts. After the dissolution of the community each one of the spouses has the right to buy the clothes he/she used to wear and the jewelry. The same applies to his/her professional tools and the papers and documents belonging to his/her family. The money for the personal clothes and jewelry falls into the community of goods (see article 1:100-103 BW).

In the near future, the system of the total community of goods will be changed into a limited community, because many legal experts think that this system does not cope with the needs of spouses and registered partners. The legislator followed this opinion.

Marriage settlements
Most Dutch people (approx. 70%) do not arrange marriage settlements. However, parties can make any settlement as long as this settlement is not in conflict with good morals or public order (article 1:121 BW). A marriage settlement must be executed by a deed passed before a civil law notary before the wedding or registration of partnership (article 1:114 and 115 BW). It can also be done during the marriage or registered partnership, if the district court has granted permission for drafting the

marriage settlement (article 1:118 BW). The notarial deeds of marriage settlements have to be filed in a public register, held at the court in the district where the partners married or registered their partnership (article 1:116 BW). There are the following major legal categories of marriage contracts (but variations are possible):

– a total exclusion of community of property;
– a limited community, e.g. a community of benefit and income or gain and loss; and
– other contracts, like the very popular 'verrekenbedingen'. A 'verrekenbeding' means that there is a total exclusion of community of property, but the partners' saved income will be shared amongst the two partners at the end of each year or at the dissolution of marriage or registration of partnership or in specific other cases (article 1:132-144 BW).[25]

There is a growing tendency, especially amongst elderly couples who have been married for a long time, to change the marriage settlements they made up when they married, some thirty, forty years before. This has to do with present tax laws. Without changing the old marriage contract to a community of goods, the taxes will be divided equally over the two halves of the community. Of course, the court has to give permission first so that possible creditors are not financially injured by this move.

8.6 De facto marriages, marriages de fait, living together without marriage

At the moment, there are no legal provisions concerning those people who wish to live together, but do not (wish to) marry. Some of them cannot marry e.g. because one of them is still married to a third party or because they are close relatives. But the great majority of them simply do not want to marry. Some couples are interpreting the cohabitation period as an experiment, as a test. Others experienced such bitter disappointments during previous marriages that they have a 'never-again-feeling' towards marriage.

However, there exist quite a few models of cohabitation contracts to be drawn up by a notary. In the Netherlands, this way of sharing a partnership is not regarded as being against good morals or public order. On the contrary, in several statutes, the government has acknowledged these de facto marriages (e.g. in the tax law of succession, in pension law and in rental law).

8.7 The dissolution of marriage in the Netherlands

According to article 1:149 BW, a marriage is terminated by:
1. the death of one of the spouses or both spouses;
2. by a divorce;
3. by a legal separation eventually followed by the dissolution of the marriage;

---

25. This new law was enacted at 1 September 2002 (Act of 14 March 2002; *Stb.* 2002, 152).

4. by the changing of marriage into a registered partnership;
5. by the new marriage or registration of partnership of the surviving partner if the court has decided that the missing husband/partner is presumed to be dead.

Most marriages are dissolved by the death of one of the spouses, but the divorce rate in the Netherlands has gradually increased in the latter part of last century. These days, one in every three marriages ends in divorce (approx. 36,000 in 2002).

Almost the same rules are applicable to a registration of partnership. The differences between them are that in case of registration of partnership, legal separation is not allowed and the registered partnership can be ended on mutual request at the Public Registrar of the local community of both partners. A solicitor or notary must also sign this request, and the partners must have made an agreement with regard to the consequences of the ending of their registration of partnership.

Divorce
A divorce may be sought by both partners (on mutual request) or by one of them by petition (article 1:150 BW). There is only one ground for divorce: the permanent disruption of marriage (article 1:151 BW). This ground for divorce does not have to be proved. The courts accept the allegation without evidence. The last decade not the divorce itself, but the legal consequences have drawn more attention, such as questions of alimony, joint parental authority, access rights and pension rights.

The marriage is not terminated by the divorce decision of the court but by the official registration in the civil registers. Either parties or one of them can request this registration. After a period of six months without registration, the divorce is no longer held valid (article 1:163 BW).

Alimony
Where one of the ex-spouses does not have sufficient income to provide him or herself with the necessities of life, nor is in a position to obtain such income, the court can give an alimony order. It has to take into account the *needs* of the person claiming maintenance and the *financial strength* of the other party (article 1:157 BW).

The present alimony limit is twelve years[26] after registration of the divorce decision, but in hard cases, the court can lengthen this period at the request of the person in need. If the marriage lasted less than five years and there are no children born from this marriage, the maintenance obligation lasts exactly as long as the marriage existed. The maintenance payments are indexed yearly.

The entitlement to maintenance ceases when the person who has this right remarries, registers as partners or starts living together with another person as in marriage or registered partnership.

---

26. Until 1995, the ex-partner had to pay maintenance to the other party all his/her life.

8.8 Legal separation and dissolution of marriage

In some cases, married partners can choose a *legal separation* (e.g. on religious grounds). The legal separation puts an end to the rights and duties of the spouses (article 1:92a BW) and to the total community of goods system, but the marriage still exists. Both parties together or one of them may request legal separation on the same ground as divorce, i.e. permanent disruption of the marriage (article 1:169 BW).

At the request of one or both spouses, the judge will decide which one will exercise parental authority over the minor children of the couple. In principle, the other parent does not lose his authority and he/she has an access arrangement. The maintenance rules in a divorce also apply in a legal separation. The legal separation will have its legal effects from the moment it has been inscribed in the registers of matrimonial acts, held at the district court. After a period of six months without registration, the legal separation is no longer held valid.

If the spouses reconcile, the legal separation ceases to exist and the (sleeping) marriage and its legal consequences revive from the moment they have registered this reconciliation in the register held at the district court. Although after such a registration the marriage revives, the validity of legal acts performed during the separation and reconciliation are judged according to the moment they took place.

The marriage of legally separated spouses can be dissolved at any time on joint request. The same may happen at the request of one of the spouses if the separation has lasted for a period of three years without conciliation. This term may be shortened to one year if one spouse cannot be expected to continue the marriage (e.g. in case of misbehaviour). Future pension rights arrangements must be made prior to the dissolution (article 1:179-181 BW).

Whatever the intentions of the spouses when they requested a legal separation, the situation is no longer a cul-de-sac, but simply a detour of three years maximum to reach the definite termination of an unsuccessful marriage.

9 Conclusions

As I have tried to demonstrate in this short overview of developments in family law in Europe and some fields of Dutch family law, the impact of human rights on the legal systems has been enormous. Special attention has been given to article 8 ECHR, because this provision appears to contain a complete code of family law and continues to exercise a considerable degree of influence upon the national judges and legislature. However, not only the European Convention on Human Rights had a great impact upon new laws, but also the International Convention for Civil and Political Rights and the UN Convention on the Rights of the Child. As was demonstrated, the legal position of children and other members of the family has changed because of the impact of these rights. In my opinion, it may be expected that we will have more and more judge-made law, because the legislator cannot follow these alterations in society in an adequate way because of dissenting political (and religious) opinions. Although there may be many differences between the

European cultures and legislations, the international conventions and especially the authority of the European Court will bring more convergence between these different jurisdictions in the long run.

The general trends in Europe are the growing individualism with respect to partnership and relatives, but more homogeneity with respect to parenthood, de-institutionalization of separation, divorce and parenthood. However, the harmonization of family law in the European countries is still far away, because of the financial, social, cultural and religious differences in the European States. Real harmonization, if ever, of family law will take many years or even decades.

With regard to family law in the Netherlands, it must be said that it has been changed and modernized dramatically in this last decade. In almost all fields of family law, the impact of fundamental rights has been enormous. Thanks to the open mind of our Supreme Court, lower courts and a modern legislator, we can conclude that our Family Code has become a modern law which can serve in this new century, at least for the coming years. Of course, this law does not reflect everyone's opinion, because some people and some (small) political parties think it is too modern, e.g. by allowing homosexuals to marry or to adopt a child. Another aspect has to be mentioned: even a modern law cannot fulfill everyone's wishes and cannot terminate all painful situations nor find solutions to bad family relationships. So, homosexual couples are (still?) not allowed to adopt foreign children, some divorced people are not able to have access to their child because the judge's order cannot be executed by the obstructive position the former partner has taken, some children are still neglected or abused (or worse) by their parents, some people suffering from a mental handicap or Alzheimer have been left by their close relatives, many married people are not happy, et cetera. It is the task of family law experts, judges, the legislator and others (social workers, etc.) to find solutions for these problems, although we must be aware that it is impossible to make everyone happy in his (family) life. Nevertheless, it is a great challenge for all the parties involved in these family issues to endeavour to create better family (law) regulations and family life.

References

C. Asser & J. de Boer, *Personen- en familierecht*, Deventer: Kluwer 2002.

Council of Europe (1970), Constituent Assembly, 21st Ordinary Session (third Part), Texts Adopted.

J.E. Doek & P. Vlaardingerbroek, *Jeugdrecht en jeugdhulpverleningsrecht*, The Hague: Elsevier Juridisch 2001.

Kees de Hoog, Clio Presvelou & Peter Cuyvers, *Family arrangements and Politics*, The Hague: Dutch Family Council (Nederlandse Gezinsraad) 1993.

'Family policy and decentralisation' (Netherlands), National replies to questionnaire, XXIInd Conference of European Ministers responsible for family affairs, Strasbourg, 21 February 1991.

The International Survey of Family Law (2000, 2001, 2002 Editions), edited by Andrew Bainham, Bristol: Jordan Publishing Limited.

M. de Langen (1990), 'De betekenis van Artikel 8 EVRM voor het familierecht', *Preadvies Deel III Handelingen Nederlandse Juristenvereniging*, 1990-I.

'Methods of child-upbringing in Europe today and the role of family services' (Netherlands), National replies to questionnaire, XXIst Conference of European Ministers responsible for family affairs, Strasbourg, 28 February 1989.

M. Rood-de Boer, Family law, in: J. Chorus et al., *Introduction to Dutch law*, Deventer: Kluwer 1993, p. 39-61.

H.G. Schermers, *The influence of the European Commission of Human Rights*, Reports of the Conference of Mordenate College, 27 September 1991, The Hague: TMC Asser Instituut 1991.

P. Vlaardingerbroek et al., *Het hedendaagse personen- en familierecht*, Deventer: W.E.J. Tjeenk Willink 2002.
40 Jaar Europees Verdrag voor de rechten van de mens, *NJCM-bulletin*, speciaal nummer, Leiden, 1990.

45 Jaar Europees Verdrag voor de rechten van de mens, *NJCM-bulletin*, speciaal nummer, Leiden, November 1995.

50 Jaar Europees Verdrag voor de rechten van de mens, *NJCM-bulletin*, speciaal nummer, Leiden, 2000.

Further Reading

Books and Articles

1   General

J. Chorus et al. (eds.), Introduction to Dutch Law, 3rd revised ed., The Hague [etc.]: Kluwer Law International 1999, 574 pages. *Overview of different fields of law with an emphasis on private law, including law on legal persons, law of succession, commercial law, civil procedure and also administrative law, environmental law, tax law and labour law. Includes an extensive bibliography of foreign language texts on Dutch law.*

F. Bruinsma, Dutch Law in Action, Nijmegen: Ars Aequi Libri 2000, 71 pages. *Dutch law from a socio-legal perspective. Emphasis on procedural law and on policy issues.*

2   Legal History

A   General and political history of the Netherlands
J.C. Blom, E. Lamberts & J.C. Kennedy, History of the Low Countries, New York: Berghahn 1999, 503 pages.
Jonathan I. Israel, The Dutch Republic. Its Rise, Greatness and Fall 1477-1806, Oxford: Clarendon 1995, 1231 pages.
E.H. Kossmann, The Low Countries, 1780-1940, Oxford: Clarendon 1978, 784 pages.

B   Institutional and legal history of the Netherlands
There is no good survey of Dutch legal history in English. One will find information in:

Raoul C. Van Caenegem, An Historical Introduction to Private Law, Cambridge 1992.
Raoul C. Van Caenegem, An Historical Introduction to Western Constitutional Law, Cambridge 1992.

In Dutch:

P. Gerbenzon & N.E. Algra, Voortgangh des rechtes. De ontwikkeling van het Nederlands recht tegen de achtergrond van de Westeuropese cultuur, 4th ed., Groningen: Tjeenk Willink 1975, 445 pages.
J.H.A. Lokin & W.J. Zwalve, Hoofdstukken uit de Europese codificatiegeschiedenis, 3rd ed., Deventer: Kluwer 2001, pages 271-311.
J.Ph. de Monté verLoren and J.E. Spruit, Hoofdlijnen uit de ontwikkeling der rechterlijke organisatie in de Noordelijke Nederlanden tot de Bataafse omwenteling, 7th ed., Deventer: Kluwer 2000, 345 pages.

3   Constitutional Law

C.A.J.M. Kortman & P.P.T. Bovend'eert, Dutch Constitutional Law, The Hague [etc.]: Kluwer Law International 2000, 212 pages. *General and useful introduction to Dutch constitutional law.*
L.F.M. Besselink, An Open Constitution and European Integration. The Kingdom of the Netherlands, SEW, nr. 6, 1996, p. 192-206.
C.A.J.M. Kortmann & P.P.T. Bovend'Eert, The Netherlands, in: International Encyclopedia of Laws. Constitutional Law, Suppl. 35, January 2000, The Hague: Kluwer Law International 1992-...
B. van Roermund (ed.), Constitutional Review/Verfassungsgerichtbarkeit/ Constitutionele toetsing. Theoretical and Comparative Perspectives, Deventer: Kluwer Law and Taxation Publishers 1993.

4   Criminal Law

General:

P.J.P. Tak, The Dutch Criminal Justice System, WODC reeks Onderzoek en Beleid, Den Haag: Boom Juridische Uitgevers 2003.
H. de Doelder, 'The Public Prosecution Service in the Netherlands', European Journal of Crime, Criminal Law and Criminal Justice (vol. 8/3) 2000, pp. 187-209. *Article about the organization and role of the public prosecution service.*

Special issues:

J. Griffiths, A. Bood, H. Weyers, Euthanasia & Law in the Netherlands, Amsterdam: Amsterdam University Press 1998. *Interesting study of the development of the law of euthanasia from a socio-legal perspective.*

5   Private Law

General:

E.H. Hondius, 'Recodification of the Law in the Netherlands: the New Civil Code Experience', Netherlands International Law Review 1982, 249-366.
P. van Schilfgaarde, 'System, good faith and equity in the New Dutch Civil Code', European Review of Private Law 1997, 1-10.

Contract law:

Arthur S. Hartkamp & Marianne M.M. Tillema, Contract Law in the Netherlands, The Hague [etc.]: Kluwer Law International, 228 pages. *Fairly detailed description of Dutch contract law.*

Tort law:

E. Hondius (ed.), Modern Tort Law: Dutch and Japanese Law Compared, The Hague: Kluwer Law International 1999.
W. van Gerven et al., Tort Law (series: Ius Commune Casebooks for the Common Law of Europe), Oxford: Hart 2000. *Comparative case book. Includes some materials (cases, texts) on Dutch tort law.*
J. Spier, The Limits of Liability: Keeping the Floodgates Shut, The Hague: Kluwer Law International 1996.
J. Spier et al. (eds.), The Limits of Expanding Liability: Eight Fundamental Cases in a Comparative Perspective, The Hague: Kluwer Law International 1998.
Two books on the comparative law of torts including Dutch law.

Family law:

John Eekelaar & Thandabantu Nhlapo (eds.), The Changing Family. Family Forms & Family Law, Oxford: Hart 1998, 634 pages. *International perspectives, not specifically about Dutch law, resulting from the World Conference of the International Society of Family Law 1997.*
Masha Antokolskaia, 'Recent Developments in Dutch Filiation, Adoption and Joint Custody Law', in: Familia, Anno II, fasc. 3-2002, pp. 781-805.
Gerda A. Kleijkamp, 'The Influence of the 1960s on Developments in Family Law in the United States and the Netherlands', in: Hans Krabbendam & Hans-Martien ten Napel (eds.), Regulating Morality, Antwerpen: Maklu 2000, pp. 213-228.

Websites

www.llrx.com/features/dutch.htm (Researching Dutch Law, By Oswald Jansen and George Middeldorp)
Useful site with general information about the Dutch legal system and many links to other sources.

www.portill.nl (portal of Dutch Internet Law libraries)
Portal that links to the different internet law libraries of Dutch universities, such as:

till.uvt.nl (Tilburg Internet Law Library)
Many general legal links; unfortunately most of the links about Dutch law are in Dutch.

www.justitie.nl/english/Themes/ (Dutch Ministry of Justice)
About a few key themes in Dutch law and policy, the Ministry of Justice gives information and links to its own publications.

www.parlement.nl (the Internet site of the Dutch Parliament)

www.government.nl (the Internet site of the Dutch Government)